INFRASTRUCTURES OF RACE

BORDER HISPANISMS

JON BEASLEY-MURRAY, ALBERTO MOREIRAS, AND GARETH WILLIAMS,

SERIES EDITORS

# INFRASTRUCTURES OF RACE

*Concentration and Biopolitics in Colonial Mexico*

DANIEL NEMSER

UNIVERSITY OF TEXAS PRESS ⬥ *Austin*

Requests for permission to reproduce material from this work should be sent to:

Permissions
University of Texas Press
P.O. Box 7819
Austin, TX 78713-7819
http://utpress.utexas.edu/index.php/rp-form

⊗ The paper used in this book meets the minimum requirements of ANSI/NISO Z39.48-1992 (R1997) (Permanence of Paper).

LIBRARY OF CONGRESS CATALOGING DATA

Names: Nemser, Daniel, author.
Title: Infrastructures of race : concentration and biopolitics in colonial Mexico / Daniel Nemser.
Other titles: Border Hispanisms.
Description: First edition. | Austin : University of Texas Press, 2017. | Series: Border Hispanisms | Includes bibliographical references and index.
Identifiers: LCCN 2016045201| ISBN 978-1-4773-1244-5 (cloth : alk. paper) | ISBN 978-1-4773-1260-5 (pbk. : alk. paper) | ISBN 978-1-4773-1261-2 (library e-book) | ISBN 978-1-4773-1262-9 (nonlibrary e-book)
Subjects: LCSH: Mexico—History—Spanish colony, 1540-1810. | Mexico—Race relations—History. | Racism—Mexico—History. | Race discrimination—Mexico—History. | Biopolitics—Mexico—History. | Mexico—Politics and government—1540-1810. | Social structure—Mexico. | Urbanization—Social aspects—Mexico.
Classification: LCC F1392.A1 N46 2017 | DDC 305.800972—dc23
LC record available at https://lccn.loc.gov/2016045201

doi:10.7560/312445

CONTENTS

## ACKNOWLEDGMENTS

OVER THE MANY YEARS I have been working on this book, numerous mentors, colleagues, and friends have supported me in countless ways, large and small. While it would be impossible to account for everything they have done for me in these pages, I want at least to recognize some of the people who did them. At the University of California, Berkeley, José Rabasa and William B. Taylor introduced me to the field of colonial Latin American studies, and each shared with me critical insights, resources, and tools that allowed me to set this project in motion. I am also grateful to Estelle Tarica and Natalia Brizuela, who were always thoughtful interlocutors, and to Ivonne del Valle, who has been exceptionally generous with feedback and encouragement for as long as I have known her.

Since 2011, I have benefited from the support of many colleagues at the University of Michigan and beyond. I am especially indebted to Gustavo Verdesio and Anna More, as well as Javier Castro, Mayte Green-Mercado, Ken Mills, Javier Sanjinés, and Ryan Szpiech, who generously read and workshopped the manuscript with me, offering detailed feedback at a key stage of the writing process. Gavin Arnall, Vicenzo Binetti, Enrique García Santo-Tomás, Juli Highfill, Kate Jenckes, Cristina Moreiras, Jaime Rodríguez-Matos, Ana Sabau, Teresa Satterfield, and Gareth Williams have offered valuable guidance, insights, and encouragement along the way. Conversations with and questions from Bram Acosta, Majed Akhter, Santa Arias, Orlando Bentancor, Jody Blanco, Larissa Brewer-García, Ximena Briceño, Derek Burdette, Kathryn Burns, Eric Calderwood, Julia Chang, Chris Chen, Pablo García Loaeza, Karen Graubart, Seth Kimmel, Josh Lund, Yolanda Martínez–San Miguel, Kelly McDonough, Jeremy Mumford, Rachel O'Toole, Jesús Rodríguez-Velasco, Olimpia Rosenthal, Karen Stolley, Nancy van Deusen, and Elvira Vilches have enriched my thinking on many different topics. They may not even know it, but their comments have made this manuscript better.

*Tlazcamati miac* to John Sullivan, Delfina de la Cruz, Victoriano de la Cruz Cruz, and Eduardo de la Cruz Cruz in Zacatecas for their time and dedication in teaching me Nahuatl, and to Martín Vega for coordinating our Nahuatl courses at the University of Michigan.

Archivists and staff at the Archivo General de Indias in Seville and the Archivo General de la Nación in Mexico City were patient and generous with their assistance, and I thank them for introducing me to the pleasures (and frustrations) of archival research. In Seville, Eva Infante, Luisa Álvarez-Ossorio, and José Luis Caño Ortigoso at the Centro Michigan-Cornell-Penn made me feel at home and provided me with valuable institutional support. In Mexico City, Karina Esparza and Christian Sperling were wonderful hosts, always receiving me warmly and accompanying me on the search for vegetarian tacos.

I am indebted to Kerry Webb at the University of Texas Press for her enthusiastic support for this project and for shepherding it through to publication. My thanks also to Cindy Buck and Angélica López, who provided assistance in preparing the final manuscript, and to the anonymous readers for their helpful feedback and suggestions.

Finally, I want to thank my friends, comrades, and family, who supported and sustained me during the writing process. I am grateful to Noor Ahmad, Paige Andersson, Javier Arbona, Amanda Armstrong, Maryam Aziz, Rachel Bernard, Jasper Bernes, Abby Bigham, Dan Buch, Jonathan Buckman, Ben Calebs, John Cheney-Lippold, Jeff Clark, Jason de León, Rachel Frey, Mary Gallagher, Lenora Hanson, Laura Herbert, Sarah Hill, Callie Maidhof, Kate Marshall, Austin McCoy, Jackie Miller, Alana Price, Magalí Rabasa, Mary Renda, Allie Seekely, Alejo Stark, Eitan Sussman, Joanna Sussman, Zhivka Valiavicharska, James Watz, and Brian Whitener for their friendship, solidarity, and dedication. Thanks to Cindy and Richard Frey, my family away from home. Of course, I owe an enormous debt to my parents. In addition to most of what I know about teaching, Sharon Feiman-Nemser also taught me how to write clearly, while Louis Nemser pushed me to draw out the contemporary political implications of my work. Thanks to Zachary Nemser for showing up at the right time. Above all, I want to thank my partner, Loren Dobkin. Without her emotional and material support, not to mention her patience and sense of humor, none of this would have been possible.

CHAPTER I IS DERIVED in part from "Primitive Accumulation, Geometric Space, and the Construction of the 'Indian,'" *Journal of Latin American Cultural Studies* 24, no. 3 (2015): 335–352; available online at http://dx.doi.org.10.1080/13569325.2015.1065798. Part of the introduction appeared as "Biopolitics in Latin America" in *The Encyclopedia of Postcolonial Studies*, 3 vols., edited by Sangeeta Ray, Henry Schwartz, José Luis Villacañas, Alberto Moreiras, and April Shemak (Malden, MA: Wiley-Blackwell, 2016), 1:178–184; copyright © 2015 by Wiley-Blackwell.

INFRASTRUCTURES OF RACE

# BEFORE THE CAMP

*Race is traditionally thought about in terms of people, but
ultimately (and originally) its politics becomes comprehensible
only when it is contemplated in territorial terms: race is always,
more or less explicitly, the racialization of space, the naturalization
of segregation.*
JOSHUA LUND, *THE MESTIZO STATE*

ON FEBRUARY 10, 1896, a ship carrying the Spanish Captain-General
Valeriano Weyler y Nicolau docked at the port of Havana, where it was
received with enthusiastic applause by crowds loyal to the Spanish
empire. Cuban insurgents had declared independence from Spain the
previous year and taken control of much of the countryside. Within a
week of his arrival, General Weyler issued what would become an infamous decree, ordering civilians living in the rural areas of the east-
ern part of the island to report to the nearest city with a garrison of
Spanish troops within eight days. There they would be housed and
protected from what Weyler later called the "Black insurgent gangs"
(*negradas insurrectas*) in towns newly ringed with barbed wire and
defensive trenches.[1] Soldiers would then comb the countryside, destroying everything that had been left behind. Anyone who refused
to comply would be considered an insurgent and summarily treated
as such. Soon the same order was applied to the rest of the island. Between 1896 and 1898, Weyler's policy of *reconcentración* uprooted half
a million civilians, and the starvation and disease it precipitated were
responsible for the death of more than 100,000, about 10 percent of
the total Cuban population at the time. Casualties were so high that
there was nowhere to bury the dead, and contemporary photographs
capture mountains of bones piling up in the island's cemeteries.[2]

Weyler's camps failed to win the war for Spain, but in a way they succeeded far beyond his expectations. For many scholars, from historians to philosophers, this episode in Spanish colonial history marks the birth of the concentration camp.[3] From there, it was rapidly adopted and deployed by other colonizing powers around the world before circling back to Europe. Weyler himself observed in his war memoir that the British and Americans who had voiced the strongest criticisms of his policies in Cuba later copied his model for their own use in the Transvaal and the Philippines.[4] The early years of the camp are thus entangled with its Spanish and, especially, colonial roots. In his enormously influential book *Homo Sacer* (1998), the Italian philosopher Giorgio Agamben suggests, in one of only a handful of references to European colonialism, that what is most important about the early *"campos de concentraciones [sic]* created by the Spanish in Cuba" is that through them "a state of emergency linked to a colonial war is extended to an entire civil population."[5] Yet these accounts also raise an important question. If (Spanish) colonialism was the camp's condition of possibility, why would it have emerged only at the *end* of a long colonial project that had already endured over four centuries?

*Infrastructures of Race* answers this question by tracing a genealogy of concentration back to the early decades of Spain's colonization of the Americas. Rather than some nefarious *deus ex machina* descending from the rafters to rescue Spain's dying imperial project, concentration had long served as one of the primary techniques of colonial governance in the Americas. The sixteenth-century conquistadors carried with them a Renaissance conception of the world that viewed the social order as intimately tied to the spatial order. Over the centuries that followed, the colonial authorities repeatedly returned to the promise of collecting and organizing human and non-human objects within architectural and urban space as the key to effective governance and a well-ordered population. When General Weyler deployed the *campo de reconcentración* in 1896, then, he was not inventing something new but drawing on a dense repertoire of forms and practices of concentration that had been developed and deployed under colonial rule since the sixteenth century.

From early on, the concentration of bodies was also intimately tied to a politics of race. As Joshua Lund sets out in the epigraph, race is as much a question of space as it is a question of people and populations. Space is the grid of intelligibility that gives race its form and makes it legible, even thinkable. As a literary critic, Lund is interested in the contributions of the Mexican literary tradition to the process of racialization in modern Mexico, which is rooted in the division of material resources as supported by the deployment of institutional violence. Race is everywhere in this corpus, he writes, "from Lizardi's *El Periquillo Sarniento* onward."[6] Though initially published just before political independence, this serial novel often stands in for some of the earliest glimmers of the emergent Mexican nation. But the intersecting politics of race and space do not begin with the project of national formation. It was during the colonial period that many of the operative categories that show up in the texts examined by Lund, from "Indian" to "Mestizo" and beyond, first began to be elaborated.[7]

Consider the Indian. This category is unquestionably central to the way race is conceptualized in many parts of Latin America today, not only because of the large indigenous population in countries like Mexico but also because the Indian is always already implied in the conventional discourse of *mestizaje* (racial mixing), which generally presumes a mixture of European and indigenous ancestry. As we all are well aware, this label is based on a geographic mistake—a confused Christopher Columbus was certain that he had reached Asia, when in fact he was still halfway around the world in what today, also as a result of his profligate naming practices, we call the Caribbean. The label was also a mistake in that it lumped together enormous human diversity into a single, homogeneous category. But the fact that it was a mistake did not prevent it from becoming naturalized. What makes it possible for an error of such magnitude to endure over so many centuries, even through revolutions based precisely on the rejection of those who first applied the name? How does it come to be not only institutionally codified but also subjectively lived? Through what mechanisms, in other words, does racial ascription produce material effects?

Today it is no longer controversial to discuss race in terms of "social construction." The social construction framework initially emerged as a response to the long-dominant assumption that racial difference was primarily rooted in real, biological variation. Measured in terms of its diffusion in both the academy and popular culture, this response has been quite successful. But social constructionism can obscure as much as it clarifies. At times, for example, it appears to cast race as illusory, operating strictly at the level of representation. Other versions either implicitly or explicitly distinguish between two levels or instances, in which a discursive or ideological veil is draped over some preexisting, objective base. While critically analyzing and high-lighting the constructed character of positive or negative meanings that may be attached to particular identities, this approach still takes for granted the fact of "difference" itself as a "natural" foundation onto which representations are, more or less accurately, grafted. In this way, racism is reduced once again to an epistemic error, based on ignorance or prejudice. Antiracist practice thus turns to correct-ing these representations, better aligning them with the objects they seek to represent, and affirming these identities and the difference they embody.

This book lays out a different argument. At the outset, I assume that race is not reducible to any prior or preexisting identity. It is not a starting point but an end product, the result of a process called ra-cialization. The racialization processes that began with the Span-ish colonial project were routed through a politics of space. That is, not only did race become thinkable in the colonial context primarily through spatial disciplines like natural history, cartography, and ur-ban planning, but racialization took place in part through physical interventions in the landscape. These colonial infrastructures consti-tuted the material conditions of possibility for colonial rule, but they also, I argue, enabled the emergence and consolidation of racial cat-egories through both ascription and subjectification. Specifically, in-frastructure projects organized around the concentration of human and nonhuman objects created new proximities that allowed "group-ness" as such to emerge. What Lund calls "the naturalization of seg-regation" requires a racially ordered space, and that space had to be built before it could be forgotten.

Rather than investigate the surfaces of colonial formations of dif-ference—how contemporaries perceived identity, how bodies were marked, how otherness was represented—this book turns instead to what I call the infrastructures of race, or the material systems that enable racial categories to be thought, ascribed, and lived, as well as the systems of domination and accumulation these categories make possible as a result. I use the word *infrastructure* in two overlapping senses. First, what often goes unexamined in theories of racialization are precisely the material dimensions of these processes, the concrete forms into which they congeal and the things on which they depend. Drawing on new scholarship on infrastructure in fields like anthro-pology, history, and geography, I argue that racialization in colonial

Mexico was made possible in part by the construction of more or less durable structures like roads, walls, ditches, buildings, boundaries, and towns, into which both human and nonhuman objects were concentrated. These interventions wove together and organized colonial territory and facilitated the composition of differentiated groups that, over time, became naturalized. While concentration is most commonly associated with confinement, it also depends on and makes possible certain forms of mobility. In colonial Mexico, the people and things that were targeted for concentration had to be displaced from one site to another, and these relocations activated new flows of people, commodities, and ideas across local, regional, and transoceanic networks. In this way, concentration combined both confinement and circulation.

Second, without disavowing the negotiability of colonial hierarchies, this book foregrounds the limits of human agency and explores racialization as a structural component of colonial domination and global capitalism. In other words, I suggest that race itself may operate as a sort of infrastructure, a sociotechnical relation that enables the ongoing functioning of specific machineries of extraction and accumulation. While infrastructure is conventionally viewed in terms of physical objects, theorists of infrastructure in the global South have advanced a notion of "people as infrastructure" that extends to the productive and reproductive effects of systems of social relations.[8] By analyzing race in terms of the "work" it does rather than the form in which it appears, this approach foregrounds historical continuities over ruptures.[9] Global capitalism was thus forged not only through violence and destruction—what Karl Marx describes as "conquest, enslavement, robbery, murder, in short, force"—but also through affirmative forms of power that produced new social relations and racialized subjectivities. The history of primitive accumulation "is written in the annals of mankind in letters of blood and fire," then, but also in bricks and paving stones, categories and classifications.[10]

## PARADIGMS OF RACE

In admittedly broad strokes, there are currently two major paradigms for addressing the question of race in colonial Latin America. The first is the *decolonial* paradigm, which has recently become influential among scholars in a wide variety of disciplines, although less so among historians. This critical work turns on the concept of the "coloniality of power" (*colonialidad del poder*), first elaborated by the Peruvian sociologist Aníbal Quijano in the early 1990s. Coloniality refers to the Eurocentric matrix of power that constitutes, in the words of Walter Mignolo, the "darker side" of modernity. The modern/colonial world was inaugurated with the conquest and colonization of the Americas, but it did not end with political independence. According to Quijano, it was organized along two intersecting axes. The first was the construction and naturalization of the idea of race as a "mental category of modernity." Initially race emerged through the distinction between colonizers and colonized, but it soon came to rest on "supposed differential biological structures." Over time, color gradually came to stand in as emblematic of racial identity. In this way, race constituted not only a tool of social classification but also a mechanism of domination, such that different identities were inscribed within social hierarchies. The second axis was the formation of a new mode of economic relations capable of articulating multiple forms of labor control into a single world system. Slavery, serfdom, and wage labor were for the first time bound together by production for the world market. Thus, for Quijano, capitalism is defined not by the hegemony of wage labor but by the articulation of variegated relations of production within a single totality.[11]

At the intersection of these historical processes was the colonization of the Americas. It was there, argues Quijano, that for the first time "a systematic racial division of labor was imposed": Indians were transformed into serfs, Blacks into slaves, and Spaniards into wage laborers and independent commodity producers. In this way, the "inferior" races were associated with unwaged labor, while the "superior" race, and indeed whiteness itself, was linked with the wage—as well as with institutional power within the colonial administration. As European colonization expanded, moreover, the colonial matrix of power was extended to other parts of the globe, and in every case "each form of labor control was associated with a particular race."[12]

Although this approach aims to provide an account of the colonial construction of race that is both epistemic and material, it nevertheless leaves us with a number of unresolved questions. It is true, for example, that Indians had to perform forced labor, but by the middle of the sixteenth century this labor, though forced, still had to be remunerated with a wage—a low wage, certainly, but a wage nonetheless. And what of those who were racialized as neither Indians nor Spaniards but as Mestizos? Here Quijano is not clear. At times he seems to suggest that Mestizos were slotted into the general pool of the un-waged along with Indians and Blacks ("the unpaid labor of Indians, blacks, and mestizos"), while elsewhere he implies their incorpora-tion into the wage ("in the eighteenth century . . . an extensive and important social stratum of mestizos . . . began to participate in the same offices and activities as nonnoble Iberians").[13] Is the argument that a shift took place between the sixteenth and the eighteenth cen-turies, such that Mestizos were initially excluded from the wage but later brought into the fold of salaried whiteness? If so, what accounts for this change? In many ways, the confusion seems to be built into the model itself, since there were simply not enough rungs on the economic ladder to correspond to the racial classifications that had emerged by that time.[14] In general, this static model cannot account for how racial ascription takes place or why the racialized meanings it produces change over time. At the same time, the material aspect of coloniality has tended to drop out of the picture, especially as the concept has been taken up by other scholars.

This shift away from materialism is especially notable given the chain of theoretical debates on questions of development and the na-tion in Latin America out of which it emerged. Quijano's theoreti-cal points of reference were, in the first place, Marxist thought, above all that of the Peruvian thinker José Carlos Mariátegui, whose foun-dational text *Siete ensayos de interpretación de la realidad peruana* (1928) engaged critical questions around the legacy of Spanish colo-nialism, the "problem" of the Indian, and the centrality of land; sec-ond, debates about "internal colonialism" within newly indepen-dent nations, as formulated by Pablo González Casanova and others in the 1960s and 1970s; third, concurrent debates about Latin Amer-ican dependency and dependency theory; and finally, world-systems theory as developed by Immanuel Wallerstein.[15] Coloniality is clearly marked by all of these debates, yet at the same time constitutes a break or departure from the political economic logic in which they were framed. For Quijano and others, coloniality is primarily a mat-ter of epistemology. As such, modernity replaces capitalism as the op-erative analytical category, with Eurocentric knowledge now consti-tuting the object of decolonization or "delinking."[16] Importantly, this shift from capitalism to modernity coincided with a historical mo-ment in which Marxism seemed to have entered into terminal crisis.

Over the last two decades, in parallel to the concept of colonial-ity, a second, *historiographical* paradigm has emerged. In this vein, many scholars have begun to reconsider the operations of race and racial classifications in colonial Latin America. Situated for the most part within the discipline of history, this literature initially appeared in response to an important body of scholarship from the 1960s and 1970s that tended to treat race as if it had a constant, transhistorical, and therefore relatively transparent meaning. A telltale sign of these assumptions was the uncritical treatment of colonial census data; the "caste versus class" debate, which sought to demonstrate the primacy of one category or the other, proceeded largely on the basis of statistical measures drawn from such sources.[17]

Taking on such assumptions as anachronistic, recent historiography has called into question the applicability of modern notions of race in the colonial period. Among many other topics, scholars have examined the experience of identity among elite and subaltern populations; questioned the extent to which racial difference in fact served to divide heterogeneous plebeian populations; reconsidered racial imagery from the eighteenth century, disaggregating often compelling visual representations from the reality of social control; traced the transatlantic reconfiguration of late medieval Iberian notions of *limpieza de sangre* (purity of blood), largely rooted in discourses of Jewish and Muslim identity, as they came to configure the racial hierarchy of the so-called *sociedad de castas* (society of castes) in the Americas; and highlighted how gendered assumptions about colonized populations and the sexual economy of reproduction contributed to early modern understandings of blood and heritability. It is now clear that the colonial matrix of identity was organized around not only phenotypical markers like skin color but also numerous other considerations, including ancestry, legitimacy, honor, language, religion, and other cultural practices. Moreover, colonial populations were not straightforwardly subjected to racial control: they continuously and strategically rejected, modified, and appropriated these categories for their own purposes. These and other important contributions have historicized the social meanings of difference in the early modern period and clarified the dynamics of identification and contestation as they played out in everyday life.[18]

Although valuable for their rich empirical detail, many of these accounts employ a theory of race that suffers from two significant analytical weaknesses. On one hand, some scholars have adopted a periodizing framework that turns on a historical break between colonial (early modern? premodern?) notions of difference and their "modern" reformulations, which generally coincide with the time of political independence in the nineteenth century. According to this view, difference in colonial Latin America should be understood as "cultural" (or perhaps "socioracial") and therefore fluid. Only in the "modern" period does it become truly "racial," meaning "biological" and fixed.[19] Yet this argument takes at face value the language of nineteenth-century race scientists without acknowledging the complexities of racial thought even during that period—it is, as the medievalist David Nirenberg observes, to remain "bedeviled by the fiction of true race."[20] Especially in the case of Latin America, for example, dominant theories of race in the nineteenth and early twentieth centuries drew more heavily on Lamarck than Mendel, and as a result the belief that environment plays an active role in producing heritable traits was common.[21] More generally, the distinction between a colonial idea of difference resting on culture (often referred to as *casta*) and a "modern" idea of race resting on biology obscures the ongoing importance of culture as well as other factors like class, genealogy, geography, and religion in more contemporary racial formations. In the end, this periodization imposes an equally anachronistic reading of "modern" race as the one it attempts to resolve for its colonial counterpart.[22]

On the other hand, the emphasis on the fluidity of identity in colonial Latin America has resulted at times in a tendency to downplay the structural character of race. By privileging descriptions of difference and highlighting what could be called the micropolitics of race, such as the elements individuals looked to as signs of identity or the practices they adopted as tools of self-fashioning, some scholars lose track of domination. This is not to say, of course, that identities were entirely fixed or that negotiation did not take place. But no system of domination is absolute, and the exception, as they say, may also prove the rule. Generally speaking, tribute was in fact collected, forced labor was in fact performed, and innumerable people were in fact made to die, as we will see, before their time. These forms of coercion were distributed in large part on the basis of race.

While I draw on certain elements of each paradigm, then, this book lays out a new approach to race in colonial Latin America by shifting from *epistemology to materiality*, and from *difference to domination*. From this perspective, race no longer appears primarily as an attribute or property of a particular body but as an effect of the material practices of power. In departing from a descriptive approach to race,

I am following a recent move by contemporary theorists of ongoing racism in the wake of what Howard Winant calls the "racial break" of the post–World War II era. If race and racism continue to structure the world system today—and there can be no doubt that they do—they cannot be reduced to the domain of biology or skin color, since these frameworks have largely (though by no means entirely) receded under the hegemony of liberal and neoliberal multiculturalism.[23] In the era of what some theorists have called "neo-racism" and others "color-blind racism," categories such as class, culture, nationality, gender, and sexuality are not only co-constitutive with but indeed can be mobilized to stand in for race.[24]

For the purposes of my argument here, what is especially striking about these formulations is how resonant they are with the early modern categories of difference that the historiographical paradigm has worked so hard to isolate. If it does make sense to talk about a strictly biological regime of racial truth, and I am not convinced that it does, then it would have to be consigned to an exceptional period, bookended on either side by the primacy of what are otherwise relatively continuous "stigmata of otherness."[25] What we are left with is a reversal of the key claim of the historiographical approach—there is, if anything, *more* resonance between the mechanisms of racial domination of the present moment and those of the early modern period, not less. In my view, it is precisely these through-lines to which scholars and critics, especially those interested in antiracist praxis, must attend.

Critical race theory has elaborated more flexible accounts of race that can acknowledge changes at the level of its signs—what properly "counts" as racial—without ignoring important continuities at the level of domination. Such an analysis must go beyond epistemology. According to Michael Omi and Howard Winant's influential "racial formation" framework, race acquires meaning through a sociohistorical process of struggle between multiple racial projects, which serve as a hinge between cultural representation and social structure. In other words, these projects articulate *"an interpretation, representation, or explanation of racial dynamics"* with *"an effort to reorganize and redistribute resources along particular racial lines."*[26] Put somewhat crudely, we might say that racial projects do the ideological work of linking the economic base to the cultural superstructure. This is a valuable account of racial domination that is simultaneously constructivist and materialist, grounded on the processes of accumulation and redistribution that contribute to the construction and dismantling of racial groupings. Yet by focusing on the distribution of already existing resources, this model not only seems more appropriate for assessing the contemporary struggles of social movements vis-à-vis what Omi and Winant call the racial state, but more importantly cannot capture the full extent of the materiality of race, because it leaves out the constitutive role of violence.

From this perspective, the materiality of race would have to be framed not only in relation to resource competition but also and crucially as a concrete relation to death. In making this claim, I am drawing on the work of critics like Nikhil Pal Singh and Ruth Wilson Gilmore, whose assessments of the violent machineries of racialization, though rooted in the contemporary United States, have helped me conceptualize the mechanisms by which this process both conceptually and materially inscribes race onto bodies in other contexts as well. "The racialization of the world," writes Singh, "has helped to create and re-create 'caesuras' in human populations at both the national and global scales that have been crucial to the political management of populations. . . . To understand this, we need to recognize the technology of race as something more than skin color or biophysical essence, but precisely as those historic repertoires and cultural, spatial, and signifying systems that stigmatize and depreciate one form of humanity for the purposes of another's health, development, safety, profit, and pleasure." Similarly, for Gilmore, racism should be understood bluntly as "the state-sanctioned or extralegal production and exploitation of group-differentiated vulnerability to premature death." Race is thus the result of a system of domination that, vampirelike, extracts the life of some in order to make others live better.[27]

Framing race and racism in terms of the uneven distribution of vulnerability is helpful for three reasons. First, it invites us to consider race broadly. These formulations do not attach race to a limited set of signs, for example, but refer instead to the production of "forms of humanity" and "differentiated groups." Although this work is historically and geographically specific, then, it opens the door to comparative spatial or temporal approaches to race that are attentive to both continuities and disjunctures. Second, it pushes racial analysis away from the sphere of difference and toward a relation of domination. If race is a matter of making some people die more in order to make others live better, then it has to be read through specific repertoires of material practices. Antiracism can no longer be a question simply or primarily of affirming and celebrating those forms of difference that have traditionally been looked down on, as some forms of identity politics would have it. Third, Singh and Gilmore frame the violence of racialization in terms of not only the production of differentiated groups but also the difference between what is or has been, on one hand, and what could be or could have been, on the other—not death but *premature* death. This is a slow violence that adds up over time, by which the conditions of the everyday conspire to make life always just a little bit more constrained. It is a violence against actual bodies, to be sure, but also against their potential, against what might otherwise be. Premature death is thus an open question, an invitation to imagine a world beyond racial domination.[28]

What does not enter into the framework proposed by both Singh and Gilmore, and what an analysis of Spanish colonialism contributes to this discussion, is the flip side of vulnerability. If the roots of modern biopolitics are found in the Christian pastorate, as the following section suggests, then we also have to be attentive to the structures of care that shaped the practices of colonial governance. Spanish colonialism, as José Rabasa reminds us, was predicated not only on the hate speech of conquest but also on the "love speech" of peaceful colonization, evangelization, and protection.[29] Both discourses involve racial ideologies and give rise to racializing projects of ascription and subjectification. In colonial Mexico, the production of group-differentiated vulnerability—that is, the process of racialization—generated forms of disposability as well as paternalistic care, premised simultaneously on conversion and extraction. These were two expressions of a single modality of power, to which I now turn.

## RACE AND BIOPOLITICS

Racialization as the politics of death cannot be detached from the biopolitics of life. According to the historical analysis that Michel Foucault first began to lay out in the mid-1970s, political modernity is characterized by the emergence of a new form of power, distinct from the sovereign power that had been dominant up to that point: "The right of sovereignty was the right to take life or let live. And then this new right is established: the right to make live and to let die." Sovereign power, "the right to take life or let live," is exercised by the sword. Faced with a given transgression of his law, the sovereign can decide to kill or not to kill, that is, to spare the life of the perpetrator. This is the full extent of the sovereign's power—a negative power not over life but strictly over death. But beginning in the sixteenth century, at the "threshold of modernity," a new form of power, borrowing and expanding on the techniques of the Christian pastorate, began to operate in conjunction with the emergence of modern capitalism. It did so first at the level of the individual, using discipline to optimize the body's forces and integrate them effectively and efficiently into various processes of production, and later at the level of the population, intervening in abstract biological processes and rhythms in order to foster life and maximize vitality. In contrast to "taking life," the negative capacity of sovereignty, the shift to "making live" captures the productive orientation of biopolitical forms of modern power.[30]

But the rise of an affirmative biopolitics, deeply invested in the production of life, does not mean that the negative power of sovereignty over death declines, disappears, or becomes entirely obsolete. Although his depiction is conceptually enigmatic, Foucault suggests that this historical shift is marked by "overlappings, interactions, and echoes." The biopolitical state never stops drawing on the techniques of sovereignty. This, importantly, is where racism comes into play. Knowledge is for cutting, as Foucault remarks elsewhere, and racism operates precisely in this way, by "introducing a break into the domain of life that is under power's control: the break between what must live and what must die." The ancient logic of warfare, by which one side confronts and must destroy another in order to survive in battle, is transformed into a new logic of biopower that operates on the basis of racial hierarchy, linking the elimination of inferior races with the improvement, optimization, and purification of life in its most general sense. Death is deployed, in other words, in the interest of life: "massacres have become vital."[31]

Although Foucault's work is almost entirely centered on Europe, as many critics have observed, this is one of the few points where he addresses the question of colonialism explicitly: "Racism first develops with colonization, or in other words, with colonizing genocide." To the extent that it is subsequently transferred to Europe, racism serves as a paradigmatic example of the "boomerang effect" by which material practices of power tested in the course of colonization are returned to and deployed in the metropole.[32] Taking this argument seriously means considering the biopolitical formations that began to emerge prior to the nineteenth century, and certainly prior to the rise of the paradigmatic biopolitical state in Nazi Germany.[33] Indeed, Foucault seems to acknowledge as much. "I am certainly not saying that racism was invented at this time," he writes in reference to the nineteenth century. "It had already been in existence for a very long time. But I think it functioned elsewhere."[34] This colonial "elsewhere" is the specter that haunts Foucault's work.

Yet space seems to disappear from Foucault's work at almost exactly the moment that the biopolitics of population emerges. Admittedly, he is somewhat ambiguous here as well. His 1977–1978 lecture course, *Security, Territory, Population*, begins by considering the material ways in which sovereign power, discipline, and biopolitics have historically organized urban space. Yet territory quickly drops out of his analysis. By the fourth lecture—the famous "governmentality" lecture that would be popularized in English long before the publication of the full course—the initial conceptual organization has been recast, the category of "territory" replaced with that of "government." The logic of this move registers clearly in Foucault's pivotal reading of Machiavelli, in which he argues that sovereignty operates primarily over territory and only secondarily over the people who inhabit it: "The territory really is the fundamental element both of Machiavelli's principality and of the juridical sovereignty of the sovereign as defined by philosophers or legal theorists." In contrast, "government in no way refers to territory. One governs things." Like the pastoral power from which they emerge, governmental techniques are thus increasingly exercised over a flocklike web of relations. Although Foucault attempts to give nuance to this historical formulation, just as he affirms that the emergence of positive forms of discipline and biopolitics did not mean the supersession of the negative modality of sovereign power, he does not return to the subject of territory in his lectures.[35]

One reason Giorgio Agamben's rereading of Foucault is helpful here is precisely that it returns to the question of space. Drawing on the work of the political theorist Carl Schmitt, Agamben lays out a metaphysical account of sovereignty that turns on the concept of the state of exception. In *Political Theology* (1922), Schmitt defines sovereignty on the basis of the capacity to decide on the exception, that is, to suspend the normal legal order. In this account, the state of exception is fundamentally a temporal category, although it is not necessarily temporary—in fact, Schmitt claims that the exception is always already embedded in the liberal constitutional order. Yet in his later work, primarily *The Nomos of the Earth* (1950), Schmitt begins to approach the question of sovereignty and the exception in spatial terms. There he argues that the international order that emerged in the sixteenth and seventeenth centuries was based on the consolidation of territorial states in Europe. The *jus publicum Europaeum*, in other words, made possible a "bracketing" of war between equivalent sovereigns. However, the production of this "internal" stability depended on the displacement of war to Europe's constitutive outsides, namely colonial space. Deemed juridically empty, this space "beyond the line" became available for occupation and was constituted as a zone where the only law was force. The shift in the form of the exception from a temporal to a spatial category decenters the figure of the sovereign, whose capacity to decide on the suspension of the rule is so central in Schmitt's earlier writings. In the sphere of imperial sovereignty, the decisionist paradigm is replaced by a depersonalized formation of sovereignty rooted in the ordering logic that gives the space of modernity its meaning.[36]

Agamben acknowledges Schmitt's analysis of the space of exception and even attaches it to the New World, "which was identified with the state of nature in which everything is possible."[37] Yet he does not follow through on the provocative implications of Schmitt's thesis linking the sovereign exception to colonial space. This thread is only later taken up by Achille Mbembe in his important work on necropolitics. By foregrounding both racism and colonialism, Mbembe expands on the work of Foucault and Agamben and clarifies the spatial underpinnings of any biopolitical regime. A global distribution of those who must live and those who must die is always already at stake in the consolidation of a politics based on the management of life and death. Likening colonial space to the frontier, he writes that "the colonies are the location par excellence where the controls and guarantees of juridical order can be suspended—the zone where the violence of the state of exception is deemed to operate in the service of 'civilization.'"[38] The convergence of space and race, the colony and the savage, is the flip side of the *jus publicum* in Europe.

Mbembe is most helpful here for conceptualizing the relation between biopolitics and space because his analysis ultimately delineates the construction of colonial space as a historical process rather than an ontological determination. Colonization is not merely the occupation of space but also its radical reorganization. Referencing the late modern occupation of Palestine, he explains:

> The writing of new spatial relations (territorialization) was, ultimately, tantamount to the production of boundaries and hierarchies, zones and enclaves; the subversion of existing property arrangements; the classification of people according to different categories; resource extraction; and, finally, the manufacturing of a large reservoir of cultural imaginaries. These imaginaries gave meaning to the enactment of differential rights to differing categories of people for different purposes within the same space; in brief, the exercise of sovereignty. Space was therefore the raw material of sovereignty and the violence it carried with it.[39]

What does "the writing of new spatial relations" look like? How—through which mechanisms—is space territorialized? Beyond conquest and military occupation, beyond the production and circulation of representations (travel writing, cartography, and so on), and beyond legal procedures and sovereign decisions, the production of territory must also, if not primarily, be understood as a process that intervenes in and shapes the landscape in material ways. Mbembe examines, for example, a number of specific techniques used by the Israeli state to "splinter" Palestinian space. A great deal of the everyday violence of occupation is aimed at dismantling infrastructures—tearing up roads and airport runways, demolishing electric grids, destroying waste disposal systems, and so on. But occupation also has a productive dimension, which includes the construction of strategic walls as well as Jewish-only roads, bridges, and tunnels that produce a three-dimensional network integrating settlements in the occupied territories into Israel proper. In other words, the territorialization of colonial space is fundamentally a question of infrastructure.[40]

## INFRASTRUCTURES OF RACE

Located at the intersection of space and materiality, infrastructure refers to the material conditions of possibility for the circulation of people, things, and knowledge. Although infrastructure has long been an object of technical study, over the last two decades the concept has begun to receive critical attention in a growing number of other fields, including anthropology, history, and geography.[41] This new scholarship has generated a number of important insights regarding infrastructure's peculiar character. For one thing, there is the issue of visibility. What distinguishes infrastructure from technology is its tendency to become normalized and fade from view, operating just "beneath" (*infra*) the surface of the phenomenal world while facilitating the operations on which that world depends. Through this assemblage of pipes, tubes, cables, wires, and tunnels flow the energy, water, waste, and data that enable, shape, and regulate the practices of modern social existence. Thus the commonplace that infrastructure becomes visible only when it fails—these enabling conditions abruptly acquire an immediate and inescapable presence precisely because of their absence.[42]

Additionally, infrastructure is a relational concept. What appears as infrastructure—what *dis*appears from view—necessarily does so in relation to specific subject positions or practices. What constitutes infrastructure for some, facilitating their circulation through space, may constitute an obstacle or object of attention for others. The anthropologist Susan Leigh Star points to the example of a person in a wheelchair, for whom "the stairs and doorjamb in front of a building are not seamless subtenders of use, but barriers." Similarly, for the indigenous laborers forced to perform the dirty and dangerous work of cleaning out Mexico City's canals, as discussed in chapter 3, these hydraulic systems were far from invisible. This differential experience of infrastructure also becomes apparent with regard to formation of communities. Infrastructures are learned, and the habitual practices that congeal around them are themselves constructive of collective norms. If familiarity can generate a shared sense of belonging to a community of users, engaging with unfamiliar infrastructures can yield the unsettling sense of being out of place.[43]

To be clear, infrastructure can serve not only as a signal of identity or belonging—not knowing how to use a particular system immediately marks one as an outsider—but also as a condition of possibility for the emergence of groupness as such, engendering social relations and structures of feeling. Reflecting on Benedict Anderson's formulation of the nation as an "imagined community," the archaeologist Bjørnar Olsen observes that what is often left out or minimized in accounts of social construction are precisely the things on which this process depends—among them infrastructural things, like "print machines, newspapers, telephone and railroad lines, roads, coastal steamers, geological surveys, post offices, national museums, stamps, maps, trigonometric points, border fences, and custom points." When this scholarship does look at things, it largely reads them in terms of representation, as symbolic of underlying meanings. In contrast, Olsen calls for a turn to "the brigades of nonhuman actors that constitute the very condition of the possibility for such large-scale social institutions to be imagined, implemented, reproduced, and remembered."[44] By shaping social relations and facilitating the consolidation of groups, infrastructure becomes a material foundation that sets in motion, guides, and sustains processes such as the formation of national identities and, as I argue here, racialization.

What is the relation, then, between infrastructure and determination? One of the major debates within twentieth-century Marxism concerned the nature of the link between the economic "base," or mode of production, and the diverse set of political and cultural products viewed as "superstructure."[45] Marx's views were far more complex than is often assumed, but the point is that architectural metaphors served to organize a social imaginary on the basis of an array of objects that were understood as either supportive or supported, either determining or determined. From the late nineteenth century on, "infrastructure" began to appear in French Marxist literature as a "somewhat incorrect" translation of the German word *basis* originally employed by Marx.[46] This metaphorical usage, however, flattens infrastructure's ambiguous character. By binding people, things, and knowledge into territorialized systems of production and circulation, infrastructure is both the condensation of an ideological project and a participant in the realization of that project. In other words, what we might call "actually existing infrastructures" are imagined, designed, and constructed by people and at the same time configure the field of possible actions and potential dispositions for human and nonhuman objects.[47]

In his influential study *The Production of Space*, first published in French in 1974, the geographer Henri Lefebvre turns precisely to the colonial Latin American city in order to reframe the schematic division between base and superstructure. In general terms, he argues, space is not an empty container or neutral platform on which social processes are straightforwardly staged, but itself a product of historically contingent social processes. Spanish colonization in particular transformed American space through an array of specific interventions. Yet the colonial city, Lefebvre insists, should be understood as not only an "artificial product" but also an "instrument of production," since it constituted part of a project aimed at facilitating new modes of extraction: "A superstructure foreign to the original space serves as a political means of introducing a social and economic structure in such a way that it may gain a foothold and indeed establish its 'base' in a particular locality." Certain material forms— roads, churches, ports, facades—are thus simultaneously superstructural and infrastructural insofar as they both express and enable relations of domination and accumulation.[48]

This duality partly explains why infrastructures, as the anthropologist Brian Larkin notes, are so "conceptually unruly."[49] If infrastructures are simultaneously produced and productive, determined and determining, critics must attend both to the processes through which they are deployed and to those that unfold as a result, as well as to their vulnerability to decay or collapse and their capacity to endure over time. This is an especially important consideration for colonial Latin American studies, since recent scholarship on infrastructure tends to privilege a limited concept of modernity rooted (as with much of the historiography on race) in the nineteenth century. No doubt this is a period characterized by post-Enlightenment liberalism, which linked circulation to progress, and by the emergence of the first large technical systems, including telegraph cables and shipping canals. But as with any periodization, this move generates certain exclusions. By the second half of the sixteenth century, for example, an assemblage of colonial infrastructures—including not only the gridded cities examined by Lefebvre but also ports and roads, way stations for llama and mule trains, dams, canals, water reservoirs for mining and metal production, and systems of standardization, among many others—was already beginning to weave Spain's American territories into a globalized world.[50] The point here is not to quibble about chronology but to highlight a structural tendency embedded in infrastructure's material form. Infrastructure does not emerge out of nowhere but tends to cohere around the accretions that precede it. "It wrestles with the inertia of the installed base and inherits strengths and limitations from that base," writes Star. "Optical fibers run along old railroad lines."[51] If this is in fact a tendency of infrastructure in general, perhaps the large-scale technical systems of nineteenth- and twentieth-century modernity that so dazzle contemporary scholars should not be detached from the historical foundations on which they rest. To repurpose Marx's famous dictum, these infrastructural pasts weigh like a nightmare on the circulation of the present.[52] They are a powerful reminder that certain material structures and practices can endure the vicissitudes of history and politics. And if race itself has an infrastructural function, it may continue to operate in this way as well.

THIS BOOK IS DIVIDED INTO four chapters that proceed in loosely chronological order, from the beginning to the end of the colonial period, and together trace a genealogy of concentration in colonial Mexico. Each chapter examines a paradigmatic case of concentration located at a specific junction of form and practice, architecture and technique—centralized towns (*congregación*), disciplinary institutions (*recogimiento*), segregated districts (*separación*), and general collections (*colección*). These cases are by no means exhaustive, nor are they intended to chart a narrative of superseding stages, such that congregation is replaced by enclosure, which in turn is followed by segregation and finally collection. Instead, the projects should be read as scaffolded, either explicitly or implicitly referring to, drawing from, building on, and reactivating those that came before them in the face of the contradictions generated by colonial rule. Moreover, these episodes capture a shift or expansion at the level of scale or complexity with regard to their racial effects, from the foundational categories of Indian and Mestizo in the sixteenth and early seventeenth centuries to the emergent theories of mestizaje and (racialized) life from the end of the seventeenth through the beginning of the nineteenth. The book thus attends to the always incomplete yet nevertheless productive techniques by which colonial institutions sought to know and manage the populations under their authority and in doing so effectively racialized them.

Chapter 1 examines the policy of *congregación*, or congregation, as implemented during the first century of colonial rule in Mexico. The colonial authorities saw the "dispersion" of indigenous communities as one of the main obstacles to effective evangelization and extraction. As the violence of the conquest, forced labor, and disease took a massive toll on the indigenous population, the "emptiness" that had been projected onto colonial space began to acquire a material character. The response of the colonial state, supported by missionaries such as Toribio de Benavente (better known as Motolinía), Diego Valadés, and Gerónimo de Mendieta, was to resettle indigenous communities into centralized, orderly towns under the authorities' watchful gaze. Laid out along a regular, orthogonal grid and inserted into regional and global markets, the congregation facilitated Christianization and the extraction of tribute and labor. But it also produced the infrastructural ground for the consolidation of the "Indian" as a meaningful category of identity. It was not only the violence of the conquest and the pillaging of the conquistadors that characterized the process of primitive accumulation, then, but also a series of productive interventions that reconfigured colonial space and racialized the bodies that inhabited it.

If the Indian was characterized by dispersion, the Mestizo emerged as a figure of unregulated and unproductive circulation. Chapter 2 turns to this racialization process by analyzing the practice of *recogimiento,* or enclosure, as developed at the Mexico City–based Colegio de San Juan de Letrán, which was established in the middle of the sixteenth century. This was a moment in which the project of evangelization was entering into crisis. Part of the problem was the difficulty that Spanish priests had in mastering the subtleties of indigenous languages and cultural practices; this obstacle was what the Colegio sought to overcome, by gathering up vagabond/Mestizo boys who were purportedly "lost" in the countryside and subjecting them to a highly regulated set of disciplinary practices rooted in a specific architectural space. Deemed reliably Christian owing to the influence of their Spanish fathers, and fluent in indigenous languages owing to their indigenous mothers, these children appeared as potential missionaries par excellence, far more effective than even the most highly trained Spaniard. Yet by the end of the century this project had collapsed under its own weight, and royal orders prohibited the ordination of Mestizo priests throughout the Americas. Enclosure could turn these children into workers and husbands, but it could not entirely erase the threat of heresy from the newly constituted Mestizo body.

Whereas the first two chapters highlight the productive work of colonial infrastructures of concentration, chapter 3 approaches the same question from the opposite direction: what happens when racial infrastructures fail? On June 8, 1692, in the context of widespread food shortages, a massive riot in the center of Mexico City left shops looted, government buildings destroyed, and the royal palace in smoldering ruins. Many colonial elites blamed the violence on drunken Indians and pointed specifically to the internal migration of the indigenous population to the city center, or *traza,* designated a non-Indian space, from the surrounding districts to which they were supposed to be consigned. In response, the viceroy enlisted a group of *letrados* (lettered elites), including the Creole polymath Carlos de Sigüenza y Góngora and the priests of the city's Indian parishes, like the Franciscan friar Agustín de Vetancurt, to develop a policy of *separación*, or segregation, that would shore up the racial order and thereby secure colonial rule. Everyone supported segregation, but segregation meant different things to different people. Some hoped to rescue the category of the Spaniard, while others were more invested in maintaining its Indian counterpart. In each case, however, what appeared on the other side of this line of demarcation was what contemporaries had begun to call the "Plebe." Defined by "mixture" and formally identical to the Mestizo according to the conventional theory of mestizaje today, this monstrous collective body emerges as the excess or residue of infrastructural collapse.

Finally, chapter 4 shows how concentration became a science. If active resistance had limited or undermined the viability of earlier concentration projects, other forms of life might prove more manageable—and no less tied to the question of race. This chapter examines the paradigmatic form of concentration during the eighteenth century: the *colección*, or general collection. Specifically, it examines the rise of imperial botany and the establishment of a botanical garden in Mexico City, which emerged as an extension of but also in contrast to its metropolitan counterpart in Madrid. Drawing on the work of Enlightenment scientists like Casimiro Gómez Ortega, Vicente Cervantes, and Alexander von Humboldt, the chapter contrasts the spatial politics of imperial botany on both sides of the Atlantic. While the Madrid garden sought to adopt new technologies like greenhouses to facilitate the acclimatization and commercialization of plants from the colonies, the Mexico City garden took advantage of the topography of Chapultepec Hill, which contained, according to its advocates, all of the diverse microclimates found in New Spain. As a result, it seemed to allow for the concentration of the totality of colonial plant life. This increasingly calculated approach to the environment and its relation to living beings, moreover, engendered reflections on human differentiation and race. If Foucault famously argues that the concept of "life" emerged from the science of comparative anatomy developed on European dissection tables, this chapter posits an alternative colonial narrative focused on the rise of a new science of racialized life in Humboldt's plant geography, based in part on his visits to the botanical gardens of the Spanish empire. There has never been a transcendent concept of life—it is always already racialized from the historical moment at which it begins to appear.

Concentration thus neither began nor ended with General Weyler's reconcentration camps. The dense repertoire of forms and practices of concentration that had developed over the course of four centuries of Spanish rule in colonial Mexico specifically and Latin America more generally converged not only in the camps of late colonial Cuba but also in multiple forms deployed by the Mexican state since political independence. In the epilogue, I examine the recuperation of these colonial techniques in contemporary Mexico. From the *aldeas vietnamitas* (Vietnamese villages) in the state of Guerrero during the "dirty war" of the 1970s to the twenty-first-century *ciudades rurales sustentables* (sustainable rural cities) deployed in the states of Chiapas and Puebla, the Mexican state continues to govern through the spatial politics of concentration. A counterinsurgency framework, extrapolating from the experience of the nineteenth-century reconcentration camp, can only partially explain these projects. It is the racialized discourse of vulnerability—the combination of disposability and care—that continues to characterize concentration today.

# CHAPTER I

# CONGREGATION: URBANIZATION AND THE CONSTRUCTION OF THE INDIAN

*To police and to urbanize is the same thing.*
MICHEL FOUCAULT, *SECURITY, TERRITORY, POPULATION*

IN A LETTER TO CHARLES V dated May 15, 1550, the Franciscan friar Toribio de Benavente, better known as Motolinía, describes space as one of the main obstacles to the so-called spiritual conquest of Mexico. Indigenous communities, he writes, are "tan apartados . . . y puestos en sitios ásperos y dificultosos" (very isolated . . . and located in harsh and difficult places), but goes on to suggest that

> esto se podría remediar en parte con hacer que se juntasen en pueblos como están en España, y no sería pequeño provecho para la dotrina y polecía humana, porque como agora están muchos dellos más viven como salvajes que como hombres, y no sabemos cómo de otra manera ellos puedan ser bien instruídos e informados en las cosas de Dios. [this could be remedied in part by gathering them in towns as they are in Spain, and it would not be of small benefit for evangelization and human order, because in their current state many live more like savages than men, and we do not know by what other means they might be instructed and informed of the things of God.][1]

Motolinía's letter activates a series of oppositions that are common to colonial discourse, such as the distinction between Spain and America, on one hand, and the human and the savage, on the other. These tropes are framed by what the Franciscan describes as the generalized "emptiness" of colonial space, which poses both a problem and an opportunity for colonial rule. The absence of a regularized spatial order impedes extraction as well as evangelization (which is obviously the main concern here), yet at the same time it makes possible and indeed necessary a radical restructuring of the territories that had only recently been incorporated into the Spanish empire.

American space was not actually empty, of course, but rather was produced as "empty" in at least two ways. First, European colonizers not only perceived the territory into which they ventured as "free" in a Schmittian sense, that is, open for occupation, but in fact occupied it on the basis of that perception. Outside of a handful of urban areas, what the Spaniards saw did not register as legitimate political communities or lands inhabited according to European norms of property and human sociability. In his work on archaeological practice, Gustavo Verdesio notes that indigenous interventions in the landscape are often overlooked because they correspond neither to familiar European models nor to a Western sense of artifice. Owing to what Verdesio calls the Western "regime of visibility," practical, effective, and often complex infrastructures, such as fisheries and irrigation systems, are rendered invisible to Western observers. They blend into the backdrop of the so-called natural world, entirely detached from human activity and agency. This effect is similar to the one that occurred with regard to indigenous settlement patterns in the sixteenth century. Forms of land occupation and social relations that did not conform to Spanish expectations were imperceptible and thus erased.[2]

Second, Spanish colonialism inaugurated a violent process of dispossession that literally "emptied" many areas of indigenous people and even, in numerous cases, of the material traces they left behind. Dispossession took various forms, the most visible being the holocaust of epidemic disease, but other policies that were far more intentional contributed significantly as well. Paradoxically, then, the restructuring of colonial space was justified on the basis that colonial space was already empty and simultaneously produced colonial space as empty and thus available for occupation. This is similar to the circular logic of a line of Spanish argumentation that justified the conquest of Mexico by claiming that the ease of Cortés's victory was proof enough of the indigenous people's natural servitude.[3]

The program of "congregation" (congregación) in New Spain, also called reducción, occupies a unique place in the production of colonial space. Much like Motolinía's proposal, this policy sought to forcibly resettle "dispersed" indigenous communities into centralized towns under the watchful gaze of the colonial authorities. Insofar as it displaced indigenous peasants from the means of subsistence and contributed to the gradual consolidation of their former lands in the hands of Spanish property owners, congregation operated as a classic mechanism of primitive accumulation, much like the enclosures Marx describes at the end of the first volume of *Capital*. In *Caliban and the Witch*, however, Silvia Federici argues that primitive accumulation involves other parallel dispossessions as well: "Primitive accumulation, then, was not simply an accumulation and concentration of exploitable workers and capital. It was *also an accumulation of differences and divisions within the working class*, whereby hierarchies built upon gender, as well as 'race' and age, became constitutive of class rule and the formation of the modern proletariat."[4] Federici's argument deals primarily with gender—she is most interested in the ways in which women were stripped of authority and their bodies naturalized as reproductive machines. Building on her insight, this chapter shows how congregation contributed to the construction of the Indian as an example of a racialization process that not only coincided with some of the classic forms of primitive accumulation seen in Marx but also functioned as a form of primitive accumulation in its own right.

What is the "Indian" but a bundle of qualities, capacities, and obligations occupying a specific location in a field of social relations? Over the course of the century bracketed on one end by the founding of Vasco de Quiroga's "hospital-towns" in the early 1530s and on the other by the official prohibition of the labor draft known as *repartimiento* in 1632, the Indian emerged as a meaningful category of identity that was both ascribed to individual and collective bodies and subjectively lived. In this way, a homogeneous population characterized, among other things, by its obligation to pay a certain amount of tribute and perform a certain amount of forced labor was fashioned out of a heterogeneous mosaic of indigenous forms of humanity. This ethnogenetic process of what could be called "primitive *mestizaje*" explodes the conventional understanding of mestizaje based on a mythical encounter between Spaniard and Indian by revealing that in fact there was no Indian at that encounter—the Indian was the product, rather, of a century of material practices that turned on the deployment of violence and care.[5]

## PERIODIZING CONGREGATION

Most historians have taken for granted that congregation proceeded in two distinct phases, the first in the mid-sixteenth century, from about 1550 to 1564, and the second at the turn of the century, from about 1598 to 1607. A distinct character is attributed to each phase—the first is often labeled a "failure," the second a "success." This historiographic trend is partly a product of the specific history of the colonial archive's formation. The final years of the sixteenth century saw the establishment of an institutional body called the Sala de Congregaciones, which was charged with carrying out the program and documenting its implementation. This documentation was stored in the Sala's own archive and later incorporated into the holdings of the Archivo General de la Nación (AGN) under the title "Congregaciones." At the AGN today, a search for "congregación" in the archive's database primarily turns up these records. As a result, it is much easier for historians to access these later instances of congregation, and this thicker archival trace has been read as a sign of efficacy and intensity. In the 1970s, however, historians like Peter Gerhard began to do the difficult work of combing through other sections of the AGN for documentation regarding earlier efforts to congregate indigenous communities. Gerhard, who identified 163 congregations that were carried out before 1570, argued that these communities constitute the majority of settlements in central and southern Mexico today.[6]

This documentary evidence of earlier congregations, however, has not substantively altered the dominant narrative, owing to the strength of a second, parallel distinction that treats the key difference between the "two phases" of congregation as a function of the institutional actor responsible for each: the first is associated with the mendicant orders, largely Franciscans and Dominicans, the second with the colonial state. Often it is suggested that the mendicants supported the first phase of congregation but opposed the second. Secularization thus serves to explain the failure of the "first phase" of the program, since it was only when the colonial state stepped in that resettlement supposedly succeeded. The implications are twofold: first, that the clergy were incapable of implementing such a program, since their obsession with the spiritual world kept them from being effective managers of the temporal; and second, that there is a meaningful analytic distinction between the religious orders and the colonial state with regard to congregation. At stake, then, are not only the historical impacts but also the political-theological foundations of this policy.[7]

This chapter proposes a different approach to congregation. Building on the work of Mexican historians like Ernesto de la Torre Villar, Marcelo Ramírez Ruiz, and Federico Fernández Christlieb, I argue that congregation should not be historiographically divided into two successive and politically discrete "phases" but treated as a single program that was enacted continuously, if intermittently and unevenly, over roughly the first century of colonial rule, from about 1530 to 1635.[8] This approach avoids the dilemma posed by communities whose congregation occurred outside of either "phase," such as the "hospital-towns" established by Vasco de Quiroga in the 1530s or the congregation of Texupa in what is today the state of Oaxaca in the 1570s, both of which I discuss later. There is also a methodological question here that has to do with defining the object of study, whether the relevant unit of analysis is "central Mexico," "New Spain," or "Spanish America" at large. After all, the *reducción general* of Peru, which began with the arrival of Viceroy Francisco de Toledo, was primarily carried out, as in Texupa, during the 1570s. Indeed, the early experience of congregation in New Spain influenced the general resettlement in Peru, and likewise the techniques deployed in Peru shaped later efforts at congregation in New Spain. In a 1604 report for his successor, for example, the Viceroy Conde de Monterrey notes that he has studied and learned from the *reducciones* in Peru. While Toledo deserves "la gloria de aver Acometido y Vencido el prim.º un yntento tan Util y tan dificultosso" (the glory of having been the first to take up and succeed in so useful and difficult an effort), he implemented the policy too rapidly and forcefully, thus provoking significant resistance. In New Spain, however, the viceroy continues, the program has been implemented "con tanta seguridad de conçiençia y suavidad" (conscientiously and smoothly) and therefore "a ressultado aqui mucho menos clamor y ruido del q̃ ubo alla" (has yielded far fewer complaints and commotion here than there).[9] As congregation was adapted over time, partly as a result of resistance and negotiation by the indigenous population, its proponents understood it as part of a general logic of early colonial rule rather than a specific policy unfolding at a specific moment in a specific place—concentration constituted both an organizing principle and a material practice of Spanish imperial reason, linked across space and time.[10]

Additionally, this approach complicates "just so" stories of secularization in colonial Mexico. Certainly, there were mendicants who opposed later congregations, but as we will see, there were also those who supported them; likewise, some opposed even the earlier ones.[11]

It could be said that the religious orders were involved in "governance," just as the colonial state was involved in "religion." But it would be more accurate to say that in the sixteenth century there was in fact no easy way to separate "governance" from "religion," that these categories were not discrete and autonomous but largely integrated within a general political rationality and corresponding set of practices. Following Foucault, I am more interested in understanding this rationality, the common elements that pertain to both the spiritual and temporal domains, than in dividing the program into coherent stages or phases through classification. Read in this way, congregation appears as a moment of what Foucault describes as the early modern intensification and expansion of pastoral power. It was primarily in colonial space, moreover, that this intensification had to occur.

### FROM PASTORAL POWER TO POLICE

In a letter to Charles V written in early 1552, the Franciscan Pedro de Gante begs the king to ensure the presence of "pastores para sus ovejas" (pastors for their sheep) and goes on to clarify that in order to do so it will be absolutely necessary to make sure that "se junten los yndios y no estén derramados por los montes" (the Indians are gathered and not dispersed throughout the forests), where they would be able to continue their idolatrous practices. In contrast, "de estar juntos y visitallos, se sigue christiandad y provecho á sus ánimas é cuerpos y que no se mueran sin fee é baptismo é sin conoçer á Dios" (by being gathered together and visited, Christianity will follow and benefit their souls and bodies, and they will not die without faith and baptism and without knowing God).[12] Gante is referring, of course, to the policy of congregation in the early years of its official backing by the colonial state. It should come as no surprise that the Franciscan would frame his call for congregation as a pastoral mechanism, not only because the trope of the pastor and his flock was common at the time but also because this imagery was embedded in the discourse of congregation from the start. After all, the etymological roots of the Latin word *congregare* are *con* (together) and *grex* (flock). To congregate quite literally means to gather and thus constitute the flock. Without the pastor who congregates—without congregation—the flock is just a dream. To put it another way, congregation is a pastoral technology par excellence.

The "pastoral power" characteristic of early Christianity occupies an important place in Foucault's genealogy of the modern state. Under the Christian pastorate, he argues, power has three main characteristics: first, it operates not over a fixed territory but on a flock in movement; second, it is essentially beneficent, the entirety of its operations dedicated to caring for the flock rather than divided up among other duties and practices; and third, it simultaneously individualizes and totalizes, treating the flock as a whole composed of individuals. For Foucault, the emergence of the modern state is tied not to a process of secularization, by which Christianity gradually disappears and is replaced by the state, but to the expansion and intensification of the pastoral beyond the sphere of the spiritual—a process of governmentalization by which the *ratio pastoralis* or "pastoral of souls" becomes the *ratio gubernatoria* or "government of men."[13]

According to Foucault's periodization, this intensification began in the late Middle Ages and accelerated during the sixteenth century as pastoral power came to supplement the sovereign's negative power over death with a positive power over life: "The essential objective of pastoral power is the salvation (*salut*) of the flock."[14] The French word *salut*, as the translator Graham Burchell notes of this passage, has both a spiritual and a temporal sense, as in the English word "safety." This double meaning is significant because it highlights the continuity between the Christian pastorate and the state's rationalization of pastoral power in the form of what Foucault calls the theory of police. While the former is aimed at guiding the flock to "salvation" in the next world, the latter, in contrast, turns to what could be called maximizing the flock's "safety" in this world. As Foucault observes, "In this context, the word 'salvation' takes on different meanings: health, well-being (that is, sufficient wealth, standard of living), security, protection against accidents. A series of 'worldly' aims took the place of the religious aims of the traditional pastorate."[15] What smooths this transition, furthermore, is the expansion of the horizon of care, which blurs together these dual senses of salvation.

Both of these dimensions of salvation are at the heart of the project of congregation, which turned on the urbanization of the indigenous population and the "geometrization" of colonial space.[16] During the Renaissance, European humanists began to recuperate the writings of classical authorities as the ideal against which to measure contemporary architecture and urban planning. Although Vitruvius's *De architectura* was not translated into Spanish until 1582, Roman architectural thought arrived via influential late medieval and early modern thinkers like Leon Battista Alberti in *De re aedificatoria*, published in Italy in 1485, and Diego de Sagredo in his vernacular *Medidas del romano*, published in Madrid in 1526. These works drew on the philosophical foundations provided by Neoplatonism as filtered through Plato's translator Marsilio Ficino, who viewed architecture as an art that was inseparable from the ideals of Platonic form. Thus, the geometrical character of the built environment, and by extension of the city, came to embody the principles of beauty, order, and reason.[17]

But this Renaissance ideal could not be realized on the Iberian Peninsula, where cities had emerged gradually, without a unified plan, and as such yielded a dense but irregular built environment composed of layers upon layers of accumulated materials. This sedimentation presented a major obstacle to utopian planners who, with few exceptions, were left to design cities in their minds instead of building them on the ground. It was only in the New World that this utopian project could effectively be implemented. The Spaniards who traveled to the Americas carried with them a set of aesthetic assumptions influenced by these Renaissance ideals as well as printed texts to aid and inspire them in their task.[18] As Ángel Rama has argued, upon crossing the Atlantic the conquistadors entered into "una nueva distribución del espacio que encuadraba un nuevo modo de vida, el cual ya no era el que habían conocido en sus orígenes peninsulares" (a new distribution of space that framed a new way of life, which was no longer the one they had known in their peninsular home). American space was perceived as *tabula rasa*, a blank slate or void on which an entirely new order could be imposed.[19]

Even where the Spanish did not perceive American space as empty— the marvelous view of Tenochtitlan afforded to Cortés and Bernal Díaz del Castillo, for example, stands out—the urban materials accumulated there appeared to have a different character than their European counterparts. In colonial space, these residues of human life were seen not as deeply rooted but as strikingly superficial, easy to sweep away and replace or reorganize. This doubt about the fixedness of pre-Hispanic materials was intensified by the catastrophic violence and death that accompanied the conquest and its aftermath, which brought the fantasy of emptiness closer to reality.

The emptiness of colonial space was thus the condition of possibility for its restructuring. A century before Descartes employed the orderly, geometrical city as a metaphorical grounding for his *ego cogito*, and a half-century before Philip II's famous *ordenanzas* on city plan-

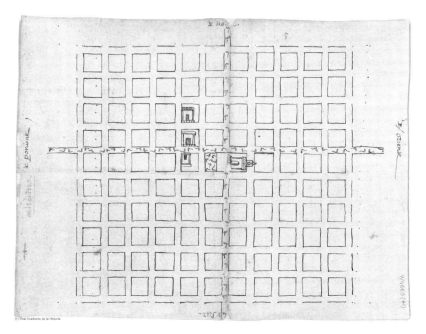

FIGURE 1.1. Map of Nochixtlan (1581). Real Academia de la Historia (C-028-008).
© Real Academia de la Historia, Madrid, Spain.

ning in the Americas were codified in 1573, the Spanish were already
deploying a colonial *ego aedifico*, plotting and building gridded cities *a cordel y regla* in the New World.[20] Mexico City was laid out
over the ruins of Tenochtitlan by a skilled *jumétrico*, a specialist in
applied geometry and topography, in 1523.[21] But it was congregation
that was primarily responsible for diffusing the grid across the colonial landscape. The map of Nochixtlan, drawn in ink by an indigenous mapmaker in 1579, offers an exceptionally clear visualization
of the spatial reorganization constitutive of this shift (figure 1.1). Unlike most of the maps that were painted around this time as part of
the information-gathering project known as the *Relaciones geográficas*, this image contains no natural toponyms but consists entirely of
a stripped-down, ten-by-eleven grid, carefully measured and laid out
for urbanization.[22] Near the center there is a church and plaza filled
with footprints, suggesting a busy marketplace; a handful of buildings occupy other nearby blocks. An axis of footprints bisects the
map, intersecting next to the central plaza and extending out from
the grid toward the edge of the paper on each side, where the car-
dinal directions are labeled. Additional lines at the edge of the grid

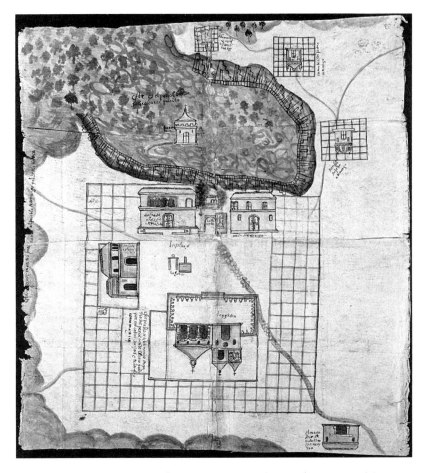

FIGURE 1.2. Map of Teutenango (1582; AGI, Mapas y Planos 33). Courtesy of the Ministerio de Educación, Cultura y Deporte, Archivo General de Indias, Seville.

suggest that it could easily be extended into the blank space that surrounds it. For Kevin Terraciano, the Nochixtlan map is more suggestive of a "colonial ghost town" than a lived space, but he acknowledges that the footprints constitute "evidence of life."[23] I would add that the skeletal trace evokes precisely the emptiness that made congregation thinkable. Each congregation was specifically required to imitate the checkerboard layout of Mexico City, and as suggested by the 1582 map of Teutenango, also painted by an indigenous *tlacuilo* (scribe), orderly grids bloomed like geometric flowers throughout the countryside (figure 1.2).

While congregation sought to make colonial space legible, the orthogonal grid was a tool that served both to represent this process cartographically and to realize it materially. The grid permits the measurement, classification, division, and apportionment of space, while facilitating the quantitative equivalencies that enable extraction, exchange, and accumulation. A gridded town composed of regular lots, for example, would allow for easier calculation of Indian tribute obligations, based after midcentury on a uniform head tax.[24] At the same time, it attempts to capture and lock down the flexible, overlapping, and rotational social relations to which it is applied. At ground level, it offers extended sight lines that facilitate the work of surveillance. The grid not only fragments, however, but also homogenizes—through spatial abstraction, it tends toward neutralizing the particularities and peculiarities of a given terrain. In the abstract, geometric space is unbounded, such that the city could at least in theory be imagined to extend its invisible lines indefinitely along the same plane, much like the Nochixtlan map. In this way, colonial space is restructured even beyond the last block of the grid, whether or not the city in fact ends up engulfing its constitutive "outsides."

## IMPERIAL METAPHYSICS AND SOFT WAX

It was not only colonial space that appeared to offer little resistance to Spanish designs. For many Spanish missionaries, the success of evangelization depended on a radical reconfiguration of indigenous life and by extension presupposed the malleability of indigenous bodies. Orlando Bentancor has suggested that the conquest was made possible in part by an imperial metaphysics that subordinated passive matter to active form. According to this Aristotelian framework, inferior matter could be "improved" and a superior form imposed through the application of certain arts or techniques. This view was operationalized primarily in terms of the exploitation of natural resources (in the case of mining, for example), but it was also applied to the "matter" of indigenous bodies. Bentancor argues that these ideas, translated into imperial reason, drove the colonization of the Americas.[25]

In this regard, congregation is no exception. As already suggested, the earliest attempts to put the spatial logic of concentration into practice in New Spain can be found in the communities established in the 1530s by Vasco de Quiroga, judge (*oidor*) in the Audiencia of Mexico and later the first bishop of Michoacán.[26] Quiroga is best known for taking inspiration from Thomas More's *Utopia* (1516) in establishing two "hospital-towns," Santa Fé de México and Santa Fé de la Laguna.[27] These towns functioned as proto-congregations insofar as they aimed to group indigenous people together into orderly, urbanized spaces and introduce disciplinary techniques as a means of caring for and Christianizing them. "Tengo muy cierto para mí" (It is very clear to me), wrote Quiroga in his *Información en derecho* (1535),

> que sin este recogimiento de ciudades grandes que estén ordenadas y cumplidas de todo lo necesario, en buena y católica policia y conforme á la manera de esto, ninguna buena conversión general, ni aun casi particular, ni perpetuidad, ni conservacion . . . en esta tierra ni entre estos naturales se puede esperar o haber, atenta a la calidad de ellos y de ella. [that without resettlement in large cities that are orderly and provisioned with every necessity, in good and Catholic order (*policia*), no sincere conversion either in general terms or even particular (cases), in perpetuity and conservation . . . can be expected or achieved in this land and among these natives, owing to the character of them and of it.][28]

Congregation is the first, crucial step toward the "salvation" of the natives. This passage clearly emphasizes the spiritual sense of this word—true and enduring conversion to Christianity and the creation of a Christian social order. But following Foucault, we can also track a temporal sense of salvation running parallel to this one. Without being resettled into orderly cities, Quiroga insists, the indigenous population will not only remain "salvajes" (savages) but simply die off, as had already begun to occur in certain parts of the Americas:

> Por falta de esta buena policia y recogimiento de ciudades . . . pues es más que verosímil que . . . nunca lo dejarán de ser ni de acabarse y consumirse de cada dia, como se han acabado y consumido en las islas é Tierra Firme por lo mismo. [Lacking good order and concentration in cities . . . it is more than likely that . . . they will never cease being (savages) or disappearing and being consumed every day, as they have disappeared and been consumed on the islands and mainland for this reason.][29]

For Quiroga, then, congregation operates not only as a valuable spiritual technique but also as the only means by which to halt the ongoing decline of the indigenous population. (It is equally true, of course, that there were other, economic objectives in mind.)[30] What is absent from his pronouncement, of course, is any sense that the Spanish may have had something to do with this phenomenon. Instead, it is the indigenous form of life itself, characterized by "el derramamiento y soledad en que viven" (the dispersion and isolation in which they live), that bears sole responsibility for and explains the natives' extreme vulnerability. Only by reorganizing colonial space and creating the infrastructural conditions for sociability, he argues, can the indigenous people be truly saved— from themselves.

Quiroga believed that the indigenous people shared with the environment they inhabited a disposition or character that opened them up to precisely this sort of transformation. As Bentancor observes, Quiroga's thought drew on the metaphysical assumptions embedded in metallurgical theories about the "improvement" of metals. His description of the natives makes this analogy explicit:

> Hay tanto y tan buen metal de gente en esta tierra, y tan blanda la cera, y tan rasa la tabla, y tan nueva la vasija en que nada hasta ahora se ha impreso, dibujado ni infundido, [There are so many people in this land, and they are of such good quality (*tan buen metal de gente*), of a wax that is so soft, a slate that is so blank, a vessel that is so new and on which nothing has so far been inscribed, depicted, or infused.][31]

Both colonial space and indigenous bodies are thus cast as a "blank slate" on which Spanish designs can be imprinted at will.

This imperial metaphysics formed the doctrinal basis for Quiroga's hospital-towns as well as for the project of congregation as it would be deployed over the course of the following century. The emptiness of colonial space and the malleability of its inhabitants were two sides of the same coin. But it was not until 1550 that what was essentially the pet project of one early colonial official acquired the backing of the colonial state and became official policy. Congregation was institutionalized partly in response to the catastrophic epidemic of 1545–1548, which contributed a sense of urgency to the work of the mendicant orders and to their collaboration with the colonial state. Although certain elements of the policy were modified over the years in response to indigenous resistance and changing conditions on the ground—there was, for example, a gradual shift of emphasis from Aristotelian "perfect communities" to infrastructural integration into both regional and world markets—the colonial authorities continued to see the dispersion of the indigenous population as one of the primary obstacles to effective colonial governance.

## INFRASTRUCTURE AND SUBJECTIVITY

Congregation turned on a series of assumptions about the relation between the human and urban space. Earlier I discussed the importance of the geometric grid, which produces a simultaneously homogeneous and hierarchically fragmented space. Here I examine the layout of the newly congregated towns according to the "Instrucción" issued by the Viceroy Conde de Monterrey in 1601, in which urban planning is conceived of as a sort of infrastructure for the emergence of a new social order that the Spanish called "police" (policía).[32] The instructions contain a set of thirty-five directives that aim to address every obstacle that might arise during implementation. They begin, furthermore, by denying any opportunity for deviation from their proscriptions, which must be carried out "sin alterar ni innovar en ellas ni en ninguna de ellas por ningún caso, aunque sea de voluntad y petición de los mismos indios, y que concurran en ella los ministros de justicia y doctrina" (without altering or innovating on any of them in any way, even at the will and request of the Indians, and even if they are supported by the secular and religious ministers).[33] In this way, the orders claim absolute authority over the procedures by which congregation is to be implemented.

Synonymous with urbanization, congregation was intended to produce rural cities with standard, recognizable characteristics. Each town would be "formado de calles y plaza y en modo de policía como la de esta ciudad de México" (centralized and ordered by streets and plaza and with police like that of this city of Mexico).[34] Here, "policía" refers not only to the social order but also to the spatial configuration of the city, specifically the checkerboard pattern of the capital's streets. The logic of congregation, in other words, posits a direct correspondence between infrastructure and social relations. In addition to these classic infrastructural elements, the instructions dictate the size of the lots (twenty-five square *varas*, or yards) as well as the hierarchical manner in which they are to be distributed, with indigenous nobles receiving those that are closer to the church and plaza. Every lot is to be located within hearing range of the church bell, ensuring that congregated life is glued together by a common set of sensory experiences.[35] The boundaries of each lot, moreover, are to be marked with a ditch (*zanja*) or wall (*mojonera*), inscribing the striations of private property into the soil. Over the homogenized space of the grid, a political character is ascribed, while at the same time the map is transformed into a symbol of the social order. Given what the Spanish saw as the indigenous propensity to dispersion, furthermore, the instructions mandate that if, after the lots are distributed and the houses built, any "empty" spaces should remain, they should be reallocated to another family and rapidly filled in:

> Porque según la ruin fama que en lo general tienen todos los pueblos de indios en esta Nueva España, sucederá muchas veces que de una casa de un indio a otra haya vacío grande, que impida la policía que se pretende . . . : en tal caso, arbitraréis en repartir el vacío a uno, o a dos más indios, para que allí hagan sus casas y . . . quede el pueblo en la mejor forma y traza que sea posible. [Because, according to the generally contemptible reputation of the Indian towns of New Spain, it often happens that between the house of one Indian and the next there is a great empty space that impedes the police that is intended . . .: in this case you will distribute the empty space to one or two more Indians, and they will build their houses there, and . . . the town will be left in the best possible form and order.][36]

Each house is to have a common set of measurements. The instructions include various requirements regarding the arrangement and organization of interior, domestic space:

> Se ha de edificar desde luego un aposento del alto que pareciere y cubierto, que tenga treinta pies de largo y doce de ancho . . . en razón de usar de compartimientos y atajos, al modo que se pueda, con que se pueda, con que se distinga la vivienda del servicio en que hubiere de haber inmundicias, y el dormitorio de los hijos del de las hijas, y se vaya recorriendo esto para ver que en todo caso lo cumplan y se introduzcan algo de policía cristiana entre ellos. [Each home should be built as high as necessary and covered, and should be thirty feet long and twelve wide . . . and it should employ compartments and partitions in every possible way, by which the living quarters will be distinguished from the outhouse, and the bedroom of the boys from that of the girls, and this should be monitored to make

sure that it is obeyed and that some Christian police is introduced among them.][37]

Congregation, in other words, did not discriminate between what today would be considered "public" and "private" domains but traversed all boundaries. It permeated and as such structured the social at large. In this concern over the separation of male and female children, for example, we glimpse an uneasy recognition of the instability of social categories such as gender among the indigenous. As a result, these categories are literally to be embedded in the architectonic structure, which operates as a foundation for the differential circulation of bodies through interior space. Similarly, the imposed distinction between living quarters and outhouse implies a categorical proximity between the indigenous and the animal, a divide that must be reinforced through some form of physical separation or barrier.

The internal division of domestic space was as important for the organizers of the colonial project as public behavior. In his influential treatise on evangelization, the Jesuit José de Acosta, who was a supporter of Toledo's *reducción general* in Peru,[38] describes the successful conversion of the indigenous as a two-step process: "Prius esse curandum, ut homines esse discant, deinde ut christiani" (first they must learn to be men, and then to be Christian).[39] One of the primary ways Acosta suggests for doing so is the following:

> Ordo vero quidam tum oppidorum tum domiciliorum, ut non veluti cuniculi occultas sedes eligant, tum vero ut in conspectu eorum omnis actio sit neque latebras petere sinantur. Ad haec permixta illa et sine ullo delectu spurca habitatio, ubi simul et maritus et uxor et filius et filia, frater et hospes et canis ipse atque sus cubat, accurate avertenda est, quantum licebit. [Establish order in their cities and homes, so that they may not make their dwellings secret, like rabbit warrens, so that their every action is observed and they are not permitted to find a hiding place. As much as possible, it is imperative to eliminate this foul dwelling without any separation, where husband and wife, son and daughter, brother and guest, even dog and sow sleep together.][40]

Disciplinary power flows, then, not only through the enclosed spaces of the home ("domiciliorum")—much as with the classic architectural forms described by Foucault and examined in chapter 2—but also and more generally through the organization of the city ("oppi-dorum"). The ordering of urban and domestic space is a necessary condition for the transformation of what are at worst animals and at best not quite humans—Acosta likens the indigenous people to rabbits living in a warren and suggests that in order for them to be converted to Christianity they first must learn to be men. Order is introduced, on one hand, through the panoptic gaze of the authorities ("in conspectu eorum omnis actio"), and on the other, through classification and separation, both analytical and spatial, such that each grouping is assigned to its own place. Thus, the son and the daughter ("et filius et filia") are sent to their own rooms within the congregated domicile. This early anxiety over mixture reveals the role that infrastructure plays in grounding the processes of subjectification. The act of separation should be seen not as managing bodies whose identities are already stable but rather as stabilizing and indeed producing these identities in the first place. Gender, for example, is constituted in part through spatial segregation.

The emergent modes of life made possible within the newly congregated towns were also secured through violent mechanisms of erasure. The colonial authorities were expected to destroy the old communities and to make sure their former inhabitants did not try to return: "Vayan derribando las viejas [casas] . . . para deshacer del todo el pueblo, y que no tengan ocasión de volverse a él; y si lo hicieren y se ausentaren, los busque y castigue para su corrección y escarmiento de otros" (Proceed by destroying the old houses . . . to entirely unmake the town, so they have no ability to return to it; and if they do attempt it and leave, find and punish them for their own correction and as an example to others).[41] This process erased thousands of indigenous place names from the map.[42] Still, the hesitation in the orders—the recognition that the indigenous might readily seek to abandon the congregations—highlights the difficulty of dismantling not just physical structures but also lived experiences and memories. This stubborn trace appears in a number of the indigenous maps painted for the *Relaciones geográficas*. The map of Teutenango mentioned earlier provides an alphabetic example in the short sentence that appears on the mountain jutting into the image just above the gridded congregation: "Este es el peñol donde solia estar el pueblo" (This is the hill where the town used to be). Similarly, a pictorial example is found in the 1579 map of Texupa (figure 1.3). The orthogonal grid of the congregated town, painted on the blank page to evoke its relocation to the flat plain, contrasts with the temple glyphs on the stylized hills that surround it. These temples indicate the original location of the communities prior to congregation, and the map thus stages the ambivalence between pre-Hispanic past and colonial present.[43] Finally, owing to this concern about the possibility of resistance, authorities were also instructed to monitor the inhabitants of the congregations carefully, tracking their movements for evidence that they were attempting to return to their old communities. The instructions offer a protocol for containing this centrifugal movement:

> El cuidado de la conservación de estas poblaciones y de que los indios no desamparen las casas y tierras nuevas, volviéndose a las viejas o yéndose a otra parte, se os encomienda y encarga en la parte que os tocare tanto como lo de la ejecución; y que de ordinario hagáis diligencia en saber si alguno o algunos indios faltan de las poblaciones nuevas que se hubieren hecho, mandando a los gobernadores y oficiales de regimiento que os lo avisen. Y visitando por vuestra persona las mismas congregaciones las más veces que pudiéredes, y habiendo entendido que se han ausentado algunos indios, pondréis mucho cuidado y diligencia en saber donde están, y si fuere fuera de vuestra jurisdicción, enviaréis por ellos con requisitoria para cualesquier justicias, que generalmente se les ordenará y mandará que la cumplan y envíen presos los que se hubieren ausentado y huido de sus pueblos. [To ensure that these settlements are conserved and that the Indians do not abandon their new houses and lands, returning to their old ones or moving elsewhere, you are ordered and charged with this matter as much as that of its initial implementation; and you should regularly make efforts to learn if one or various Indians are missing from their newly built settlements, ordering the governors and council officials to advise you. And visiting in person these congregations as many times as you can, if you learn that some Indians have run away, you will invest much care and effort in discovering where they are, and if it should be outside of your jurisdiction, you will send for them by means of a summons to any and all justices, ordering and commanding them to capture and return those who have abandoned and run away from their towns.][44]

In this and other ways, the regularized layout and the practices it enabled facilitated new and intensified forms of surveillance and control over the indigenous inhabitants.

FIGURE 1.3. Map of Texupa (1579). Real Academia de la Historia (C-028-010). © Real Academia de la Historia, Madrid, Spain.

Early critics of the project offer an indirect sense of the oppressive experience of congregation. A 1561 letter to Philip II by the provincials of the three mendicant orders, for example, notes that indigenous inhabitants frequently complained about the specific forms of disciplinary oversight to which they were subjected in the congregated towns: "Dizen agora que los emos engañado, que no a sido sino para contar los cada dia, como se haze, y añadir les triuutos y serurise dellos los christianos" (Now they say that we have tricked them, that it was done only so the Christians could count them every day, which they do, and increase their tribute and take advantage of them).[45] If the extraction of tribute and labor rests precisely on the capacity not only to locate but also to calculate the size of the indigenous population, then to be congregated is to be perpetually counted, to become an object of quantification.

Foucault writes that the regime of police transforms both the town into "a sort of quasi-convent" and the territory as a whole into "a sort of quasi-town."[46] The infrastructural reach of congregation, similarly, extends beyond the boundaries of the newly urbanized space. Diego Valadés, a student of Pedro de Gante, published his *Rhetorica Christiana* (1579) about three decades after the policy began to be implemented. He opens a chapter on the life of the indigenous population under Spanish rule with a description of the project of congregation:

> Postquam Religiosa non sine magno labore per mōtes & deserta dissipatos Indos congregauerunt & ad vitae societatem conuocauerunt mores & instituta vitae rerum familiarium ac domesticarum rationem illis sollicite tradiderunt. Primum autem, locorum futuris aedificiis viis & itineribus metatio condecens facta est: necnon agrorum distributio ex praescripto Regiae maiestatis & senatus facta est. Antequam enim quidquam tentaretur, primū consulto opus fuit, ad eiusmodi consilia coetusque incultorum hominū instituēdum ad salutem illorum tam corporalem quam spiritalem & commodum eorum, qui cum illis commercia tractaturi in posterum essent. [After the clergymen, not without great effort, had congregated the Indians, who were dispersed throughout the forests and deserts, and assembled them in social life, they carefully taught them the customs and ways of life concerning family affairs and domestic accounts. But first an appropriate design of the locations of future buildings, streets, and highways was made; and likewise a distribution of lands by the order of his Royal Majesty and the Ayuntamiento. Before anything was attempted, first it was considered what should be instituted regarding the assemblies and gatherings of uncultured men, for their corporeal and spiritual well-being, as well as the convenience of those who will engage them in exchange in the future.][47]

For Valadés, congregation is a disciplinary project that aims to remake not only the space of the countryside but also the character of its inhabitants—thus the emphasis on instituting "proper" social and familial formations, ways of life, and so on. His description articulates a lettered project that proceeds, according to the chain of sequential indicators (*postquam-primum autem-antequam*), in the following order: first, a careful reflection regarding the goals of congregation, that which the indigenous are to become and how; second, the prudent design of a space adequate for such a disciplinary task; and finally, the concentration of the dispersed indigenous population into these newly built locations. For Valadés, then, the urbanized space of the congregation explicitly emerges from an ideological project and serves an equally ideological purpose. Infrastructure is both determined and determining, both a product and productive of colonial governance.

In this description, furthermore, the architectural and infrastructural dimensions of the project appear to have solidified since the initial institutionalization of congregation in the 1550s. Beyond the vague references to cities and sociability that are found in the writings of earlier supporters of the policy, Valadés highlights a number of specific elements that compose the centralized town. He is interested in the buildings and streets that internally make up the town, but also in the roads that connect it externally to others ("aedificiis viis & itineribus"). Here the congregation is not merely a warehouse for indigenous bodies, or an autochthonous "perfect community" along the lines of Quiroga's classically inspired utopian towns; rather, it is a single point in a larger network defined by circulation. That circulation is the goal is reinforced by the distribution of lands among the indigenous inhabitants as well as the emphasis on the exchange ("commercia") of goods and ideas.

Over time the extension of this infrastructural network was woven into the fabric of congregation. By the early seventeenth century, officials known as *jueces demarcadores* were tasked with paying close attention to routes and nodes as they laid the groundwork for future resettlements: "Considerareis los caminos que pasan por las tales caveceras, o, sujetos y distritos y á que partes van, y si son caminos Reales y si estan despoblados o, tienen pus° donde hagan las Jornadas o, si pueden poner Ventas o, mesones para acomodar el camino" (You shall consider the roads that pass through such head-towns, subject-towns, and districts, as well as where they lead, whether they are

Royal roads and whether they are uninhabited or have towns within a day's journey, or if they can set up Inns to make the trip more comfortable). All of this was to be depicted graphically in a map (*pintura*).[48] The location of new towns, moreover, would be determined on the basis of the economic geography of the territory, with the need for indigenous labor and commodities taken into account. The question was whether it would be "forçossa o conveniente" (necessary or convenient) to establish a congregation at a given location,

> o para xornada de caminantes o passaxe de algun rio o para el veneficio o lavor de alguna quantiossa cosecha que aya alli o en la vecindad que de sal que de grana o cacao o otro genero semejante que importe riqueça particular de el pueblo o grosedad comun destas provi.[as] y de el comercio gnral de ellas. [either because it is a day's journey for the traveler or for the crossing of some river or to facilitate the preparation or production of some substantial crop there or in the area, whether salt or cochineal or cacao or another similar type, which generates wealth in the town or the general abundance and commerce of these provinces.][49]

A visual representation of the congregation's integration into an infrastructural network designed for the circulation of commodities through an increasingly globalized market is found in the 1582 map of the district around the town of Zumpango (figure 1.4). Like other examples from the *Relaciones geográficas* described earlier, this map was painted by an indigenous tlacuilo and contains a variety of pictorial elements common in Nahua cartography, such as hill and water glyphs. It also displays the gridded streets characteristic of the congregated town. The map evokes circulation and extraction in two main ways. First, the city streets as well as the roads connecting the *cabecera* (head-town) of Zumpango to the smaller towns around it are marked with footprints, a traditional glyph indicating movement. Here it suggests circulation, both within the main town and between it and its *sujetos* (subject-towns) displayed on the map. Notably, each town is labeled with not only its name, written in alphabetic text, but also the number of tributaries, written in Roman numerals. In this way, the map serves as both a representation of the human "resources" of the region and a tool with which to tap into them. Second, the map highlights one route in particular by marking it with the prints not only of human feet but also of horses' hooves.

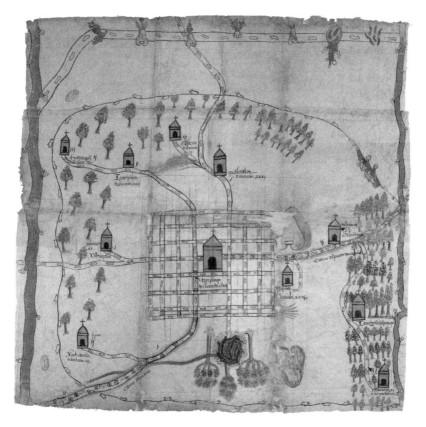

FIGURE 1.4. Map of the district of the mines of Zumpango and its jurisdiction (1582). Real Academia de la Historia (C-028-011). © Real Academia de la Historia, Madrid, Spain.

This route runs from the corner at the bottom left, labeled "camino de mexico" (road from Mexico City), through the center of town, and exits the page at the right edge, where it is labeled "camino del puerto de acapulco" (road from the port of Acapulco). Acapulco, of course, was the Manila galleon's point of departure and arrival; the goods it delivered were then taken by way of Mexico City and the port of Veracruz on to Spain. The congregation of Zumpango, in other words, was situated along the principal trade route whose commodity flows linked Europe and Asia.

At the same time, the order of congregation as infrastructure is inseparable from an expansive project oriented toward future development. In this sense, as Valadés seems to suggest, it is not merely buildings but *future* ("futuris") buildings and roads, for example, that are designed and placed. The communities in Valadés's description are becoming less and less the "perfect communities" of Quiroga's utopian ideal, which contain everything they need within themselves and remain separate from the outside world, and increasingly nodes integrated into an expansive system of extraction, production, and circulation.

## BIOPOLITICAL CARE AND RACIALIZED POPULATIONS

According to Silvia Federici, it was the population decline of the sixteenth century that gave rise to the earliest forms of biopolitical governance in Europe. To encourage population growth, praised by political theorists like Jean Bodin and Giovanni Botero, early modern states launched a "true war against women" that sought to dispossess them of control over their bodies and transform them into machines for reproduction. But Federici also examines the catastrophic demographic collapse that followed the conquest of the Americas and argues that the response in the colonies took a different form. "While the response to the population crisis in Europe was the subjugation of women to reproduction, in colonial America . . . the response was the slave trade."[50] No doubt the slave trade did constitute one response to the decline of the indigenous population in colonial Mexico, but the two paths are not mutually exclusive, as she suggests. In fact, Spanish colonialism gave rise not only to the necropolitics of conquest but also to new biopolitical techniques that sought to protect the declining indigenous population. The colonial project, in other words, involved more than making bodies die—it also aimed to make them live, though not in the ways they might have chosen.

One of the main objectives of congregation, as we saw with Vasco de Quiroga, was precisely to "conserve" the indigenous population, which for colonial officials meant, in the first place, fostering the basic conditions for demographic growth. This was a major concern in the instructions left by the Viceroy Conde de Monterrey to his successor. Congregation, he claimed, would encourage communities to labor more productively in "la cultura del campo y crianza de gallinas y todo genero de grang^a" (the cultivation of the countryside and the raising of chickens and all types of animals) and thereby provide the basis for the "augmento grande" (great increase) of the population. At a more intimate level, the supposed dispersion of the communities, which made it necessary for the men to travel consistently, also impeded efficient reproduction. "Y q̃ con sus ordinarias y largas ausencias y caminos hazen poca cohabitacion con sus mugeres y en disposicion muy cansada y malsana q̃ es occasion de no multiplicarse las familias como pudieran" (Because of their frequent and long absences and travels, they perform little cohabitation with their wives and in a very tired and unhealthy disposition, and as a result these families do not multiply as they might).[51] The viceroy was thus concerned not only with configuring domestic space in particular ways, as examined earlier, but also with fostering productive relations in the bedroom. Sex, of course, is the "pivot" between individual and collective bodies, and its control links the disciplined behavior of the attentive (and presumably well-rested) husband, on one hand, with demographic "multiplication," on the other.[52]

More urgent than optimizing indigenous sexual and reproductive practices, however, was countering the catastrophic effects of disease. Although there is no scholarly consensus regarding the precise degree of population decline, it is clear that the epidemics of the sixteenth century constituted a "veritable holocaust" for the indigenous population.[53] Earlier I discussed Vasco de Quiroga's hospital-towns as the foundational moment of the program of congregation that unfolded over the first century of Spanish colonial rule in the Americas. Foucault argues that in early modern Europe the hospital was in fact detached from the institution of medicine—unlike its contemporary counterpart, it was not concerned with treating illness but with assisting and warehousing the poor. "Until the eighteenth century the ideal person of the hospital was not the patient, there to be cured, but the poor person on the point of death. . . . One used to say in those times—and with reason—that the hospital was the place where one went to die."[54] Rather than doctors, hospital personnel were largely religious actors dedicated primarily to facilitating spiritual salvation. To some degree, this privileging of the soul over the body was reproduced in sixteenth-century Mexico. As the historian of medicine Francisco Guerra has shown, the decree of the fourth Lateran Council of 1215 ordering physicians, on pain of excommunication, to stop treating patients who refused to confess, "on the grounds that salvation of the soul was more important than bodily care," reappeared in the First Mexican Council of 1555.[55]

But Quiroga's hospital-towns and the congregations to which they gave rise operated according to a very different logic than their counterparts in Europe—their objective was not only to save indigenous souls at the moment of death but also, to the greatest possible extent, to care for infected indigenous bodies. Indeed, a new social theory of medicine, tied to the specificity of colonial space, was articulated alongside this project. Based on the social order of police, this theory paid less attention to balancing the bodily humors of the individual, which was central in the Galenic medicine that dominated the period, than it did to the capacity of an infrastructure of human sociability to ameliorate the harmful effects of diseases and other disorders.[56] Urbanized space and the dense human communities it sustained thus came to be seen as enabling the delivery of care—or perhaps, more accurately, as facilitating mutual aid and "hospitality" (a word that, not surprisingly, shares an etymological root with "hospital").[57] This model was not based, as Foucault suggests, on the exclusion of those bodies identified as sick but rather on the concentration of and care for *potentially* sick bodies—conceptualized in increasingly racialized terms.

In Europe, urban hospitals and the religious actors who ran them exercised an important welfare function, but the need for and attention to care appeared qualitatively different in the Americas. There, especially during the first half of the sixteenth century, the magnitude of demographic catastrophe was entangled with the apocalyptic vision of the missionaries who were tasked with bringing Christianity to the New World, especially the Franciscans.[58] Motolinía, a member of the order, likens these epidemics to one of the plagues of Egypt:

Estaba toda esta Nueva España en extremo muy llena de gente, é como las viruelas se comenzasen á pegar á los indios, fué entre ellos tan grande enfermedad y pestilencia mortal en toda la tierra, que en algunas provincias morian la metad de la gente, y en otras poco menos, porque como los indios no sabian el remedio de las viruelas, antes como tienen de costumbre, sanos y enfermos, bañarse á menudo, con esto morian como chinches, y muchos de los que murieron fué de hambre, porque como todos enfermaron de golpe, no podian curar unos de otros, ni habia quien les hiciese pan; y en muchas partes aconteció morir todos los de una casa y otras, sin quedar casi ninguno, y para remediar el hedor, que no los podian enterrar, echaron las casas encima de los muertos, ansi que sus casas fué sepultura. [All of New Spain was extremely full of people, and as smallpox began to infect the Indians, deadly illness and pestilence were great among them all across the land. In some provinces half the people died, and in others a little less, because the Indians did not know the treatment for smallpox, and instead, as was their custom, the healthy and the sick bathed together frequently, and because of this they died like insects. Many died of hunger, since when everyone became ill all of a sudden no one was left to cure them or make their bread. In many parts it happened that all the members of a household would die, leaving almost no one behind, and to remedy the stench of those left unburied, they demolished the houses upon the dead, so that their houses were their graves.][59]

For Motolinía, mass death is less a result of the disease itself than of the lack of assistance in the aftermath of an outbreak. Someone has to care for and feed the sick and bury the dead, to provide the sacraments and carry out the last rites. Would the indigenous die like "insects" (*chinches*) or human beings, embedded in the sustaining webs of mutual aid? Earlier I cited Motolinía's 1550 letter to Charles V calling for congregation as a mechanism for the construction of "polecía humana" among the indigenous people. Under the right conditions, the spatial proximity of the new towns' inhabitants would contribute to the emergence of a new set of social relations characterized not by "savage" anomie but by "human" sociability. The hope was that this socialization would lessen the devastation wrought by the epidemics. Moreover, the constant, watchful presence of the pastor would facilitate the delivery of appropriate care.

The clearest elaboration of this argument appears in the later writings of Gerónimo de Mendieta, who, like Motolinía, was a member of the Franciscan order and supporter of congregation. In a letter to the archbishop of Mexico written in 1589, Mendieta briefly describes the grave problems posed by the decline of the indigenous population in New Spain. The most important task of the authorities, he writes, is to "ampar[ar] y def[ender] á los indios de todo lo que es contrario á su conservación y segura vivienda" (protect and defend the Indians from everything that is contrary to their conservation and safety). If the plagues continue, he goes on, "forzosamente han de ir, como van, cada día á menos, y se han de acabar" (their numbers will necessarily continue to decline, as is happening every day, and they will disappear). Along with the letter, Mendieta enclosed a *memorial* containing a number of policy recommendations to respond to the crisis.

These same recommendations had already been delivered to King Philip II by Pedro Calderón, vicar of the Convent of San Francisco in Madrid, to whom Mendieta had dispatched a copy the previous year.[60]

Included in this packet was a document in which Mendieta laid out five main arguments in favor of congregation: first, to remove the opportunity for the indigenous to return to their idolatrous past, since "los mismos lugares remotos y apartados de conversación les pueden traer ocasión para ello" (the very places that are remote and isolated from conversation may offer them occasion for it); second, to ensure missionaries' ability to administer the sacraments and more generally watch over their flock effectively; third, to care for them when they fall sick; fourth, to establish police (policía); and fifth, to improve conditions of safety (seguridad) in the community.[61] Although at first glance there appears to be a clear division between spiritual concerns (the first two items on the list) and temporal ones (the remaining three), in fact the spiritual and temporal overlap in complex ways.

Consider Mendieta's third argument, which could have been written as a direct response to the concerns raised by Motolinía a half-century before. If depopulation and dispersion prevented the delivery of medical care and sustenance—as Motolinía had suggested with regard to the plagues that accompanied the conquest of Mexico—Mendieta called for establishing social density among the indigenous through congregation. Only this would ensure a minimum of effective care for both body and soul:

> 3ª Para que se pueda mirar por ellos cuando caen enfermos, y curarlos corporal y espiritualmente, porque en las pestilencias que de muchos años atrás sin cesar han ido picando en unas partes ó en otras, han muerto muchas por falta de comida y socorro, por estar todos caídos y no tener vecinos que les diesen una sed de agua, pues de creer es que morirían hartos de ellos sin confesión, por no tener quien llamase al ministro de la iglesia. [Third: So that they can be looked after when they fall ill, and cured in both body and spirit, because as a result of the epidemics that have been spreading for many years without pause, first in some areas then in others, many have died for lack of food and assistance, as everyone is ill and there is no neighbor to give them a drink of water, and it is clear that many would die without confession as they have no one to call the minister from the church.][62]

The question of disease returns later in the document, where Mendieta sets out to rebut a series of what he sees as common arguments against congregation. One of these arguments is precisely the claim that grouping indigenous bodies together only accelerates contagion: "En las poblaciones se suele pegar más la pestilencia de unos á otros" (In populated areas disease tends to spread more easily). In Spain, the *contra* argument continues, people regularly flee the cities for less populated areas when epidemics strike. But the situation in the Americas, Mendieta responds, is exactly the opposite:

> Entre los indios no se tiene esta experiencia, sino antes lo contrario, que en los lugares remotos los ha llevado la pestilencia tan bien y mejor que en las poblaciones, á causa que en lo poblado han tenido ayuda y socorro de los españoles . . . lo cual no tenían en los lugares remotos, y así morían más comunmente. [Among the Indians we do not have this experience but rather the opposite, that in remote places disease has hit hard and worse than in the populated areas, because there they have had the help and assistance of the Spaniards . . . which they lack in remote areas, and as such they die more frequently.][63]

Disease operates differently in colonial space. Assistance outweighs contagion, and an effective response trumps prevention.

Here Mendieta gestures at a second, parallel distinction between Old and New Spain. Like many of his contemporaries, the Franciscan recognizes that the diseases unleashed by the conquest seem to strike only at the indigenous population, and he suggests that if Christians have a unique obligation to care for their neighbors, Spaniards similarly have a unique capacity to care for the indigenous sick. Claudio Lomnitz observes that what distinguishes the epidemics of Europe from those that plagued the Americas was precisely the fact that their effects broke down neatly along racial lines. Smallpox strictly affected the indigenous; the Spanish were almost entirely immune. This distinction initially appeared to contemporaries as a sign of the power of the Christian God. Some missionaries believed that disease was a form of divine punishment for the idolatrous practices of the indigenous, while others (including Mendieta) saw it as a sign that God was punishing the Spaniards for their own sins in the New World. Either way, "the very fact that plague discriminated by race was proof of a mysterious connection between Spanish power and divine justice." Whereas in Europe the plague was seen as a sort of great leveler, striking down the poor as well as the rich (though the latter might escape to their country houses), in the Americas the only casualties were indigenous. According to Lomnitz, this discrimination consolidated the idea that the Spaniards, as a "noble caste," were closer to God.[64] But while congregation was a pastoral technique aimed at a population defined by vulnerability—in this case, the *potential* for infection—this distinction also performed a parallel racializing function on their indigenous counterparts.

Mendieta's first claim about the unique ability of Spanish missionaries to provide care owing in part to a racialized immunity to disease is supported by a second claim that goes a step further: namely, that human sociability itself is the most effective response. Whether disease constitutes a natural or divine disorder, the introduction of police seems to promise continuous and decentralized care. Mendieta's anecdote about the inhabitant who offers thirst-quenching water to his sick neighbor evinces precisely the sort of hospitality that activates the congregation as "hospital." Although the Franciscan was concerned about the persistence of idolatry in indigenous communities, one perhaps unintentional implication of his theory of care is that it indirectly supported the use of indigenous medical practices, which were often violently repressed because of their presumed connection to idolatry.[65]

Congregation thus constitutes the material condition of possibility for hospitality, which for Mendieta serves to mitigate the harmful effects of not only disease but criminality as well:

> 4ª Para que con la comunicación que hay en las poblaciones se vayan poniendo en más policía; y para que en esto les puedan ayudar los ministros de la justicia y de la iglesia, conforme á lo que arriba se tocó.
>
> 5ª Para que posean con más seguridad lo que tuvieren en sus casas y sembraren ó plantaren junto á ellas; y si fueren en algo agraviados tengan cerca el recurso y remedio, porque en el campo están ocasionados á que ladrones y malos hombres les hagan violencias, y para el daño que recibieren tienen lejos el remedio.
>
> [Fourth: So that with the communication of the settlements they begin organizing themselves in policía; and so that the ministers of justice and the church can help them in this, in accordance with what was stated above.
>
> Fifth: So that they possess with more security whatever they

might have in their homes and sow or plant on their land; and if
they should be harmed in some way they have recourse and remedy
nearby, since in the countryside they are vulnerable to violence committed by thieves and evil men and the remedy for the harm they
might receive is far away.][66]

For each malady, in other words, congregation offers the same form of
care: mutual aid based on the activation of human sociability. Policía
is sustained by "comunicación," which refers, beyond mere conversation, to a specific configuration of social relations that purports to
mark the boundary between human and animal, between civilized
and savage life. It is an everyday practice, in other words, that does
not merely name an existing distinction but indeed calls it forth, ex-
cluding the "malos hombres" who hover at the boundaries of the human and solidifying their counterpart, those who constitute not so
much "good" men as simply "men." In sixteenth-century theology
and law, furthermore, "communication" also implied circulation—
the exchange of words and ideas as well as goods and money.[67] The
ordenanzas through which congregation was implemented explicitly
linked "comunicación de unos con otros" to the fulfillment of basic needs.[68] What was at stake, in other words, were the dense social
relations that grew out of a particular spatial and indeed economic
order based, in this example, on agricultural production and private property. What Mendieta's text makes clear, then, is that "communication" cannot take place in a vacuum, a neutral space of fric-
tionless and unimpeded harmony. Rather, like all naturalized social
practices, it is embedded in a particular terrain—in other words, it requires infrastructure.

In Mendieta's proposal, there is little difference between conta-
gious disease, on one hand, and social crime, on the other. The police made possible by congregation acts not so much to *prevent* these
evils as to remedy or resolve a problematic situation after it has already occurred, as it inevitably will. Police is associated with response rather than preemption. Implicit in this mode of governmentality is an acknowledgment that social disorders like epidemic
disease must be understood to some degree as a given, beyond the capacity of either the colonial state or its delegated actors to eliminate
entirely. But they might be managed using certain techniques. In
part this assumption is linked to the Franciscans' apocalyptic mille-
narianism—if disease was a divine punishment for sin, as Motolinía

and Mendieta believed, then human will was incapable of preventing it. But there is another tendency here, one that in certain ways prefigures the biopolitical apparatus that Foucault sees emerging in eighteenth-century Europe, which aimed to "maximiz[e] the positive elements" and "minimiz[e] what is risky and inconvenient, like theft and disease, while knowing that they will never be completely suppressed."[69] Although the capacities of sixteenth-century medicine were of course limited, congregation nevertheless aimed to produce a population uniquely vulnerable to disease as a racialized object of colonial governance.

## LABOR, RACE, AND THE FRAGMENTATION OF THE *ALTEPETL*

I have suggested that the logic of congregation turned on a correspondence between infrastructure and social relations. If the restructuring of colonial space facilitated the subjectification of the indigenous population through the application of discipline, it is important to consider the racializing effects of these processes, specifically with regard to the emergence and consolidation of the category of "Indian" over the first century of colonial rule. The point of departure for tracing this process is the indigenous *altepetl*, which served as the basis of many of the early colonial institutions that were established after the fall of Tenochtitlan. The ethnohistorian James Lockhart has defined the altepetl as an "ethnic state" consisting of a specific territory, a set of named constituent parts, a dynastic ruler or *tlatoani*, and a special ethnic god.[70] Composed of two Nahuatl roots, *atl* (water) and *tepetl* (mountain), the etymology of the word points to its territorial conditions of possibility—without a "physical location," the altepetl was unthinkable.[71] But it was not territorial in the same way as the modern state or even the ancient city-state. Its constituent parts, called *calpolli* or *tlaxilacalli*, were often distributed over a significant geographical space and oftentimes the calpolli associated with different altepetl were interspersed within a single area. In other words, the altepetl did not have strict linear boundaries or a unified jurisdiction but was composed of noncontiguous networks that could stretch over significant distances.

The altepetl also constituted the primary unit of identity, characterizing how indigenous people thought of and situated themselves within social relations, both before and for decades after the conquest. It goes without saying that the indigenous did not identify as "Indians" before the arrival of Europeans, but neither did they think of themselves in terms of language groups—as "Nahuas," for example. Instead, they identified on the basis of their altepetl—as Tenochcas (from Tenochtitlan), say, or Tlatelolcas (from Tlatelolco). Even at the level of the calpolli, there appears to have been a relatively autonomous sense of ethnic identity; as Lockhart puts it, "The ethnic pride so characteristic of the altepetl is seen at the calpolli level too."[72] The altepetl was thus not only an ethnic but also a multiethnic state, whose subdivisions are visible even in pictographic texts.[73]

In the decades immediately following the conquest of Mexico, the altepetl continued to serve as the foundation of economic extraction, which essentially sought to establish a new layer of colonial authority over the existing, pre-Hispanic structures.[74] Conquistadors were rewarded for their service with an *encomienda*, a grant of both tribute and labor provided by the indigenous commoners of a given altepetl and coordinated through its tlatoani. Initially, tribute included commodities like maize, cotton cloth, cacao beans, wood, turkeys, tomatoes, chiles, salt, wheat, and fodder, while quantities were directly negotiated and *encomenderos* sought to extract as much as possible.[75] Although indigenous tributaries remained nominally "free," in practice the boundary between encomienda servitude and slavery was generally blurry and often explicitly violated—at times indigenous held in encomienda were branded and sold as slaves, but in any case conquistadors saw themselves as entitled to essentially unlimited quantities of labor.[76] The intensity of exploitation under encomienda heightened the indigenous population's vulnerability to disease and frequently left them without the means of social reproduction. Moreover, production declined along with the population, and to make up for it encomenderos demanded a greater percentage of whatever production remained.

By the mid-1540s, and especially after the plague of 1545–1548, the encomienda was beginning to exhaust itself as an effective mechanism of accumulation. In the final years of the decade, the colonial authorities began to regulate the encomienda and in the process also contributed to the restructuring of the altepetl through such practices as the formal demarcation of static boundaries and the denomination of cabeceras (head-towns) and sujetos (subject-towns). They also began to standardize tribute, mandating payment in the form of money and maize instead of the multiple commodity forms that had previously been used, while replacing decentralized negotiations between encomendero and tlatoani with a uniform head tax.[77]

In parallel to these changes regarding tribute, the dominant system of labor control was altered as well. A royal order in 1549 prohibited the extraction of labor through encomienda, and the following year—the very same year that Motolinía was writing his letter to the king and congregation first began to be implemented with the backing of the colonial state—the forced labor draft known as *repartimiento* was imposed. "The date follows so closely the prohibition of labor services in encomienda," writes the historian Charles Gibson, "that an immediate causal relation may be supposed."[78] Instead of the encomienda model in which a specific altepetl provided essentially unlimited labor to its encomendero, repartimiento channeled a standardized percentage of the indigenous tributary population (initially 1 to 2 percent, depending on the season) into work that was ostensibly in the public interest: either agricultural or mining labor for individual Spanish owners or massive public works projects (often infrastructures like roads and drainage projects) for the colonial state.[79] Whereas under the encomienda indigenous labor was performed without remuneration, repartimiento labor had to be paid a wage, however small. These reforms broke the monopoly of the encomenderos over indigenous labor and inserted indigenous laborers more directly into a market system of production and consumption. More generally, the result was a gradual shift from forms of extraction deeply rooted in and tied to the space of the altepetl to a more generalized form of extraction operating over the indigenous population as a whole.

The congregation served as an access point where Spanish capital could tap directly into repartimiento labor. In addition to accelerating the circulation of goods (commerce) and of ideas (conversion), then, resettlement facilitated the exploitation of the indigenous population. The reterritorialization of the indigenous population into rural cities paradoxically contributed to the emergence of an increasingly deterritorialized "Indian" as a meaningful category of identity, detached from the altepetl that had previously served as its anchor and instead constituting a racialized, relatively mobile, laboring population.

Congregation facilitated the reconfiguration of the altepetl form and, in parallel, of indigenous subjectivity in three ways. First, resettlement at times brought together indigenous communities from different ethnic and linguistic groups.[80] This was primarily the case in less centralized areas, but historians have documented various cases even in and around central Mexico. Toward the end of the 1550s, for example, the Otomí-speaking community of Teocalhueyaca and the Nahuatl-speaking community of Tenayuca were congregated together at Tlalnepantla. The congregation of Teutenango, the map of which I discussed earlier, brought together speakers of Nahuatl and Matlatzinca.[81] Second, even within a single language group, if communities came from different altepetl, the congregation would have been experienced as a "mixed" space, since, as we have seen, the altepetl was the basis of indigenous identity.

Third, even when congregation was implemented within a single altepetl, it still tended to destabilize prior identity formations. The first step of resettlement was to designate one of the calpolli that made up the altepetl, usually the most populous one, as the cabecera and the rest as sujetos. In the pre-Hispanic altepetl, the relation between constituent units had been nonhierarchical; under Spanish rule, cabecera status came with certain privileges. Not only were many important institutions, such as the church and the market, located in the cabecera, but they were often built by obligatory labor provided by the inhabitants of its sujetos.[82] Under congregation, furthermore, those settlements designated sujetos were frequently relocated to their cabecera. In the second half of the sixteenth century, even as early as the 1550s, many sujetos began to seek cabecera status for themselves in order to acquire these privileges, thus boosting the number of recognized cabeceras while at the same time accelerating the fragmentation of altepetl identity and altering the very meaning of the altepetl.[83] In all of these ways, congregation laid material foundations that brought heterogeneous indigenous groups into spatial proximity, weakened prior regimes of identification, and enabled the emergence of a new subjectivity based on the idea of the Indian as a single, homogeneous type.

The shift from an altepetl-based identity attached to specific territory to a more generalized, racial identity inhering in the body is also evident, finally, in the changing terminology that indigenous people employed to refer to themselves in a collective sense. Obviously, there was no equivalent to the word "Indian" in indigenous languages before the conquest. "When it came to collectivities," argues Lockhart, "the writers of Nahuatl documents from the sixteenth century forward . . . emphasized the narrow ethnicity of the local altepetl and calpolli-tlaxilacalli rather than broader ethnic categories. They tended to do so even when the contrast between indigenous and Spanish was specifically at issue."[84] The earliest usage that most closely approximates the word "Indian," found in the mid-sixteenth century, is *nican tlaca* or *nican titlaca*, that is, "people here" or "we are people here." The centrality of location in this expression ("here") reflects the territoriality of the altepetl. By the beginning of the seventeenth century, however, a different word was increasingly being used in its place. Initially, Lockhart suggests, the word *macehualli* (pl., *macehualtin*) referred to social class—"commoners," in contrast to *pipiltin*, or "nobles." But by the seventeenth century Nahuatl speakers were using it in a way that was more or less equivalent to "Indians."[85] This change is front and center in the indigenous historian Domingo de Chimalpahin's discussion of the congregation policy, written in Nahuatl in the early seventeenth century:

> x. tochtli xihuitl. 1606. años. ypan in in yancuic xihuitl. yhuan ypan in yancuic metztli henero. yn ohuacico. yn ohualla ycedulatzin. yn itlanahuatiltzin. yn tohueytlahtocatzin Rey Don felipe tercero. yn ipampa yn quin nepa omochiuh congrecacion y nohuian ypan altepetl. ceceyaca cece yn itlahuillanalpan yn itlatititzalpan motenehua. ysojetos. in campa. inyeyan. ymonoyan in macehualtzitzintin. yn quaxochtli. quitztoca. in quaxochpiaya. yquaniloque. mochintin tlaliloto. ytzontecompa. yn altepetl. yn inpopohuian. auh yc cenca innetoliniliz. mochiuh. yn macehualtzitzinti. auh iuh quimocaquilti. yn tohueytlahtocauh. Rey. ye ōxiuhtica. nepa nohuian omochiuh yn congrecacion. ynic axcan ohualmotlatitlani ohualmotlanahuatilli yn tohueytlahtocatzin. y iuh quihualmitalhui. Yc nitlanahuatia. yntla quinequizque mochintin. macehualtin. yn ohualliquaniloque. yn imaltepeuh ypan yn inpopohuian yntla oc ceppa mocuepazque. ma mocuepacan. ca yyollocacopatiz. yntla quinequizque mocuepazque yn campa inyeyan ymonoyan catca. auh aocmo huel iuh mochiuh. aocac omocuep yn macehualli. ça iuh omocauhque yn oncan oyquaniloque. auh ça cana yn omocuepque. yn campa inyeyampa. macehualtin. [10 Rabbit year, 1606. In the new year and new month of January, the cedula and order of our great ruler the king don Felipe III came and arrived here, concerning the *congregaciones* that were carried out a little while back in the [various] altepetl all around. In each one, each of its dependencies, called sujetos, where the *macehual-*

*tzitzintin* were and dwelt, looking to and guarding their boundaries, were all moved and taken to be settled in the headtown of the altepetl to which they belonged; through this the *macehualtzitzinti* suffered great afflictions. But our great ruler the king heard about it two years after the congregaciones were carried out everywhere, so that now our great ruler has sent a message here and given orders, saying "I order that if all the *macehualtin* who were moved in the altepetl to which they belong want to go back again [to where they came from], let them go back; it is to be by their own free will if they want to return to where they used to be and live." But it could no longer be done, none of the *macehualli* went back, but stayed where they were moved to; only in rare cases did the *macehualtin* return to where they had been.][86]

The congregation thus served as the infrastructure that made possible the consolidation of a system of economic extraction drawing on a newly generalized Indian population and at the same time activated the emergence of a new form of subjectivity in which certain people were able to think of themselves as Indians. By naturalizing this identity, the reorganization of life that enabled it, brought about through the deployment of both violence and care, was erased, much like the place names that dropped off the map, to which Chimalpahin's *macehualtzitzintin* could never return.

## CONCLUSION

In Marx's classic account at the end of the first volume of *Capital*, primitive accumulation primarily takes the form of violence—"conquest, enslavement, robbery, murder, in short, force, play the greatest part." By documenting these vectors of dispossession, Marx challenges the "nursery tale" histories of bourgeois political economists like Adam Smith, for whom the emergence of capitalism is merely a story of hard work and thrift, on one hand, and idleness and "riotous living," on the other. In this morality tale, the capital relation, according to which "free" individuals enter into voluntary contracts with each other, appears both natural and eternal. In contrast, Marx's history of primitive accumulation emphasizes the role of violence in creating the conditions in which capitalist accumulation can begin to unfold according to its own logic, that is, without supplementary forms of extra-economic coercion.[87] Still, as Jason Read observes, the expropriation of the means of production is not enough to guarantee the operation of a new mode of production governed by an entirely different set of social relations.[88] Marx himself shows that peasants dispossessed from the English countryside did not proceed immediately and voluntarily to the factories but became vagabonds, wandering from town to town and trying to survive by other, informal means. As a result, laws were passed—what Marx calls "bloody legislation"—that sought to transform these disorderly bodies into a pool of potential laborers. In the last instance, of course, the law always depends on force (thus, "enforcement"), but there is a *productive* aspect to it as well: "It is not enough that the conditions of labour are concentrated at one pole of society in the shape of capital, while at the other pole are grouped masses of men who have nothing to sell but their labour-power. Nor is it enough that they are compelled to sell themselves voluntarily. The advance of capitalist production develops a working class which by education, tradition and habit looks upon the requirements of that mode of production as self-evident natural laws."[89] Primitive accumulation requires not only the destruction of previously existing social life but also the creation and normalization of new forms of subjectivity both individual and collective. Among other factors, argues Read, it requires the introduction of "new forms of police to transform disenfranchised peasants and artisans into subjects of labor."[90] Primitive accumulation proceeds, then, in two acts: one negative, through dispossession and destruction; the other positive, via the construction of new social relations adequate to emergent forms of production.

This chapter has examined one of these "new forms of police" that contributed to the restructuring of colonial space and indigenous bodies in New Spain during the first century of colonial rule. It was not only the violence of the conquest, the pillaging of the conquistadors, or the forced extraction of the encomienda that characterized primitive accumulation, but also a three-way process of spatial restructuring that, first, constructed a network of infrastructural elements to facilitate the circulation of bodies, commodities, and knowledge; second, set in motion the transformation of indigenous social relations and the consolidation of a new form of racialized subjectivity; and third, generated newly productive forms of extraction tied to this emergent category of racial identity. Congregation laid the material groundwork for the emergence of new forms of extraction, circulation, and subjectivity that would endure even beyond the formal end of Spanish colonial rule.

This analysis of the congregation of indigenous communities has two final implications that are worth clarifying. First, the general logic of congregation reveals a deeply biopolitical concern with the production and management of indigenous life—a process that I have called the construction of the Indian—from the earliest moments of the colonial project. Certainly, Spanish colonialism drew effectively on necropolitical techniques that served to gather and redirect structural violence toward targets deemed especially pernicious while simultaneously accelerating the extraction of precious metals and souls. This negative politics of death is especially pertinent in analyzing the colonial space of exception.[91] However, it is equally important to acknowledge the productive aspect of certain techniques of colonial governance that aimed to intervene at the level of indigenous life.

If the problems of effective colonial governance made congregation necessary, the sixteenth-century holocaust, which contemporaries like Quiroga, Motolinía, and Mendieta believed might effectively empty New Spain of inhabitants, made this policy uniquely urgent. Of course, sixteenth- and early seventeenth-century actors did not have access to the eighteenth-century statistical instruments that Foucault sees as a defining feature of biopolitics proper. Likewise, before the development of modern medical techniques in the nineteenth century, there was little effective treatment for epidemics like smallpox. Still, between approximately 1530 and 1635, a great deal of information about what could be called an emergent Indian population (as well as the space it inhabited) was collected, systematized, and archived by colonial institutions. And regardless of the effectiveness of the medical care that was delivered, there is little doubt that proponents of congregation were invested in saving, to the best of their ability, not just indigenous souls but Indian bodies as well.

What does it mean to take seriously the claims of its advocates that congregation was not (or at least not only) a cynical land grab but an act of love? The point is not to reproduce the "white legend" mythology, of course, but to consider care as a key logic of colonial biopolitics. José Rabasa has shown how in the colonial context "love speech" operates not in opposition to racist hate speech but rather as its Janus face. "Hate speech is pervasive, indeed, constitutive of colonial situations, but the implantation of colonial rule and the subordination of colonial subjects cannot be reduced to a modality of hate speech. 'Love speech' is as central to colonization as spurting offensive yet injurious stereotypes. The challenge is to understand love speech as a powerful mode of subjection and effective violence."[92] And beyond these speech acts, congregation shaped this colonial politics of love into a new and enduring spatial order.

The second implication of this analysis is that congregation constituted the material condition of possibility for the construction of the Indian as a socially meaningful category of identity. Race is not constructed through discourse alone—it is deeply material, directly implicated in capitalist accumulation, and not only entangled with but also facilitated by the organization of space and the built environment. In this reading, race refers not to some objective or prior form of "difference" but to the product of a series of racializing procedures operating at the level not only of representation but also of materiality and infrastructure. The infrastructures of race, then, are the material conditions of possibility for processes of racialization that both ascribe categories of identity to bodies and populations and enable these identities to be subjectively experienced and lived.

# CHAPTER 2

# ENCLOSURE: THE ARCHITECTURE
# OF MESTIZO CONVERSION

*Mestizos were not born but made.*
KATHRYN BURNS, *COLONIAL HABITS*

IN FRANCISCO CERVANTES DE SALAZAR's Latin dialogues, published in 1554 for use at the newly established Royal University in Mexico City, two local residents, Zuazo and Zamora, lead a Spanish visitor, Alfaro, on a guided tour of the city. Praising its magnificent buildings and notoriously straight streets, the group comes to the western edge of the *traza*, or city center, where Zuazo points out a building he describes as a "colegiū . . . promiscuorum puerorum" (college for boys of mixed blood), the Colegio de San Juan de Letrán. Who are these "mixed" children, wonders Alfaro, and his guide responds: "Hispano indos. . . . Orbatos, qui nati sūt ex hominibus Hispanis & Indicis feminis" (the Spanish-Indians. . . . Orphans, born of Spanish men and Indian women). Questioned about what the children do while "conclusi" (enclosed) there, Zamora responds: "Legūt, scribunt, & quod est potius, in his quae ad Dei cultum pertinent, instituuntur. . . . Liberalibus qui ingenio valent, caeteri qui non perinde, mechanicis & circunforaneis artibus incumbūt" (They read, write, and, better still, they are trained in those matters that pertain to the worship of God. . . . Those endowed with talent apply themselves to the liberal arts; others, not equally endowed, to handicrafts and jobs about the marketplace). Following the drainage canal that loops around to the other side of the church and convent of San Francisco, the guides point out the Colegio de Nuestra Señora de la Caridad for Mestiza girls, who are similarly disciplined, trained in the "muliebres artes" (womanly arts), and prepared for marriage.[1]

The humanist Cervantes de Salazar was deeply influenced by Renaissance urban planning and interested in the infrastructures, such as roads and drainage canals, that made the city function. His work reflects the view, elaborated in the previous chapter, that the geometric space of the city was directly related to social relations. The well-ordered grid constituted a material infrastructure that enabled certain forms of calculation and extraction and promoted the social order that colonial commentators called *policía*. But Cervantes de Salazar's description of the Colegio serves as a useful reminder that discipline also operates—and perhaps operates most effectively—at the micro level of architectural space. The colonial politics of *recogimiento*, which refers in short to the overlapping practices of capture, enclosure, and subjectification, is thus founded on a concrete spatial order.

This chapter analyzes the racialization of the Mestizo by tracking the rise and fall of what I call the project of Mestizo conversion—that is, the conversion of Mestizo bodies as a means of converting Indian souls—at the Colegio de San Juan de Letrán over the second half of the sixteenth century. Founded in 1547, the Colegio emerged as an urgent political project—vital to the interest of the state, as Cervantes de Salazar believed—and was one of the only institutions of its kind to receive the direct endorsement and support of both the Crown and the pope.[2] It also served as a model for imitations throughout the Americas. Constituted as a mechanism of spatial politics, the Colegio was aimed at capturing unregulated and unproductive bodies and reterritorializing them as part of a newly productive colonial order. The objects of concentration, in this case, were conceptualized through the common early modern trope of vagabondage and "lost" children, but in colonial space these figures also took on the racialized character of the mixed-race body, initially framed in genealogical terms as "hijos de españoles e indias" (children of Spanish men and Indian women).[3]

At the outset, the Colegio was split between two largely opposing projects, each one foregrounding a different side of this genealogical equation. The first was tilted more toward the Spanish (father) and essentially sought to mold these boys into reliably non-Indian subjects trained to enter the colonial workforce as wage laborers and reproduce the social order by serving as the anchors of stable family units. Partly as a result of these social processes, the status of the Mestizo as nontributary *in spite of* his indigenous origins was secured.[4] It was not only Mestiza girls, then, but Mestizo boys as well who became targets of gendered processes of subjectification. This project, which endured at the Colegio well into the seventeenth century, was largely successful at carving out a subordinated position for these "dis-placed" bodies within the so-called *república de españoles* (republic of Spaniards), a social space defined in opposition to Indianness.[5]

The second project, which has received far less scholarly attention despite the fact that it was unique among the disciplinary institutions of New Spain, was tilted more toward the Indian (mother) and organized around reinvigorating so-called spiritual conquest. The Colegio was established during a moment of crisis for the evangelization project. By the middle of the sixteenth century, many clergy had begun to feel that Christianity had not taken hold among the indigenous population as deeply as they initially believed. Once seen as innocent and predisposed to the new faith, the Indian now appeared as two-faced and deceptive, holding on to idolatrous beliefs and practices beneath a cultivated Christian facade. The "racial baroque" thus gave rise to an emerging distinction between external appearance and internal essence, and many blamed the Spaniards' inability to see through these illusions on their failure to learn indigenous languages and cultures.[6] At midcentury, when the Colegio was founded, the vagabond/Mestizo was envisioned as the embodiment of a potential to constitute a new cadre of specialized missionaries par excellence. Reliably Christian due to their Spanish fathers, and with an intimate knowledge of indigenous languages and cultural practices due to their Indian mothers, they would be far more effective than even the best-trained Spaniard. Yet by the end of the century the Mestizo aroused such profound suspicion that the project of Mestizo conversion was largely abandoned.

An account of recogimiento at the Colegio and the project of Mestizo conversion is crucial to understanding the process by which the Mestizo emerged as a racial category in its own right. Discipline was premised on certain assumptions about the possibility of "reform," but what came to be viewed as the limitations of the Colegio's spaces and procedures yielded a new science of the racialized body, grounded in a gendered reading of mixed ancestry that sought to disentangle and account for the complex and interwoven matrix of influences on human development. The construction of the Mestizo body thus took place at the nexus of religion, blood, and gender. According to the historian María Elena Martínez, the second half of the sixteenth century was marked by heightened attention to the role of the mother in shaping the identity of the child as well as the consolidation of an authoritative discourse regarding the transmission of inheritable characteristics through the blood. As colonization extended the Iberian concept of *limpieza de sangre* to the Americas, what had initially referred to the absence of Jewish and Muslim ancestors (*raza*) was gradually reconfigured into a hierarchical system of classification based on relative proportions of Spanish, Indian, and African blood. "At the start of the seventeenth century," argues Martínez, "the category of mestizo, like that of Indian, was deeply embedded in discourses of religious conversion and being linked, more often than not implicitly, to the concept of limpieza de sangre."[7] The racialization of the Mestizo, then, may be best explored at a site like the Colegio, which stands at the intersection of colonial evangelization and genealogical analysis.

This chapter argues that the Mestizo, like the Indian, was not the object but the product of the spatial politics of colonial rule. "Mestizos," as Kathryn Burns observes in the epigraph, "were not born but made."[8] Yet in this case it is important to carry the argument a step further, since the standard narrative of mestizaje also treats the Mestizo as an unintended product of colonialism. According to that account, the Mestizo is a primarily *biological* consequence of the "mixture" of two previously "pure" groups. Although few scholars explicitly accept this account, it nevertheless forms the implicit background for much of the research on the colonial period, as in the assumption that the conquest unleashed a purportedly "natural" process of racial mixture that registered demographically in the form of an emerging "Mestizo problem." Over time, this story continues, the growing Mestizo population gradually destabilized the binary character of colonial society, organized around a spatial and institutional divide between Spaniards and Indians. Not surprisingly, much of the historiography on the Colegio is framed in precisely this way.

A second approach attempts to mediate this demographic background with a weak form of social constructionism. Here the point of departure is the acknowledgment that, in contrast to the assumptions of the biological framework, the Mestizo did not appear overnight. It was only when the Mestizo population grew so large that it was impossible to ignore that colonial commentators were forced to fashion a language and corresponding set of meanings with which to make sense of it. At first glance, this seems to be a useful example of social construction, since the generation-long time lag demonstrates that the discursive superstructure does not map neatly or directly onto the biological base. In the end, however, this formulation reproduces the same demographic essentialism as the conventional mestizaje narrative because it continues to assume that even if there is no language to represent the Mestizo, there is still, in the end, a biological Mestizo, an object of discourse for both the colonial authorities and the contemporary historian. Demographics remains the motor of history. As Joanne Rappaport insightfully observes, "There is still a tendency in the historical literature to tacitly accept the transparency of 'caste' designations as some sort of essential yet fluid marker of difference: in other words, that even if we (and colonial officials) cannot determine to which casta an individual 'really belonged,' there is a sense that an answer does exist, albeit just beyond our grasp."[9]

It is time to rip up mestizaje's demographic base. My account of the racialization of the Mestizo takes as its point of departure not the purported biological reality of racial mixture but the material infrastructures of concentration and circulation that were implemented under colonial rule. The disciplinary space of the Colegio, embedded in its architectural dimensions and more generally in the built environment of Mexico City, played an early and important role in the construction of the Mestizo, not only as a cluster of attributes but also as a specific corporeality to which these attributes could be ascribed.

## THE RACIALIZATION OF THE VAGABOND

Like the Indian, the Mestizo first emerged as a problem of spatial control. Rather than dispersion, however, the Mestizo appeared as a problem of circulation, and this process of racialization was routed through the figure of the vagabond. Marx's discussion of this figure in his classic account of the history of primitive accumulation at the end of the first volume of *Capital* provides a useful point of entry here. As noted in the previous chapter, the violent separation of the peasants from the means of production in feudal Europe did not give way smoothly and automatically to the constitution of a proletariat willing to sell its labor power for wages. Instead, it produced a floating population that had to be compelled to work, not indirectly through what Adam Smith called the "invisible hand" of the market but directly through the violence of the state:

> The proletariat created by the breaking-up of the bands of feudal re-tainers and by the forcible expropriation of the people from the soil, this free and rightless proletariat could not possibly be absorbed by the nascent manufactures as fast as it was thrown upon the world. On the other hand, these men, suddenly dragged from their accus-tomed mode of life, could not immediately adapt themselves to the discipline of their new condition. They were turned into massive quantities of beggars, robbers and vagabonds, partly from inclina-tion, in most cases under the force of circumstances. Hence at the end of the fifteenth and during the whole of the sixteenth centuries, a bloody legislation against vagabondage was enforced throughout Western Europe. The fathers of the present working class were chas-tised for their enforced transformation into vagabonds and paupers. Legislation treated them as "voluntary" criminals, and assumed that it was entirely within their powers to go on working under the old conditions which in fact no longer existed.[10]

Primitive accumulation, then, consists of not only violent social dislocations on a mass scale but also the production of new, workerly subjectivities. Uprooted from the land, this formerly self-sufficient population appeared as a contradiction of the emerging social order that had produced it. To resolve this contradiction, the vagabond had to become the worker. Although the historical process that Marx de-scribes for late-fifteenth- and sixteenth-century Europe occurred in parallel to the rise of the vagabond as a problem of governance in New Spain, the colonial case differs in at least two important ways.

First is the question of race. As noted in the introduction, in the 1960s and 1970s scholarship on race in colonial Latin America was largely framed by the "caste versus class" debate, which revolved around evaluating the relative weight of each of these factors in de-termining social position over the course of the colonial period. Some historians argued that class came to trump race by the eigh-teenth century, while others believed that race remained dominant until political independence. The details of the debate are less impor-tant here than the fact that in this context race and class were treated largely as independent variables rather than as intersectional categories within an interlocking system of oppression. The concept of intersectionality, elaborated by Black feminist scholars and activists in the 1980s, highlights the ways in which categories such as race, class, and gender may in fact be mutually constitutive and suggests that in a given scenario gender can do the work of race, for example, or race the work of class. The figure of the vagabond in sixteenth-century Mexico, as Laura Lewis observes, is a useful case through which to analyze these entanglements.[11]

For Marx, the category of "vagabond" refers primarily to social class—the material result of the expropriation of the means of production. But it is also associated with a series of practices—including the lack of a fixed domicile, formal employment, or stable family relationships—that are easily translated into naturalizable qualities and dispositions. (Even Marx accounts for the emergence of the vagabond in part by referring to "inclination.") As ideas about the poor and destitute in Spain were transferred to the Americas in the mid-sixteenth century, however, this process of naturalization became explicitly racialized in the figure of the Mestizo, to which social concepts like legitimacy, abandonment, and orphanhood were attached.[12] Although vagabondage could be and was ascribed to other groups as well, it was *especially* ascribed to Mestizos, whose mixed ancestry served as a convenient "explanation" for their social practices.[13] The peasants who in Marx's account of primitive accumulation in England and France were "turned into vagabonds" were turned, in New Spain, into Mestizos as well.

The second difference revolves around the question of sovereignty. For Marx, primitive accumulation produces the proletariat primarily through the deployment of sovereign power. Numerous examples of "bloody legislation" in England and France during this period subjected vagabonds to being whipped, branded, imprisoned, enslaved, exiled, and executed in order to force them to accept "the discipline necessary for the system of wage-labour."[14] Foucault would call this a negative form of power, one that operated strictly through the decision to take life or let live. But in colonial Mexico, primitive accumulation took place through productive mechanisms as well. Supplementing the wide array of punishments deployed in Europe was an additional layer of individualizing care that sought to remake these unproductive bodies using disciplinary techniques. Repeated royal decrees in 1533, 1555, 1558, and 1569, for example, called for the authorities to seek out vagabonds "que anden perdidos" (who are lost)

and to "recoger[los], y dar tutores, que miren por sus personas, y bie-
nes" (gather them, and give them tutors, who look after their persons
and things) by capturing and concentrating them "en Colegios los va-
rones, y las hembras en casas recogidas" (in Colegios for the males,
and casas recogidas for the females).[15] Here infrastructure bridges the
gap between the various meanings of the verb *recoger*—capture, en-
close, subjectify—and clarifies the mechanisms by which the colonial authorities, in seeking to address this newly emergent problem
of governance, produced the Mestizo as a racialized body.

We can begin to trace the racialization of the vagabond by attending to the way social categories blur into genealogical designations in
early descriptions of the Colegio. One early and vigorous supporter
was the Franciscan Juan de Zumárraga, bishop of Mexico, who described the institution soon after its establishment in a 1547 letter to
then-prince Philip II:

> En esta ciudad . . . se han comenzado a recoger en un colegio de la
> doctrina cristiana, todos los niños huérfanos, hijos de españoles e in-
> dias, que andaban perdidos por los campos, sin ley ni fe, comiendo
> carne cruda; y ha sido Dios servido que con el recogimiento que agora
> tienen hacen tanto fructo y aprovechamiento en el servicio de Dios,
> que sería gran bien sustentallos y ayudalles, para que esta tan justa
> obra no caya. . . . Estos huérfanos, que son hijos y descendientes de los
> españoles que morieron en su servicio en la conquista y conservación
> desta tierra y por ser muertos nunca fueron galardonados. [In this
> city . . . they have begun to gather/enclose in a Colegio of Christian
> doctrine all of the orphaned children, sons of Spanish men and Indian
> women, who were lost in the countryside, with neither law nor faith,
> eating raw meat; and God has been served that with this enclosure
> they now benefit and progress in the service of God, and it would do
> much good to sustain and aid them, so that such a righteous project
> does not fail. . . . These orphans are the sons and descendants of the
> Spaniards who died in the service of the conquest and conservation of
> this land and because of their deaths were never honored.][16]

This passage makes it clear that for Zumárraga the problem of the
vagabond in New Spain cannot be reduced to the familiar discourse
of the orphan in Europe. For one thing, the bishop frames this social category in historically and regionally specific terms, a consequence of the conquest of Mexico and its political aftermath. But
the more important consideration is one of descent. If vagabondage

was explained away in Spain through reference to a purportedly "voluntary" idleness, as with the Gypsy, in New Spain a different discourse coalesced around the involuntary consequences of mixed ancestry.[17] The children of a Spanish man and an Indian woman were intimately linked to the category of the vagabond for two main reasons. First, owing to the belief that no Spanish man in his right mind would marry an Indian woman, these children were apparently seen as predisposed to illegitimacy and abandonment; and second, the fact that colonial society was organized around a spatial divide between Spaniards and Indians left these children without a fixed social location, giving rise as a consequence to assumptions of unregulated mobility that corresponded to the characteristics of the vagabond. This is why, as Rappaport effectively shows, Mestizos have a tendency to "disappear" in the documentary record.[18] In Zumárraga's letter, these "lost" boys seem to be destined to wander the remote countryside without direction or purpose, "free" not only from parental authority but also from human and divine law. Cast from the sphere of social relations, these children enter into a state of nature, prior to the consolidation of human civilization and symbolized by the consumption of raw meat.

If Zumárraga's letter voices the support of the ecclesiastical authorities and the Franciscan order for the Colegio, another document from the same period signals the endorsement of the colonial state. In 1550, the outgoing viceroy, Antonio de Mendoza, made note of the Colegio in the instructions he left to his successor:

S. M. y la Emperatriz, Nuestra Señora, que está en la gloria, me mandaron por muchas veces que yo diese órden como los hijos mestizos de los españoles se recogiesen, porque andaban muchos dellos perdidos entre los indios. Para remedio desto y en cumplimiento de lo que sus Majestades me mandaron, se ha instituido un colegio de niños donde se recogen no sólo los perdidos, mas otros muchos que tienen padres los ponen á deprender la dotrina cristiana, y á leer y escribir, y á tomar buenas costumbres. Y asimismo hay una casa donde las mozas de esta calidad que andan perdidas se recogen, y de allí se procura sacallas casadas. [His Majesty and the Empress, Our Lady, who is in heaven, directed me many times to give the order for the Mestizo boys of the Spaniards to be gathered/enclosed, because many of them are lost among the Indians. To remedy this and comply with what their Majesties ordered, a Colegio has been established in which not only the lost boys but many others who have parents are deposited to learn Christian doctrine, and to read and write, and to take on good customs. And likewise there is a house where the girls of this quality who are lost are gathered/enclosed, and from there they are married off.][19]

Although Mendoza's language resonates in many ways with the description in Zumárraga's letter, there is a subtle but important difference regarding what it means for the children in question to be "lost." On one hand, the bishop's formulation ("andaban perdidos por los campos") foregrounds the question of geographical space or terrain. The key issue here is the association between rural space and the state of nature, the constitutive outside of the "civil" space of the city. On the other hand, the viceroy's expression ("andaban . . . perdidos entre los indios") highlights the social space that defines the "lostness" of the children who are targeted for capture and reform. Here the problem is not that the children are wandering the countryside, entirely disconnected from human society, but that they are integrated into the *wrong* social formation. For Mendoza, these children are not literally but *transitively* "lost" owing to their presence among the indigenous population. Not "lost," in other words, but "lost to." These are the foundations of the trope of the "lost" Mestizo child—abandoned by his father, left to his Indian mother—who is then "collected" (*recogido*) and inducted into the Colegio. The project is thus doubly gendered, as it aims not only to recover the Mestizo children from their supposedly Indian mothers and deliver them into Spanish society and its paternal "law," but also to refashion Mestizo subjectivity according to a gendered division of education and labor.

Having drafted these instructions for his successor, Mendoza left for Peru, where as viceroy he continued to promote the establishment of Colegios for vagabond/Mestizo children. The project of recogimiento focused on the vagabond/Mestizo may have both begun and reached its apex in New Spain, then, but the "Mexican model" was quickly extended to other parts of the Spanish empire, including Guatemala, New Granada, and Peru.[20] The generalization of this spatial politics thus coincided with the racialization of the vagabond and the emergence of the Mestizo.

## DISCIPLINARY SPACE AND RECOGIMIENTO

In 1552, five years after its foundation, one of the deputies of the Colegio de San Juan de Letrán, a Spaniard named Gregorio de Pesquera, traveled from Mexico City to Seville to make an appearance before the Council of the Indies. Pesquera had been in the Americas since the 1530s, first participating in the conquest and later collaborating with the infamous Fray Bartolomé de Las Casas in Chiapas and Vera-paz before establishing himself in the capital of New Spain. There he became involved with the Colegio as one of its directors and perhaps even its founder, and it was the Colegio that brought Pesquera back to Spain, where he hoped to convince the Crown to commit its re-sources to supporting the institution. Along with his presentation to the Council, he also submitted an anonymous report, or *memorial*, detailing the daily life of the approximately 200 children who lived there, the rules and regulations to which they were bound, and the intended objectives of the project. Both the Council and the Crown evidently found Pesquera and the memorial believable and the Cole-gio worthy of support. On October 23, 1552, the Council forwarded the document to the king along with its own letter of support recom-mending an annual subvention of 2,000 ducats, which was approved.[21]

The anonymous memorial highlights the importance of space to the project of recogimiento, a word that had a variety of meanings in the early modern Iberian world. We have already seen the verb *reco-ger* used to refer simultaneously to the acts of gathering and enclos-ing people or things. The noun form thus describes the point at which this spatial concentration occurs. The two levels of recogimiento I want to highlight here are the *architectural*, or a physical enclosure organized through both external and internal partitions, and the *sub-jective*, or the withdrawal into—and simultaneously the production of—the interiority of the self as a space of reflection in which the soul may come into harmony with God. The point is not only that re-cogimiento operates at multiple spatial levels, but also that there is an interaction between them. Although insufficient in itself, physi-cal enclosure was thought to contribute to and indeed enable certain forms of spiritual practice, grounding the subjective in the architec-tural. Over time the hermetic seclusion of the *recollectio*, favored by Franciscan mystics seeking to escape from worldly stimuli, took on solidly physical dimensions as it coalesced into the recogimiento or enclosure behind thick walls as a means of separating the external space of the world from the internal space of the sacred.[22]

Each of these levels is apparent in the memorial presented by Pes-quera. First and foremost, it explicitly notes the need for the build-ing to have "altas paredes porq̃ no se huyan los niños q̃ estan recogi-dos alli" (high walls so the children who are enclosed there do not flee). And if they should nevertheless find some way to escape, a bailiff (*alguacil*) will not only "buscar los niños q̃ se uyen" (find the children who run away) but also bring back "los demas q̃ hallare pdidos y bagamundos a la dha casa" (any lost and vagrant children who may be found to this house). Revealingly, the Colegio's agent was authorized to carry out this task "por fuerça" (by force) if necessary. In moments like these, the recogimiento begins to resemble a prison, and the "recogidos" inside inmates. But it also underscores the authorities' recognition of the difficult project that faced them and the forms of resistance that were likely to emerge in response. The building's walls thus constituted the architectural foundation of recogimiento, without which the project of subjectification would have been impossible.

High walls do more than keep children *in*—they also serve to keep *out* worldly distractions, thereby producing an interior space that can be subjected to careful regulation and surveillance. For its part, this internal ordering contributes to the process of subject formation by embedding practices and routines in the space of the everyday. The memorial offers glimpses of the composition and consolidation of this disciplinary space within the Colegio's walls:

> Los niños . . . tengan dormitorio largo de una pieça, y en el aya camas de una parte y de otra de madera encajada como tablado y de ancho de siete pies y atajado con una tabla ancha entre la cama de cada uno demanera q̃ duerma cada uno por si y todos juntos. Esta la sala desocupada por medio, tienen seis lamparas q̃ arden desde q̃ anocheçe hasta q̃ amanesçe sin cessar. En el dormitorio quatro, en la enfermeria una, en las necesarias una. Estan los maestros y disçipulos dentro deste dormitorio. Ay treinta y seis veladores cada noche desde las ocho y media hasta la ora q̃ amaneçe, y estos an de ser de los mas fieles, cada vela es ora y media por una ampolleta y velan seis niños paseandose los tres contra los otros tres, y van reçando el rossario. Y en levantandose hechan con un ysopo agua bendita por todas las partes del dormitorio un niño en cada vela de las seys. Estos veladores tienen cuidado de cubrir a los niños y mirar no haya alguno mal recaudo hasta q̃ amanece. Y uno de los seis veladores de la vela postrera tañe en amanesçiendo una campanilla por todo el dormitorio con q̃ despierta a todos los niños. [The children have a dormitory that is the length of a room, and in it there are beds made of fitted wood like a plank, seven feet wide and separated by wide boards between each bed such that

every child sleeps by himself and all together. The room is empty in the middle, and there are six lamps that burn continuously from dusk to dawn: four in the dormitory, one in the nursery, one in the lavatory. The teachers and disciples are also in this dormitory. There are thirty-six watchers every night from 8:30 until the hour of dawn, and these are to be the most reliable. Each night watch lasts an hour and a half according to an hourglass and six children circle the room in opposite directions in groups of three, and they recite the rosary as they walk. When they get up one child of every six sprinkles holy water with an aspergillum in every part of the dormitory. These watchers take care to watch over the children and make sure that nothing bad happens until dawn. And as dawn breaks one member of the final watch rings a little bell throughout the room to wake up all of the children.]

I have cited this passage at length because it is representative of the document as a whole insofar as it captures the imbrication of built environment, material culture, and bodily practice, the way routines were organized around and calibrated to a specific architectural space. Consider, for example, the description of the night watches or *velas*. This was a spatially situated practice, with the field of action defined and circumscribed by the walls and objects that composed it. Six students took part in each vela, which lasted an hour and a half—time was measured, and broken up, by the hourglass. At the beginning of each watch, one of the participants circled around the perimeter of the dormitory with an aspergillum, sprinkling holy water and blessing each corner of the room. Forming themselves into two groups of three, the students continued circling the room, one group clockwise and the other counterclockwise, praying the rosary and watching over the rest of the sleeping children, until their shift ended and the next one began. If this practice was aimed at securing the dormitory from sinful or otherwise diabolic intrusions, it also served to synchronize the children's movements and actions and repeatedly demarcate the room as a space of care through vigilance.

Equally important was the partitioning of internal space, a dimension that involved not only architectural details and spatial practices (such as the demarcation of the dormitory) but also the intentional use of material culture. The beds in the dormitory, for example, were divided between two areas, separated from each other by an open space in the middle, which made it easier to account for each child.

Moreover, the beds were separated by wooden dividers. These designs established a space that was simultaneously integrated, part of a single, common dormitory, and doubly partitioned, with two areas for the beds and within each area separate compartments for each child. And these formal qualities had an explicit function: as the memorial puts it, the intention was for each child to sleep "cada uno por si y todos juntos" (every one by himself and all together). Such pastoral power simultaneously totalizes and individualizes, assuming responsibility for the safety of the flock as a whole (*omnes*) and at the same time the health and well-being of each and every individual member (*singulatim*). As Foucault observes, it is not enough for the shepherd to know where every sheep is at any given moment, but everything they have done and may do, any good or evil acts they have carried out or may perform, also falls under his purview. He must know not only their "public sins" but also "what goes on in the soul of each one, his secret sins, his progress on the road to sanctity."[23]

The shepherd's knowledge of the soul of each member of his flock thus comes from the deployment of a closed space of continuous surveillance and an array of truth procedures. Disciplinary space underlies subjective recogimiento. Designed to give voice to the children's innermost thoughts, these mechanisms were woven into the fabric of daily life at the Colegio. Consider, for example, the memorial's detailed description of the steps for ending the day and going to bed:

> Y luego entran los mayores y medianos en un lugar q̃ p̃ ello tienen diputado con el dho preceptor y se hincan de rodillas un paso apartado uno de otro y una candela puesta delante en una linterna metida, y el preceptor o preceptores detrás q̃ los puedan ver, medio a escuras, p̃ se recoger un cuarto de ora en silencio apartados del ruido q̃ an traido y traen todo el día, a pensar en sus pecados, y en la misericordia de dios. Y acavado haze señal el principal preceptor, y sacan la lumbre, y lebantanse halli tornales a dezir alguna cossa p̃ les aparejar á contriçion y a comfisión y a los demas sacramentos p̃ dignamente los rescevir y p̃ emendar la vida. [And then the oldest and middle children enter with the preceptor into a determined place and kneel down at a distance of one pace from each other with a candle in a lantern set out in front of them and the preceptor or preceptors behind to watch over them so that, in the dim light, they may gather their thoughts (*se recoger*) for a quarter of an hour in silence, separated from the commotion of the day, and contemplate their sins and

God's compassion. And when this is complete the main preceptor gives the signal, and they take the light and stand up, and the preceptor says a few words to ready them for contrition and confession and to receive the rest of the sacraments with dignity and reform their lives.]

The distribution of bodies and objects in space is central here. On one hand, the configuration of the students' kneeling bodies, forming a regular line with a specified amount of space between them, and the preceptor behind; on the other hand, the positioning of objects, specifically the light source, set at the front of the room so as to backlight the students' bodies under the watchful eyes of the preceptor. The preceptor's gaze works on the children's shadowy forms, coaxing them to inner reflection, contrition, and finally confession. Such spatial distributions thus operate through a double enclosure: within the walled-off architectonic enclosure of the Colegio, the child is guided toward enclosing himself within the intimate recesses of his mind. Yet the ultimate goal here is not the practice of self-reflection per se, but the externalization of this truth of the self through confession. The children's public and private lives, their bodies and souls, are thus bared to the preceptor.

But it was not the preceptors alone who watched over the students—the students themselves participated in the apparatus of surveillance, multiplying and dispersing the sight lines of the disciplinary gaze. After morning prayers, the memorial states, "se levanta uno [de los niños] en pie y toma una tabla en q̃ estan los nombres de todos escriptos y llama a todos p̃a ver si falta alguno" (one of the children stands up and takes a list on which the names of all the children are written and calls each one to see if anyone is missing). Similarly, four officials were appointed to inspect the entire house, "y han de dar cuenta de lo que se hizo fuera o dentro, si hubo cosa mala o de pecado" (and they shall give an account of whatever happened, whether inside or outside, if there was anything bad or sinful). Here the institutional gaze was not only personified but regularized and decentralized as well. Any student who had learned to read could check the names off the list, such that beyond being integrated into the disciplinary apparatus the students had to some degree also become interchangeable. There is not necessarily a tension between the individualizing power of confessional truth procedures and the normalizing power of subject formation, since these mechanisms serve to produce the individual and at the same time the collective subject—the sheep and the flock.

## FROM CONFINEMENT TO CIRCULATION

We have seen how the emergence of the vagabond as a crisis of spatial governance is, in colonial space, racialized in the figure of the Mestizo. The colonial authorities sought to "fix" the vagabond/Mestizo in part by capturing and enclosing him behind the "altas paredes" (high walls) of the Colegio. But the project of Mestizo conversion went beyond mere confinement. The Colegio was more a factory than a warehouse, designed to transform idle, parasitic children into productive adults. Like congregation, recogimiento aimed not to prevent circulation altogether but to order and regulate it, making it useful to the colonial project.

As noted earlier, the memorial describes two tracks for children at the Colegio. The first was a straightforward effort to train them in a variety of specific vocations and insert them into the colonial wage economy:

> Los offiçios son camareros q̃ barren riegan limpian el dormitorio y hazen las camas, y las limpien y sacuden, y lampareros q̃ limpian y adereçan y açienden las lámparas, y enfermeros q̃ tienen cuidado de la enfermeria, y de los enfermos, y cozineros q̃ hazen la comida, y refitoleros q̃ limpian y varren y adereçan las mesas y sirben y dan la comida y la çena, despenseros q̃ traen la comida y la compran y la dan a guissar, y porteros. [The vocations are *camareros*, who sweep, mop, and clean the dormitory and make the beds, and clean and dust them; and *lampareros*, who clean and fix and light the lamps; and *enfermeros*, who take care of the nursery, and of the sick; and *cocineros*, who cook the food; and *refitoleros*, who clean and sweep and set the tables and serve lunch and dinner; and *despenseros*, who purchase, collect, and store the food; and *porteros* (i.e., doormen).]

By performing these tasks, the students would learn to "servir a sus amos en todo lo que les mandaren" (serve their masters in whatever they demand) and in the process contribute to the social reproduction of the Colegio. Beyond training the children in a specific set of tasks, then, the overarching objective was to transform them into obedient and productive subjects. Adopting a gendered position in the

colonial *oikonomia*, these "lost" boys turned "hombres" were defined by their capacity not only to perform waged labor but also to
constitute stable family units, which acted, as the Colegio's walls had
previously done, as a hedge against backsliding, a return to the prior
state of idleness: "Les encaminen en como se casen y tengan casa y
ganen de comer pā sy y pā su famillia como no tornen a ser pdidos y
vagamundos como de antes" (They are directed toward getting married and having a house and earning enough for themselves and their
family to eat so as to avoid once again becoming vagabonds and lost
as before). It was not only Mestiza girls who were made into subjects
of domesticity, then, but Mestizo boys as well.[24]

Although most of the children were thus channeled into wage labor, the memorial in fact privileges a second track: to participate in
the ongoing evangelization of the indigenous population. The initial
phase of the "spiritual conquest" of the Americas had been charged,
especially among the Franciscans, with a millenarian optimism that
had led early missionaries to believe that the pace of Christianization would be rapid. By midcentury, however, some critics had begun
to see cracks in the facade of Christianity and decry the blindness of
their predecessors. Above all, they blamed the clergy's insufficient
knowledge of indigenous languages and cultures for the failure of
Christian teachings to take hold and for the indigenous people's ability to continue to perform their traditional practices without being
caught. When Gerónimo de Mendieta arrived in New Spain in 1554,
for example, he noted that there were still few priests who spoke indigenous languages and that as a result conversion was difficult:
"Yo que escribo esto llegué á tiempo que aun no habia suficiencia de
frailes predicadores en las lenguas de los indios" (I who write this arrived at a moment when there were still insufficient friars capable of
preaching in the languages of the Indians).[25] A systematic approach
to ethnographic and linguistic knowledge production and diffusion
was undertaken to fill in these gaps.

Of course, such a project would require an enormous amount of
time, energy, and resources. The Colegio seemed to offer a significantly easier alternative. If Mestizo children could be effectively captured, enclosed, and reformed—if, in short, they could be subjected
to recogimiento—it might be possible to accelerate or even bypass
entirely the slow, difficult, and expensive work of training Spanish
priests effectively in indigenous languages. Drafting Mestizo children for the task of evangelization would make fluency not a distant

goal but the point of departure. The memorial frames the objective of the Colegio as creating a path of study

> para que los q̃ se inclinaren a letras, o a ser eclesiasticos o religiosos lo sean por q̃ de alli salgan psonas q̃ aprovechen en los naturales, por q̃ sabran las lenguas de ellos y ayudaran mucho mas q̃ los q̃ de aca van, uno mas q̃ diez, por ser naturales, y tener la lengua y conocer y saber las flaquezas y conditiones dellos pã convertir y atraer, enseñar y conservar en la fee y doctrina, y seran pã mas travajo y supliran la falta q̃ ay de religiossos y de sacerdotes alla en muchas maneras y no desearan venirse aca por ser alla su patria, y por q̃ se compadesceran mas de las necessidades de los yndios y les doleran mas sus travajos por ser sus naturales, y entenderlos an mejor q̃ los q̃ de aca van, q̃ de cien se vuelven los noventa aca. [so that those who are inclined to letters or to become ecclesiastics or mendicants may do so, and thereby train people who will be of great use among the natives (*naturales*), because they will know their languages and be of far more help in converting, attracting, teaching, and conserving them in faith and doctrine than those who are from here (i.e., Spain), ten times more effective, because they are natives (*naturales*) and know the language and are familiar with their weaknesses and character, and they will be willing to do more work and in many ways make up for the lack of regular and secular clergy there (i.e., New Spain), and they will not seek to return here because their homeland is there, and because they will feel more compassion for the needs of the Indians and will be more moved by their work because they too are natives (*naturales*), and they will understand them better than those who come from here, of which ninety out of every hundred return.]

This dense passage clarifies two important points about the specificity of the Mestizo missionary. First, for Spanish priests, learning one or more indigenous languages was always a difficult and often insurmountable barrier, even with the help of grammars and dictionaries. The students of the Colegio, on the other hand, already knew everything they needed to communicate effectively with the indigenous population. Additionally, beyond such language skills, their knowledge of the Indians' "flaquezas y conditiones" would allow them to frame their evangelizing rhetoric in the most convincing way and recognize the temptations and backsliding tendencies of the already converted. The Mestizo missionary thus embodied the dual potential of effectively attending not only to the initial moment of conversion but also to the ongoing "conservation" of the faith against the constant threat of apostasy.

This is not to say that the Colegio was framed in opposition to the Sahagunian project of ethnographic capture.[26] On the contrary, Mestizo students might be able to assist such a project in various ways, potentially even by teaching indigenous languages to future missionaries. The memorial proposes linking the Colegio to the Royal University in order to train a new cadre of language instructors, "ordenandolo de manera q̃ se enseñen todas las lenguas en la dha Cassa pā q̃ de alli salgan algunos Predicadores pā enseñar tanta diuersidad de lenguas de gente como ay en aq̃llas provincias" (organizing it so that all the languages are taught in this House in order to train some Preachers capable of teaching all the diverse languages of the people of those provinces). Although this institutional link was never implemented, the children were nevertheless drafted to help the friars with their translations, grammars, and dictionaries. The Colegio's official constitution, approved in 1557, required students to spend one to two hours a day "en la traducción de las lenguas de los naturales de la dicha Nueva España en nuestra lengua castellana, en artes y vocabularios" (on the translation of the languages of the natives of this New Spain into our Castilian tongue, into grammars and dictionaries).[27]

But the passage also indicates, second, that the Mestizos' privileged capacity for missionary and pedagogical work went beyond linguistic and cultural fluency—a subtle bond further linked these potential shepherds to their flock. Spanish-born priests might be frustrated or overwhelmed by the significant needs of the indigenous population, but Mestizos would feel a profound sense of empathy with their Indian parishioners that would evoke a sort of emotional resonance, such that even pain would be mutually experienced and generate feelings of compassion among the priests. The memorial clarifies the source of this bond by using the word "natives" (*naturales*) in two distinct ways. In the first instance, following common practice for the period, the word refers to the indigenous population that would make up the congregations of these missionaries-in-formation. A distinction is elaborated between the "personas" formed in the Colegio and then sent out to the missionary field, and "los naturales" they will encounter there. In the second and third instances, however, the valence of the word shifts, and "naturales" begins to include the missionaries themselves. They are linked, apparently, by an affinity of birthplace, a connection that goes beyond mere familiarity with indigenous languages and cultures. Comparing Spanish-born to locally born priests—recall that the "here" of the memorial is Spain and the "there" is New Spain—the document suggests that a single priest trained at the Colegio will be as effective as ten from Spain. The reasons are twofold: first, since people inevitably long for their homeland, 90 percent of the missionaries who travel to the New World will eventually return to the Old; and second, a shared birthplace gives rise to an affective bond, one that not only makes the work less taxing but also produces a profound compassion in the missionaries for their compatriots. In these ways, the Colegio expands the evangelization project in both absolute and relative terms, producing new priests to send into the missionary field while making the clergy as a whole more effective in its spiritual work. These "natural" skills make the Mestizo not only an *object* but also the ideal *subject* of conversion.

What is interesting here is that, if it were not already clear that the students at the Colegio were meant to be Mestizos, the passage would resemble an argument for *indigenous* priests. This, of course, was one of the initial objectives of the well-known Colegio de Santa Cruz de Santiago Tlatelolco, founded by the Franciscans in 1536 not only to educate and Christianize the children of the indigenous nobility but also to produce indigenous subjects capable of serving as missionaries themselves. Robert Ricard has argued that "the college had been founded not merely to train translators, copyists, and Latinists, but above all to train priests. It was to have been the first native seminary of the New World." In this respect, it proved a failure. Opposition emerged quickly and came from both the secular clergy and other religious orders, such as the Dominicans. In 1544, for example, Domingo de la Cruz and Domingo de Betanzos wrote to Charles V to persuade him against the education and ordination of Indians, arguing that they were as yet insufficiently Christianized and would as a result end up spreading heretical beliefs. Even the initially enthusiastic Zumárraga had changed his mind by the early 1540s.[28]

The figure of the Mestizo changes the terms of this debate, and it is possible that the Colegio de San Juan de Letrán emerged in part as a response to the strong opposition to the Colegio de Santa Cruz. The Mestizo seemed to contain the same valuable capacities as the Indian, but with the added advantages of a genealogical counterweight against idolatry and an apparently "natural" tendency to be followed and imitated by the indigenous. The memorial continues:

> Y desta manera se acortaran los grandes males q̃ estos hazen y hazian en los yndios, y los robos y muertes y fuerças, tomandoles las mugeres e hijas a los yndios e haziendo otros graves e innormes pecados. Y sin haber ni tener cuenta con missa ni doctrina ni confesarse; ni aun saber q̃ cossa es ser Chrianos, blasfemando con sus malas obras y exssemplos el nombre de nrō s°ʳ, y aun siendo causa q̃ muchos o todos los naturales yndios q̃ los veen, y con quien conversan y tratan, lo blasphemen y huyan del por su causa, y animando a otros q̃ hagan lo q̃ ellos y sean como ellos y peores. [And this is how the great evils that they do and did among the Indians will be reduced, and the robberies and killings and violence, taking their wives and daughters and committing other grave and enormous sins, and without accounting for it through mass or instruction or confession; without even knowing what it means to be Christians, blaspheming with their evil acts and examples in the name of Our Lord, and even causing many or all of the Indian natives who see them, and with whom they speak and exchange, to blaspheme and flee from Him, and animating others to do what they do and be like them and even worse.]

Instead of the affective bonds noted earlier, in this passage the Mestizo-Indian relation appears as one of violence and exploitation. In this respect it resonates strongly with colonial legislation that, as we have seen, constructed the vagabond as a racial problem and in the process cast the Mestizo as a population to be managed by the colonial state. Much as with what we would call "race relations" today, this art of government is framed as mediation between collections of people who are presumed to belong to coherent and differentiated groups but is in fact a racializing procedure that contributes to the formation of these groups. At first glance, then, the memorial appears to contain a contradiction: on one hand, the Mestizo (missionary) experiences a "natural" affinity with the Indian; on the other hand, the Mestizo (vagabond) exudes a "natural" enmity for the Indian. Upon closer inspection, however, both characterizations share the same mimetic structure, according to which the Mestizo acts as a mirror in which the Indians see themselves reflected and toward whom they are drawn ("todos los naturales yndios que los veen y con quien con-

versan y tratan . . . hagan lo que ellos y sean como ellos y peores").
In other words, what is valuable about the Mestizo—his capacity to
serve as a model for the indigenous—is precisely what makes him
dangerous.

In endorsing Pesquera's request and forwarding it to the king, the
Council of the Indies summed up the work of the Colegio as follows:

> Muchos mestizos y otros muchachos que andan perdidos se reco-
> gen allí y son doctrinados, y unos salen para oficios y otros para reli-
> giosos. . . . aquellos niños, después de enseñados en la fe y en nuestra
> lengua, lo comunican con los otros naturales, y de esta manera parece
> que cumple vuestra Majestad gran parte de la obligación que tiene a
> enviar ministros a aquella tierra para la conversión de ellos. [Many
> Mestizos and other lost boys are gathered and enclosed there and
> are taught Christian doctrine, and some become laborers and others
> clergy. . . . Those children, after learning the faith and our language,
> will communicate them to the other natives, and in this way it seems
> that your Majesty fulfills a great part of his obligation to send minis-
> ters to that land for their conversion.][29]

In effect, the project of enclosure does not end with confinement but
generates new and productive forms of circulation as well. Mestizo
conversion is played out in three steps: first, the capture of "lost" vag-
abond/Mestizo boys and their enclosure in the orderly space of the
institution ("se recogen allí"); second, the application of discipline
to transform these vagabonds/Mestizos into Christianized subjects
("son doctrinados"); and third, the redeployment of these "new men"
into the colonial economy, either as wage laboring and gendered subjects of production and reproduction or as idealized subjects of evangelization within the missionary field ("unos salen para oficios y
otros para religiosos"). Unlike the disordered flows of the vagabond/
Mestizo, however, this circulation is policed—territorialized, carefully regulated, channeled through institutional points of entry, and
oriented toward a specific set of objectives.

At the time the memorial was delivered, this project was beginning to bear fruit, with the anonymous author personally testifying
that in the five short years since the Colegio's foundation "yo dexe
mas de Veynte moços hechos frailes" (I left more than twenty children [who had] become friars) in the Franciscan and Dominican orders. But this window of opportunity would not stay open for long.

## THE DECLINE OF MESTIZO CONVERSION

By the last quarter of the sixteenth century, only one of the Colegio's dual tracks remained. The shift is apparent in the documentation of a meeting between Archbishop Pedro Moya de Contreras and Viceroy Martín Enríquez that took place in April 1579. To resolve a number of administrative problems at the Colegio, the archbishop proposed turning it over to the Jesuit order, which had a proven track record of administering such institutions: "Es tan peculiar a la compañia doctrinar muchachos, que se vee y tiene experiençia, q̃ exçede a todos" (The Jesuit order is well suited to teaching boys, and it is apparent and proven that they exceed all others).[30] The viceroy disagreed. Although he recognized the Jesuits' abilities in this regard, he argued that transferring the institution to them would end up quickly consuming its resources and prestige, as well as erasing the Colegio's history and presumably the objectives for which it was founded: "Dentro de pocos ao[s] no oviese mem[a] de su fundaçion" (Within a few years no memory of its establishment will remain). Instead he recommended staying the course, perhaps adding an instructor or two but without making major changes. This call for continuity, however, was situated within a partial history of the institution:

> Porq̃ este colejio la prim[a] fundacion fue para criar y domar mochachos perdidos como son los q̃ para esto estan fundados en españa y otras partes. Y aunq̃ despues de la prim[a] fundacion pareçio q̃ era bien q̃ oviese alg[os] studiantes atento a la necesidad q̃ entonçes Avia en la tierra porq̃ ni Avia scuelas ni colejios la speriençia mostro ser de poco provecho porq̃ al fin quiere mas Recogimi[o] el estudio q̃ ay por la m[r] parte donde ay multitud destos mochachos. [This Colegio was initially founded to raise and tame lost boys, like those that have been established for this purpose in Spain and other parts. And although after its initial establishment it seemed good for there to be some students, given the need that existed at the time since there were neither schools nor Colegios in the land, experience showed it to be of little benefit since, in the end, study requires more recogimiento than there generally is with the multitude of these boys.][31]

Although the viceroy had indeed noted that the walls of the building that housed the Colegio were collapsing in a letter to the king several years earlier, here the failure of recogimiento is primarily subjective.[32] Even within the walls of the institution, the distracting "multitude" of boys makes substantive education largely impossible. As a result, the pedagogical aspect of the Colegio is minimized and at the same time decoupled from evangelization. Indeed, what is most notable in this account of the Colegio's history is that, despite the viceroy's concern for conserving the "memory" of the institution, the project of Mestizo conversion has been entirely erased. To the viceroy, the institution looks more like a reformatory dedicated to the formation of workers than a center of study dedicated to the formation of lettered subjects.[33]

Like Antonio de Mendoza before him, Viceroy Enríquez was sent to Peru soon after, clearing the way for Moya de Contreras to move forward with the implementation of his own vision. But the Colegio was not transferred to the Jesuits. The figure of the Mestizo, it seems, no longer embodied the positive potential that had animated the project of Mestizo conversion three decades before. If the notion of "reform" continued to resonate, it did so only in relation to the recogimiento and transformation of "lost" boys into productive workers. In structural terms, the Mestizo had been inserted into the "republic of Spaniards." Far from an egalitarian measure, however, this shift represented a form of differential inclusion—it meant being almost Spanish but not quite. Not surprisingly, this was also the period in which the Mestizo began to be associated with a specific location in the colonial economy—mostly artisans (though they were largely excluded from important guilds), as well as laborers and servants. If the Indian was constructed, as chapter 1 shows, in large part through the obligation to pay tribute and perform a certain amount of forced labor, the Mestizo emerged as non-Indian—not subjected to these forms of direct extraction—and was inserted into a structural position in the colonial economy as a relatively stable supply of waged labor power.[34]

Although the Jesuits did not take over the direct administration of the Colegio, they certainly had ideas about the direction it should take. A different future for the Colegio was articulated by the Jesuit Juan de la Plaza soon after the meeting between the viceroy and the archbishop. Having spent five years as *visitador*, or inspector, in Peru, he arrived in New Spain in early 1580 and was appointed provincial later that year. Due to his familiarity with the spiritual terrain in both viceroyalties, Plaza was viewed as a resource by the ecclesiastical authorities and as a result was invited to contribute a series of *memoriales* that were discussed during the conciliar meetings of the Third Mexican Council. Plaza's reports lay out his vision for the church in New Spain, a vision that draws heavily on the ideology of the Counter-Reformation.[35]

The first of Plaza's memoriales was concerned with seminaries. For most of the history of the Christian church, there had been no organized system for the education and training of priests. Only at the Council of Trent did the church codify the need for seminaries in all dioceses where no such institution existed. Opening with an architectural metaphor drawn from the Book of Kings, Plaza explains that the stones used to build the Temple of Solomon were fully worked ahead of time in the quarry and only later brought to the construction site and set in place. As a result of this careful preparation, the materials fit together perfectly and it took just seven years to complete the magnificent temple. These rocks, writes Plaza, are like priests who must be carved and polished before being placed in the walls of the "templo vivo y espiritual" (living, spiritual temple) of the church. Specifically referencing the Council of Trent's 1563 decree, he compares seminaries to these metaphorical quarries. Before that time, the main option for candidates aspiring to the priesthood was to approach a bishop directly and study under him while living in his home. This practice was common in Spain, Plaza observes, and had produced many ministers cheaply and effectively. But the Counter-Reformation church aimed to standardize, improve, and expand these educational pathways by ordering the establishment of seminaries "donde, desde pequeños, se crian e ynstruyan en virtud y letras ministros que puedan hazer este officio con edificación del pueblo y fructo de las ánimas" (where, from the time they are little, ministers who will be able to perform this work for the edification of the people and the health of their souls are raised and instructed in virtue and letters). Plaza acknowledges that such an effort could be costly, but points out that, at least in New Spain, much of the institutional base already exists:

> Aviendo pensado y mirado, con attención, el medio que podía aver para la institución destos seminarios, me pareze, si no me engaño, que ay más commodidad en este reyno, que en algún otro de los que yo he estado; porque en esta ciudad de México está fundado y dotado, con bastante renta, el collegio de S. Juan de Letrán que llaman, en esta ciudad, en la qual se podría fundar este seminario. Vues-

tras Señorías Illustrísimas verán las difficultades que en ello ay, y de mi parte supplico pongan todas las fuerças possibles, para vencerlas. [Having attentively reflected on and considered the means for establishing these seminaries, it seems, if I am not mistaken, that there is more to offer in this kingdom than in any of the others where I have been; because in this city of Mexico there is a Colegio that they call San Juan de Letrán that is endowed with sufficient resources, in which this seminary could be founded. Your Illustrious Lordships will consider the difficulties involved in this, and for my part I beg that you make every effort to overcome them.][36]

One way to interpret Plaza's vision for the Colegio would be as a confirmation of the project contained in the original plan laid out in the anonymous memorial three decades before. The institution would be dedicated, in this light, to forming priests who would be able to continue the work of evangelization. Their training would likewise begin at a young age, but these boys would differ in an important respect from their predecessors—they would not be Mestizos. Before traveling to New Spain, Plaza had been involved in debates about the ordination of Mestizos in Peru. He made two arguments against this practice. While, on one hand, he disparaged their abilities with the claim that they were "poco aptos para ministerios eclesiásticos, porque tienen muchas costumbres de las madres que los crían" (not suited to be ecclesiastical ministers, because they have many customs from the mothers who raise them), he at the same time captured the visual dimension of racial domination: "Comúnmente tienen los españoles y especialmente los eclesiásticos y religiosos, mucha aversión con ellos, porque son muy conocidos en el color" (Spaniards and especially the secular and regular clergy commonly feel a great aversion toward them, because they are very distinctive in color).[37] Despite any structural similarities, then, Plaza's reimagined Colegio de San Juan de Letrán would represent an entirely different project—one in which the Mestizo would play no part.

Although many of his recommendations were taken into account, the bishops did not heed Plaza's proposal for the Colegio. Apparently its crumbling adobe walls were not as well built as his metaphorical Temple of Solomon. Yet it is worth considering the two proposals I have highlighted here as a measure of the shift in attitude toward the Mestizo. On one end of the spectrum, we have the viceroy, for whom the Colegio had been recast as a reformatory; on the other end is the

provincial, who saw it as a potential seminary, the material foundation for implementing the decrees of Trent in the New World. What
unites these two very different projects is the sense that the Mestizo
could no longer be trusted on the front lines of the "spiritual conquest." What locked in the failure of recogimiento was an emerging
account of the mixed-race body that turned on the matrix of gender,
religion, and blood.

## THE GENDERED BODY POLITICS OF THE MESTIZO

Plaza's work in general, especially his view of Mestizo ordination, reveals the significant influence of another member of the Jesuit order,
the renowned José de Acosta. Plaza met Acosta soon after arriving in
Peru and was impressed, promoting him just three months later to
rector of the Colegio de San Pablo and five months after that to provincial. During the five years Plaza spent in Peru, the two worked together closely, participating in church events and collaborating on a
set of rules for the Colegio for indigenous caciques.[38] Plaza was also in
Peru while Acosta was composing his influential missionary treatise
*De procuanda indorum salute*, which was completed in 1577, though
not printed until 1588. As the most authoritative argument advanced
against Mestizo ordination in the sixteenth century, Acosta's text
also served as the most effective rebuttal of the memorial that Gregorio de Pesquera had presented to the Council of the Indies at midcentury. While Acosta's own missionary activities and writings were
focused primarily on Peru, his work had a significant impact on religious and secular thought and official policy far beyond. In fact,
his rejection of Mestizo ordination in *De procuranda* resonated even
more strongly in New Spain than in Peru. Plaza seems to have helped
transfer Acosta's ideas to New Spain, and this influence is reflected
in his proposal for reenvisioning the Colegio.[39]

In *De procuranda*, as in the earlier memorial, the potential of
the Mestizo missionary is linked to his fluency in indigenous languages—sorely lacking among many of his Spanish counterparts,
whom Acosta describes as "muti ipsi et elingues" (mute and without a tongue).[40] This linguistic familiarity is necessary for the pastor to enter into an effectively dialogic relation with his flock. On one
hand, only by speaking indigenous languages can the priests' words
reach the hearts and souls of the indigenous parishioners. "Valde
enim mihi persuadeo ita futurum brevi, ut evangelium Christi ad

animos istorum penetraret et vires suas expromeret, quod in ho-
diernum diem plurima ex parte tantum auribus indicis insonuisse
non etiam intima cordis penetralia pulsasse videtur" (I am entirely
convinced that in this way the gospel of Christ will quickly pene-
trate their souls and reveal its power, since until now it appears that
more often than not it has only echoed in the Indians' ears without
striking deep within their hearts).[41] On the other hand, understanding indigenous languages allows the pastor to know and watch over
his flock, whose own words reflect the sincerity of their conversion,
externalizing the internal truth of the soul. The faithful are those
who "fidem corde concipiunt et ore confitentur" (conceive faith in
the heart and confess it with the mouth), but Acosta insists that most
Indians are precisely the opposite: "specie et voce christiani, animo
et re obstinati infideles" (Christians in appearance and name, but in
their soul and in reality obstinate infidels).[42] These concerns resonate with the emerging baroque architecture of the self, which conceived of surfaces as deceptive and increasingly treated them with
suspicion. In the colonial context, specifically, what I have elsewhere
called the "racial baroque" gives way to a situation in which the Indian subject, split between external appearance and internal essence,
is constructed as "newly inscrutable and permanently suspicious."[43]

Acosta thus sees linguistic abilities as crucial both for transmit-
ting Christian faith to the indigenous population and for monitoring
the results of that evangelizing labor, the only possibility of overcoming the stubbornly racialized gap between illusory and sincere conversion. After all, the priest must administer the sacraments, take
confession, and recommend appropriate penance. How can he possi-
bly confess an indigenous parishioner, asks Acosta, without understanding the language? Catching a word here and there is clearly insufficient: "Cum confessionis integritas ex iure divino sit, eum non
esse idoneum poenitentiae ministrum, quem propter imperitiam
dimidium et eo amplius necessario latet, perinde enim est ac si tan-
tumdem non audiret" (Given that the integrity of confession falls under divine law, he who out of ignorance of the language misses half of
a confession is not capable of being a minister, since this is the same
as if he heard nothing).[44] Confession must be complete in order to be
effective.

In light of these weighty implications, Acosta judges the use of interpreters to be inadequate. The insertion of an intermediary might
threaten the integrity of confession by making the penitent reluctant

to divulge a complete and detailed list of sins in front of a peer, while any words he or she does speak are likely to be confused in their passage from mouth to mouth and language to language. Moreover, a translation error risks compounding the sins of those who confess—especially during Last Rites, when even a small mistake could result in eternal damnation. Yet Acosta's sharpest critique of the use of interpreters has to do with the nature of the interpreters themselves: "Atqui interprete utuntur plerumque, vel infido, vel imperito, qui vix intelligat ipse, quae audit, vix etiam exponere norit, quae intelligit, utpote indus ipse quoque, *vel ab indis prognatus*, qui neque res, neque sermones nostros satis plerumque callet" (But most often the interpreters who are used are either infidels or ignorant, and themselves barely understand what they hear, and when they do understand they barely know how to explain it, since after all they are Indians *or descendants of Indians*, who often know neither our matters nor our language sufficiently well).[45] The Jesuit asserts that many interpreters are simply too ignorant to understand what is being said, let alone formulate an accurate translation. But beyond the issue of competency is the far more significant danger that the interpreters themselves may be "infidels." Positioning such people next to the minister, depending on them as the medium through which the word of God is delivered to the community, could put the project of evangelization at risk. The logic of the racial baroque compounds this anxiety, since, as noted earlier, even the most "obstinati infideles" (obstinate infidels) are capable of fashioning and maintaining a deceptively Christian appearance. Finally, Acosta foregrounds descent as the critical framework for assessing the reliability of the interpreter. Alluding to the concept of limpieza de sangre, which treats blood as a vector for idolatry, he condemns not only "Indians" but "ab indis prognatus" (descendants of Indians) as well. Contrasted with the former, the latter can refer only to Mestizos. It is an interesting formulation, since, as we have seen, the language originally employed about the Colegio was "hijos de españoles." Here the project described by the Colegio's officials has been reversed—rather than the reliable descendant of a Spanish (father), predisposed for missionary service, the Mestizo is now cast as an unreliable descendant of an Indian (mother), a threat to the spiritual health of those around him.

María Elena Martínez shows that Spanish concerns about the heritability of indigenous idolatry in the late sixteenth century coincided with "the construction of indigenous women's bodies as vehicles for contamination."[46] Acosta's reference to "descendants of Indians" in his critique of interpreters reflects this sense of the increasing centrality of the indigenous mother in shaping the character of her children, whether Indian or Mestizo. This does not mean that the father was cast as irrelevant, but that his role—like that of the mother—was framed in a newly circumscribed way. In a passage explaining the Indian's apparent resistance to evangelization, Acosta lays out an explicitly gendered account of identity formation:

> Est haereditarium esse impietatis morbum, qui ab ipsis matrum visceribus ingenitus, ipso uberum lacte nutritus, paterno et domestico exemplo confirmatus, tum diuturna consuetudine et legum publica auctoritate munitus, nullo modo nisi copioso christianae gratiae munere et magna doctoris evangelici atque indefessa cura sanari queat.
> [It is a hereditary idolatrous sickness that, engendered in the belly of the mother and nourished from the milk of her breast, strengthened by the example of the father and the home and then fortified by long-lasting custom and the public authority of law, can in no way be cured without abundant Christian grace and the considerable and indefatigable work of the evangelical doctor.][47]

Beyond the discourse of heredity, what stands out in this passage is the clear division of reproductive labor, which links the mother to the body and nature, on one hand, and the father to education and culture, on the other. It is important to note that early modern medical theory treated breast milk as an altered form of blood that returned to its original state after consumption. Writing around the same time as Acosta in his *Diálogos familiares de agricultura cristiana* (1578–1580), Juan de Pineda asserted that "naturaleza lleva su tenor continuado de que como en el vientre nos compuso de sangre y nos mantuvo de sangre, ansí después de nascidos nos mantuvo con leche, que es sangre blanqueada" (nature maintains a continuous order in that, having been composed and maintained by blood in the belly, similarly after birth we were maintained by milk, which is whitened blood).[48] While Martínez suggests that blood tended to function as a metaphor for inheritance that worked through the "conflation of culture and biology," Acosta's clear differentiation between corporeal and pedagogical influences may have been an exception—an attempt not to conflate but to disentangle the combined forces acting on and shaping the child's development.[49]

Acosta applies a similar model in the case of the Mestizo. Having rejected the use of interpreters, he examines three proposed solutions to the key problem of the lack of indigenous language skills. The first is the political line of the Crown, which would force the indigenous population to learn Castilian. Acosta observes that such a policy would be difficult if not impossible to enforce, and the failure of repeated royal decrees to achieve the desired effect leads him to characterize them as "verbis nudis" (empty words). Who would denounce those Indians who chose to speak Quechua in their own homes? The second proposal would promote, also by decree, the use of "lenguas generales," like Quechua in Peru or Nahuatl in New Spain, in an attempt to reduce the scope of linguistic diversity of the Americas. Again Acosta concludes that this outcome, though desirable, would prove equally difficult to achieve by means of a simple mandate and in any case would take a long time to implement. In the meantime, he argues, missionaries must dedicate themselves both to mastering indigenous languages and to teaching their own language to the Indians.[50]

The third and, at first glance, most reasonable proposal would harness the capacities of Mestizos ("mixto genere"), born of a Spanish father ("patre hispano") and an Indian mother ("matre inda"). In laying out this argument, Acosta reproduces the claims that had been mobilized thirty years before at the Colegio de San Juan de Letrán. As fluent speakers of indigenous languages who furthermore are deeply knowledgeable about indigenous cultures, he suggests, these Mestizos could serve as excellent teachers for Spanish priests and perhaps even excellent "ministros sermonis" (ministers of the word) themselves. As long as they demonstrate honesty and virtue, moreover, major doubts about the reliability of their Christian faith might be resolved by the knowledge that Christian instruction will have been imparted to them from a very young age and, perhaps more importantly, by their Spanish fathers: "Cum ab hispanis progenitoribus fidem ecclesiasticamque consuetudinem haereditario fere iure retineant" (From their Spanish fathers they have retained their religious faith and education by an almost hereditary law).[51]

Acosta notes that at one point he supported this proposal, but has since changed his mind: "Certissima magistra experientia copiose monstrat non posse nos, nec debere sollicitudinem omnem nostram studiumque deponere indigenarum praesidio fretos" (Experience, that most proven teacher, abundantly demonstrates that we cannot and must not place all of our solicitude and zeal in the aid of those born in the Indies).[52] Such efforts, he now writes, should be treated as "periculosa" (dangerous). In saying this, Acosta may have been thinking about political rebellions such as the Mestizo "mutiny," which had been foiled just a few years before his arrival in Peru.[53] It is equally likely, however, that his attention was on the missionary's especially sensitive position in relation to the Counter-Reformation expansion of the faith and the potentially heretical indigenous population. In any case, what most interests me here is the gendered discourse of identity that actively sustains this racializing shift: he describes these Mestizos as "tantam apto sermoni hominum . . . quorum mores non aeque apti sint. Fere enim indorum ingenia et mores redolent, quorum et lacte et consuetudine educati sunt" (men who are well suited for language, but whose customs are not so suitable. For they are generally redolent of the nature and culture of the Indians, due to the milk and customs with which they have been raised).[54] Over and above their language abilities, Acosta foregrounds the dangers posed by their corrupting ways: "Plus obesse corruptis moribus, quam verbo sano proficere" (There is more to be hindered by their corrupt manners than gained from their good word).[55] Here, as in the earlier example of indigenous children, the Mestizo child's development has two elements: the natural, on one hand, and the cultural, on the other. The parallel structure of Acosta's description ("ingenia et mores . . . lacte et consuetudine") generates the twinned pairings of nature-milk (*ingenia-lacte*) and culture-customs (*mores-consuetudine*), once again distinguishing between the gendered mechanisms of subject formation that operate over the body of the child. Although parallel, these pairings are not necessarily equivalent. That the traces of vice supposedly retained by the adult Mestizo are described as a bad odor or aftertaste suggests that milk performs the critical work in this operation.[56]

Equally important in Acosta's elaboration of the Mestizo's development, however, is the disappearance of the father and his "paternal example." In the case of the Indian child, as we saw earlier, the long-term disciplinarity of *mores-consuetudine*, backed by the public authority of the state, falls under the patriarchal jurisdiction of the father-governor. Yet the Mestizo child has been abandoned by his father and separated from the force of law. Only one actor remains: the indigenous mother, figured metonymically by the product of her breast.[57] Nature is privileged to the point that the efficacy of culture is naturalized—any pedagogical influence the mother may have is conflated with or subsumed by the bodily processes through which material substances pass from her to her child. In this way, Acosta constructs a language of corporeal materiality to resituate the discourse of subjectivity in the face of the difficulties facing the Spanish colonial project at the end of the sixteenth century.

## CONCLUSION

We have seen how Acosta's reflections on Mestizo ordination were taken up by Juan de la Plaza and inserted into discussions about the future of the Colegio from 1580 on, but this does not account for the full extent of the Jesuit's influence on the matter. Already in 1578, the year after *De procuranda* was completed, Fray Rodrigo de Loaysa, an Augustinian missionary with years of experience in Peru, traveled to Spain to present a series of legislative requests directly to Philip II. As with Acosta, language was one of his main priorities. The Indians are not being Christianized, he asserts, because the priests who are supposed to instruct them do not speak their languages. There is not even a school where these languages are taught. Spanish priests arrive, learn "una docena de vocablos" from a *confesionario*, and are sent into the field. "Los que no saben la lengua" (Those who do not know the language), he concludes, "son predicadores mudos" (are mute preachers) and cannot "descargar la conciencia de Vuestra Magestad" (unburden Your Majesty's conscience).[58]

But Loaysa presses the king further. In stark contrast with the supporters of the project of Mestizo conversion three decades earlier, he demands a prohibition on the ordination of Mestizos, regardless of any new legislation requiring knowledge of indigenous languages:

Es gran inconveniente ordenar mestizos y ponerlos en doctrina siendo tan mal doctrinados. Debía de mandar Vuestra Magestad los obispos tuviesen gran moderación en ordenarlos, y si alguno se ordenase, no se pusiese en doctrina hasta ser muy aprobado y conocido por muy virtuoso, porque tenemos experiencia que han hecho mucho daño. [It is a serious problem to ordain Mestizos and place them in *doctrinas* being so poorly educated. Your Majesty should have ordered the bishops to use great moderation in ordaining them, and if one were to be ordained, that he not be placed in *doctrina* until he has been very much proven and known to be very virtuous, because our experience shows that they have done great harm.]

If the arguments in Loaysa's appeal to the king sound familiar, it is because he apparently based them on the substantial authority of Acosta's missionary treatise.[59] Moreover, though he does not go into details concerning the bad "experiencia" with Mestizo priests, he was probably familiar (like Acosta) with the project of Mestizo conversion, since the "Mexican model" of the Colegio de San Juan de Letrán had been exported to Peru. As early as 1550, the Dominican friar Domingo de Santo Tomás wrote to the Council of the Indies proposing to establish a house for Mestiza girls, and the following year an enclosure based on this model was set up in Lima. More concretely, a royal decree in 1554 ordered the same authorities to replicate the gendered approach that had been implemented in Mexico City, creating one Colegio for Mestizo boys and another for Mestiza girls. Viceroy Antonio de Mendoza probably played a direct role in this transfer of recogimiento practices, since after overseeing the establishment of the Colegios in New Spain he was reassigned to Peru in 1550.[60] Loaysa may have been referring to these or similar projects, then, but regardless of the specific rationale, his arguments reflect the changing view of the Mestizo and the possibility of "reform."

Philip II was convinced. On December 2, 1578, soon after the visit, royal decrees were issued to the colonial authorities on precisely the subjects Loaysa had raised. One required that all priests sent to indigenous parishes speak the local language. A second generalized and extended to the rest of the Indies a decree from the previous year that the king had issued to the bishop of Cuzco prohibiting Mestizo ordination. "Nos somos imformado q̃ aveis dado ordenes a mestizos y a otras personas que no tienen sufficiencia para ello" (We are informed that you have ordained Mestizos and other people who lack suitability for it), wrote the king to Moya de Contreras, the archbishop of Mexico. "Os ruego y encargo que mireis mucho en ello y tengais en el dar las dhas ordenes el cuydado q̃ de vrõ buen celo y xpiandad se comfía dandolas solo a personas en quien concurran las partes y calidades necessarias, y por agora no las dareis a los dhos mestizos de ninguna manera" (I request and charge you with examining the matter seriously and with taking the care that your good Christian zeal merits in conferring these orders, granting them only to people in whom all the necessary aspects and qualities are present, and for now not granting them to Mestizos at all). In this way, both language requirement and Mestizo prohibition were made official colonial policy throughout the Americas.[61]

In New Spain, the prohibition was especially effective.[62] There is little question as to the views of the bishops toward the end of the sixteenth century, despite the fact that Philip II overturned his prohibition in 1588 and the legislation from the Third Mexican Council, approved in 1591, included a loophole allowing Indians and Mestizos to be ordained. Stafford Poole cautions us to remember that the final version of these laws, which were modified by the Roman Curia, does not necessarily index the attitudes of the religious authorities who drafted them, or for that matter those who implemented them. The bishops of New Spain clearly intended to exclude Mestizos (along with Indians and Mulattoes) from the priesthood altogether, and there is little indication that Rome's intervention had a significant effect on their attitude. This is not to say that no one who was identified as Mestizo was ever ordained, of course, but it was an exceptional occurrence.[63]

Yet the relative efficacy of the prohibition may be less important than the object toward which it was directed. There is a tendency to reduce race to a matter of exclusion, but racialization also operates through inclusion—forced, material, and differential inclusion. What is at stake in these debates over Mestizo ordination is not a morality tale about discrimination against a marginalized group (either as a condemnation of its occurrence or a celebration of its overcoming), but the construction of individual and collective bodies and the disciplinary processes of subjectification that inserted them into structures of domination and exploitation. Despite their differences, all the parties to the dispute, from the bishops of New Spain to the Roman Curia, agreed about one thing: the specificity of Mestizo bodies that were, as Larissa Brewer-García suggests, *"materially different* from Old Christian bodies."[64] In this sense, the "mixed" body gradually emerged not through the "mixture" of blood but through a process of "purification" by which the Mestizo was conceptually detached from Spanish—and I would add Indian—corporeality.

This material difference emerged in large part through the spatial politics of enclosure at institutions like the Colegio. For a time, the vagabond/Mestizo—the body without a "place," expressed through unregulated mobility—seemed to contain at least two possible futures. One tilted more toward the Spanish side of the genealogical equation, aimed at producing wage laborers and stable family units that would sustain both the production and reproduction of the colonial order. The other tilted more toward the Indian side, seeking to harness the Mestizo's "natural" familiarity with indigenous languages and cultures to overcome the biggest obstacle to effective evangelization. By the end of the century, however, only the first path remained open. Recogimiento, it seemed, could carve out a subordinated space within the republic of Spaniards but could not erase what Acosta called the Mestizo's "genere obscuri" (obscure origin)—a genealogical bond, materialized through specific bodily substances such as breast milk and blood. As a result, the Mestizo could no longer be trusted to perform the extraordinarily sensitive task of mediating between the post-Tridentine orthodoxy and an Indian population increasingly characterized as predisposed to idolatry and imitation.

If Francisco Cervantes de Salazar situates the Colegio firmly within the infrastructural space of the ordered city, Juan de la Plaza's metaphor of the Temple of Solomon helps us consider the bodies that passed through the Colegio as part of an infrastructural system as well. Each priest is a meticulously carved and polished stone, carefully set into the wall of the church, part of a system of social and material relations that underpins and enables the practices of everyday Christian life. Plaza's apt imagery captures the ways in which subjects are integrated into infrastructural systems. Yet it also suggests that the Mestizo fit not into the walls of Plaza's spiritual temple, but instead into the foundations of the urban economy.

# CHAPTER 3

# SEGREGATION: SOVEREIGNTY, ECONOMY, AND THE PROBLEM WITH MIXTURE

*How may a space be said to be at once homogeneous and divided, at once unified and fragmented?*

HENRI LEFEBVRE, *THE PRODUCTION OF SPACE*

ON THE AFTERNOON OF JUNE 8, 1692, in the context of widespread food shortages, a massive riot broke out in the central plaza of Mexico City. By nightfall, the stalls of the marketplace had been looted and burned and numerous government buildings, including the viceroy's imposing palace overlooking the plaza, had been reduced to smoldering ruins. It was not only the walls of the palace that were shattered as a result of the violence but the facade of colonial hegemony as well, and the authorities were shocked at the ease with which the urban and mostly indigenous underclass had overpowered them.[1]

The quasi-official history of the riot is a long account written several months later by the prominent Creole intellectual Carlos de Sigüenza y Góngora.[2] Sigüenza situates the event in the context of a generalized decline of Spanish imperial sovereignty, highlighting pirate attacks and commercial competition from European rivals in the Caribbean and Pacific as well as indigenous uprisings along New Spain's northern frontier.[3] But the breakdown of the social order in Mexico City was most immediately precipitated by a highly localized and deeply material crisis—the breakdown of urban infrastructure. According to Sigüenza, what set in motion the cascading series of events that culminated in the riot was precisely an infrastructural failure. One year before the riot, the sky filled with clouds and an unseasonably heavy rain began to fall. The waters overflowed the canals and flooded the city. Sigüenza is careful to note that this crisis, while triggered by an accident of nature, resulted primarily from human failure. "Si las muchas asequias que tiene Mex.ᶜᵒ no estubieran en estta ocasion asoluadas todas, buque tienen para hauer reseuido toda estta agua y condusidola a la laguna de Tescuco, donde quanta general mentte viene de las serranías se recoje siempre" (If the many canals of Mexico City had not been obstructed on this occasion, they are capacious enough to have received all of this water and channeled it into Lake Texcoco, where however much generally comes off the mountain ridge is always collected). It was the failure to maintain the city's hydraulic infrastructure, keeping the canals clear and functional so they could contain and redirect the flows of water, that created the conditions for the disaster. The riot, Sigüenza writes, was "[el] fuego en que, en la fuersa de la ambre, se transformó el agua" (the fire into which the water was transformed by the stress of hunger).[4]

Beyond the failure of the city's hydraulic infrastructure, however, was a more generalized infrastructural collapse. The colonial order, as we have seen, was based on the assumption of a more or less direct correspondence between infrastructure and social relations. In the case of congregation, for example, the concept of *policía* linked the geometric space of the centralized town to a series of Christian practices that the indigenous population was intended to adopt. The same assumption grounded the overarching framework of colonial governance from the mid-sixteenth century on—the model of two separate "republics," one for "Spaniards" and the other for "Indians," each organized around a distinct set of institutions, rights, and obligations for its members. Although the republics were primarily administrative, ecclesiastical, and juridical structures, they also took on a spatial form, visible not only in the congregated town but also in the segregated order of the capital of New Spain. At the moment of its foundation over the ruins of Tenochtitlan, Mexico City was laid out according to an orthogonal grid as well as a segregated plan that divided the Spanish center (*traza*) from the Indian districts (*barrios*) that surrounded it—a simultaneously homogeneous and fragmented space, as Lefebvre suggests in the epigraph. Early descriptions of the city highlight the canal that physically separated the two zones, as well as the defensive architecture of the traza's fortresslike buildings meant to stand in for walls as protection from the hostile native population.[5] Yet the riot underscored the fact that by the end of the seventeenth century many of the city's indigenous inhabitants had relocated to the traza.

Along with the spectacular punishment of the riot's purported leaders and the prohibition of the indigenous alcohol known as *pul-que mezclado*, the colonial state's most important response was the effort to secure the infrastructural order by once again segregating the city along racial lines.[6] The viceroy requested a collection of official *informes* (reports) from members of the colonial elite, including Sigüenza himself, along with the seven priests entrusted with overseeing the Indian parishes or *doctrinas*. As one of the main architects of the segregation policy, Sigüenza outlined a "linea de separacion" (separation line) demarcating the Spanish traza and dividing it from the Indian barrios, a boundary that was eventually incorporated word for word into the viceroy's final order.[7] Sigüenza's report has tended to overshadow those of the parish priests in terms of scholarly attention, largely owing to his importance as a Creole intellectual figure, but in this case his intervention may have been less significant than his reputation might lead us to believe. Although the formal, external contours of segregation were taken directly from Sigüenza's report, this chapter suggests that it was in fact the ministers, and especially the Franciscan friar Agustín de Vetancurt, whose interventions—including their informes as well as other documents called *padrones* or ecclesiastical censuses—not only register the decline of the infrastructure of segregation but also model the biopolitical techniques of population management that were consolidated in the wake of the riot and over the course of the following century.[8]

Earlier chapters have underscored the "positive" work of colonial infrastructure—its capacity to create the material conditions that both enable the unfolding of everyday life and facilitate the construction of racialized (and other) categories and subjectivities. This chapter approaches the matter from the opposite direction. What kinds of racial categories, subjectivities, and theories are fashioned not through the construction of durable structures but through their collapse? How do new material forms and practices emerge to rescue and replace those that have entered into crisis? And what kinds of racializing processes might be set in motion as a result? The segregation documents track the response of colonial elites not only to the political crisis precipitated by the riot but also to the more general decline of the infrastructure of separation on which Spanish colonial rule had been established over the previous two centuries. The reports thus lay out a political analysis, building a theory of crisis capable of explaining what went wrong and attempting to resolve it. Across the board, the informes called for segregation, although they did not always agree about what this meant. In one version, segregation would attempt to rescue the Spaniard, while in the other, it would turn toward the Indian. In both cases, however, what appeared on the other side of the line of demarcation was what contemporaries called the "Plebe."

At first glance, the Plebe appears to refer straightforwardly to a category of social class. In *The Limits of Racial Domination* (1994), the historian R. Douglas Cope offers a careful reading of everyday life among the urban poor of Mexico City during the seventeenth century. What effectively secured the colonial order during this period, he argues, was not the racial hierarchy known as the *sistema de castas* but the patronage system that congealed around employment networks and practices. If the 1692 riot marked a powerful rupture when plebeian solidarity was able to overcome these divisions, it was short-lived—within days, fissures resurfaced and the potential for collective political action was undermined.[9] Cope's meticulous study has been widely influential, yet the distinction he draws between race and class may obscure more than it reveals. He asserts, for example, that what distinguished the Mexican Plebe from its European counterpart was its "racially mixed nature." By this he means that it was a heterogeneous mass, composed of people who belonged to numerous racial categories: "Indians, castizos, mestizos, mulattoes, blacks, and even poor Spaniards."[10] I want to suggest, however, that this can also be read as a statement about the ways in which class can become racialized in specifically colonial contexts. In other words, perhaps the Plebe is better understood not as a category that encompasses many races and thus constitutes a "mixed" group, but as a collective embodiment of "mixture" itself. In a society dominated by limpieza de sangre, mixture acts as a racializing marker.

Even the purported heterogeneity of the Plebe does not necessarily secure its nonracial ground. The construction of the Indian that I examine in chapter 1, for example, operates in much the same way, by producing new proximities that create the conditions in which groupness as such may emerge. Epistemic and material violence do the initial work of neutralizing or synthesizing vast heterogeneity, fashioning and dispersing new identities and subjectivities by suturing together cultural representations and social structures. From this perspective, despite their significant differences, the "work" that the category of the Plebe does for colonial Mexico formally resembles that which the Mestizo does for post-revolutionary Mexico.

One of the first things that stands out about the segregation documents is how clearly they register an obsession with "mixture": words like *mezcla, mixtura,* and *conmixtión,* along with a host of other terms without a common etymological root but nevertheless designating a confused, blurred, or jumbled state, are everywhere. This makes sense, given that the "mixed" can only be defined in relation to the "pure," which is in turn the object of segregation. This chapter thus traces the racializing construction of the Plebe in late-seventeenth-century Mexico by closely attending to the formations of "purity" and "mixture" embedded in the segregation documents. The historian Natalia Silva Prada suggests that it was only around the time of the riot that this category began to take on a concrete social meaning.[11] If this is the case, the segregation documents offer a glimpse into the mechanisms through which this process occurred. The Plebe, I argue, emerges as a spatial and indeed an infrastructural category—like the floodwaters overflowing the banks of the city's garbage-filled canals, it is an excess or residue, the result of infrastructural failure. The ministers' efforts to rescue the figure of the Indian end up producing the Plebe as surplus population, a terrifying new subject that is beyond redemption and will therefore require new forms and practices of concentration to contain.

## COUNTERINSURGENT HISTORY AND RACIALIZED GOVERNANCE

It was to Sigüenza that the viceroy immediately turned in order to set the segregation of Mexico City in motion. On July 1, a message was sent to the Creole asking him to draw up a plan for dividing the city into Spanish and Indian zones by defining the "terminos que le pareciesen mas convenientes" (boundaries that seem most advisable). In his response, dated four days later, Sigüenza sketched out a "linea de separacion" in the form of a narrative itinerary, devised from a textual and material excavation of the colonial city's original layout. For Sigüenza, in other words, urban planning was not only a cartographic operation but also an eminently historical one.[12]

In her groundbreaking study of Sigüenza's work, Anna More traces the emergence of a Creole discourse of governance in response to the crisis of Spanish imperial sovereignty of the late seventeenth century. What makes Sigüenza's work exemplary is his historical approach, manifested specifically in Sigüenza's collection of books, manuscripts, and artifacts dealing with the indigenous and colonial past. This "Creole archive," More argues, stood in for a hermetic law and allowed Sigüenza to elaborate a form of patrimonialism that was tied not only to local knowledge but also to a notion of citizenship based on pure Spanish descent. This racial project thus aimed not to undermine Spanish rule but to shore it up by placing the administration of empire in the hands of capable Creoles who would manage and control the indigenous and mixed-race population far more effectively than the traditional structures of authority—structures that, as the riot had demonstrated, were at this point completely exhausted. By fashioning a spatial foundation for this racial project, furthermore, Sigüenza's segregation proposal serves as one of the clearest examples of this discourse of governance.[13]

Sigüenza turns to the historiography of conquest and the archives of colonization to link the segregated city to the foundational moment of the colonial order: "Que fuese esto, lo dicen los Historiadores de la manera siguiente" (That this was the case is stated by the Historians in the following manner). Referencing the work of Antonio de Herrera, Juan de Torquemada, Francisco López de Gómara, and Bernal Díaz del Castillo, as well as "los primeros libros capitulares de esta ciudad" (the first charters of this city), which he had personally saved from the burning archive on the night of the riot, Sigüenza aims to document that Cortés called for a separation between the Spanish traza, on one hand, and the Indian barrios, on the other, when he set out to "rebuild" (as he put it, borrowing Herrera's terminology) Mexico City over the ruins of Tenochtitlan. It was the legitimate fear of a hostile indigenous population, the Creole asserts, that led to this division and to the fortification of the Spanish center. Yet this defensive architecture had not prevented the indigenous population from infiltrating the traza and revealing its "innata malicia" (innate malice) for the Spaniards in a series of devastating insurrections. In 1537, 1549, and 1624, and now in 1692, he writes, this Indian "multitud" (multitude) had merged with other members of the urban poor to form a "gigante cuerpo" (gigantic body) that had nearly overthrown the Spanish colonial order.

Sigüenza's segregation proposal thus reverses the pastoral logic of the original policy of separation, as codified in the sixteenth-century legislation on congregation. According to this doctrine, as we have seen, Indians were kept apart in order to protect them from purportedly malicious elements, including Spaniards, Mestizos, and others, as a means of facilitating their Christianization. Following the 1692 riot, however, Sigüenza calls for the center of the city to be reserved for "Spaniards" alone, with everyone else removed to the city's peripheral districts and transformed into surplus population. Rather than protecting Indians, in other words, the original doctrine of separation was reconfigured and infrastructurally redeployed to protect a counterinsurgent bloc of Spanish/Creole "citizens" defined by revanchist proto-whiteness—the very same "vezinos" who formed the companies of soldiers that set about patrolling the city as the sun rose over its smoldering ruins.[14] As More observes, the segregation proposal thus outlines a spatial foundation for a new racial order that pits "an elite identified by its Spanish descent against an alliance of the city's casta and indigenous subjects."[15]

As one of the main architects of the segregation order, as well as an important figure in the field of colonial Mexican studies, Sigüenza's intervention has received more scholarly attention than those of the parish priests who were also asked to participate. But this differential reception may also have to do with the different projects they envisioned. While the priests remained caught up in "traditional forms of colonial governance" based on pastoral care, writes More, Sigüenza outlined a "new form of administrative knowledge, disinterested in ecclesiastical quarrels over jurisdiction."[16] Certainly, the Creole discourse of racial governance staked out ground that would become increasingly salient over the course of the eighteenth century. Yet focusing on his report alone can make it difficult to see the ways in which Sigüenza's proposal in fact depended on the work of the ministers as well. Indeed, it is the ministers, far more than Sigüenza, whose interventions register the full extent of the ongoing breakdown of social and spiritual infrastructure that, in their view, had begun long before the riot, and who proposed a series of biopolitical techniques that would come to characterize the practice of colonial governance at large. Foucault reminds us that the state may be most productively seen as a "modern matrix of individualization, or a new form of pastoral power."[17] In this respect, the pastorate may not have been so traditional after all.

## SOVEREIGNTY AND THE DISAPPEARING INDIAN

The emergence of new biopolitical techniques in the sixteenth and seventeenth centuries corresponds to a shift concerning the finality of the law. Foucault argues that sovereign power is synonymous with the law, whether human or divine, and articulates itself primarily in terms of good and evil, right and wrong. The objective of sovereignty, moreover, is the "common good," which refers precisely to a scenario of obedience in which those who are subject to the sovereign's law acknowledge and comply with it. Yet with the rise of governmentality, the law begins to be articulated in terms of efficacy as well, operating instrumentally or tactically to guide its objects toward a "suitable end." No longer reducible to the violence of justice or the image of the "good" society, the law comes to operate as a technique aimed at conducting the objects of governance in such a way as to maximize the potential within them.[18]

About three weeks after the riot, on June 21, the viceroy circulated a statement on the many problems that had arisen because of the Indians living in the traza of Mexico City. Previous attempts to address this problem had failed, but now the task had acquired a new urgency: "Y porque con la ōcasion de su mouimiento, ācaecido a los ocho del corriente, incendios tumulto y saqueo en que incurrieron, pareçe que Ynsta mas la resolucion de lo referido" (Given the event that occurred on the eighth of this month, and the fires, rioting, and looting that they committed, it has become more urgent to resolve this matter).[19] The viceroy requested a meeting of the Real Acuerdo, an official body composed of himself along with officers of the Audiencia of Mexico, to deliberate and decide on the best way of moving forward. Five days later, the Real Acuerdo issued its own statement regarding the segregation order. It opens as follows:

La lei 19. lib. 6. ti.° 1. de la novisima Recopilacion de yndias dispone que para que los yndios aprobechen mas en cristiandad y policia se deve ordenar q̃ viban juntos y concertadamente, pues desta forma conocerán sus perlados y atenderan mejor a su bien y dotrina y porque asi conviene mandamos que los Bireies y governadores procuren por todos los medios posibles sin acerles opresion y dandoles a entender quan util y probechoso sera para su aumento y vuen govierno como esta ordenado. [Law 19, book 6, title 1 of the recent *Recopilación de Indias* mandates that for the Indians to live according to Christianity and police they must be made to live together and in an orderly manner, and in this way their prelates will know them and better attend to their well-being and Christianization. Because of this we order the viceroys and governors to ensure (this) by all possible means without oppressing them, informing them of how useful and beneficial it will be for their growth and good government as it is ordered.][20]

The passage references the *Recopilación de leyes de los reynos de las Indias* (1680), a compilation of royal legislation pertaining to colonial matters that had been published just over a decade before. In one sense, this collection was intended to pare down the unwieldy mass of casuistic legal positions that had accumulated over nearly two centuries of colonial rule. Yet it can also be read as an attempt by the Habsburg monarchy to respond to the crisis of imperial sovereignty by reaffirming the juridical discourse of early colonization.[21] The law in the passage just cited corresponds to a 1538 decree issued by Charles V that established the dualist social order of the two republics, a framework that would be taken up in the policy of congregation. As in the case of congregation, one of the main objectives of these policies, captured in this passage, was to insulate the indigenous population from harm or contamination, whether from disease or malicious actors like Mestizos. The protection of the "vulnerable" Indian formed the ideological core of the sixteenth-century spatial order. Confronted by a profound crisis a century and a half later, the authorities turned back to the legal foundation of the spatial order on which colonial rule was installed and through which it was reproduced. In the words of the Real Acuerdo, the segregation of the city should be executed "a la letra de la citada lei" (to the letter of the cited law).[22]

According to the ministers, however, the problem was that, upon entering the traza, the Indian seemed to disappear, slipping out of the cold embrace of the law. In his well-known treatise *Teatro mexicano* (1698), Fray Agustín de Vetancurt, minister of the parish of San José and chronicler of the Franciscan order, gives an account of the reign of each of the viceroys of New Spain. His succinct (and unflattering) description of the government of the Viceroy Conde de Galve, who by this time had left office, deals entirely with the riot and captures this interruption of sovereign power: "Estando [los indios] en los corrales de las casas de la ciudad escondidos, sin que justicia secular ni eclesiástica los conozcan, amparados de los dueños de las casas que no consienten que se éntre por ningun modo en los corrales, viven como moros sin señor" (Hidden in the courtyards of the city's houses, out of reach of secular and ecclesiastical authorities, protected by the owners of the houses, who do not permit entry to the courtyard under any circumstances, they live as Moors without a lord).[23] The city's architecture of impunity breaks down the relation of obedience between the sovereign and his subject and constitutes a space of exception where the force of sovereign law is not permitted to materialize—at least with regard to Indian migrants to the traza, who were subject to a racially specific set of civil and church institutions.[24]

In the previous chapter, I highlighted what Joanne Rappaport has called the trope of the disappearing Mestizo. Lacking a fixed social position and genealogically divided between the republic of Spaniards and the republic of Indians, the Mestizo tended to drop out of the documentary record and otherwise fade from view. A parallel trope is taken up and rearticulated here by the ministers, yet it is no longer the Mestizo but the Indian who has disappeared. What one of the ministers refers to as "la instabilidad, de los indios" (the instability of the Indians) is tied to the materiality of urban life in two ways.[25] On one hand, the priests insist that Indians seek to avoid the gaze of the authorities through the strategic use of material culture and bodily practices. As the Franciscan friar José de la Barrera, minister of the parish of Santa María la Redonda, asserts in his informe, "en poniendose el indio capote, zapatos, y medias y criando melena, hetelo meztizo, y á pocos días español libre del tributo, enemigo de Dios, de su iglesia y de su Rey" (by putting on a cape, shoes, and leggings and growing out his hair, we behold the Indian as Mestizo, and in a few days a Spaniard, free from tribute and an enemy of God, his church, and his king).[26] Similarly, the Augustinian friar Bernabé Núñez de Páez, of the parish of San Pablo, calls for the viceroy to enforce existing sumptuary laws that made it illegal for Indians to wear capes, "porq Parece que les infunden soberbia y con las mantas, son mas humildes y obedientes y no pareceran meztiços" (because it seems to fill them with arrogance, while with *mantas* they are more humble and obedient and they do not look like Mestizos).[27] The minister attributes this affective force to the object itself, since it apparently does not occur to him that his parishioners might intentionally adopt another persona as an added layer of disguise. On the other hand, clothing also serves as a metaphor for the capacity of the urban environment to obscure the Indian from the authorities' gaze. The Franciscan Fray Antonio de Guridi, minister of the parish of Santiago Tlatelolco, asserts that it is common for an Indian who has committed a crime in his town to flee and find "abrigo" (cover; literally, a coat or jacket) in Mexico City, "donde vive a su salvo sin temor de

Dios, sin poder ser conocido de Justicia Secular ni Eclesiastica, porq̃ los yndios son tan parecidos así en los nombres como en los trajes y caras" (where he lives freely and without fear of God, without being identified by the secular or ecclesiastical authorities, because the Indians are so similar in terms of their names as well as their clothing and facial appearance).[28] Lost in a sea of bodies dressed in similar clothing, the Indian body is represented as being insulated from the law.

The trope of the disappearing Indian had an architectonic foundation as well. According to the ministers' informes, those Indians illicitly residing in the traza occupy obscure and hidden spaces, such as "corrales, desvanes, patios, paxares y solares de españoles" (courtyards, attics, patios, lofts, and lots belonging to Spaniards).[29] It is especially easy for the Indians to "esconderse [y] ocultarse" (conceal and hide themselves) in the houses of Spaniards, writes Barrera,

> donde ay tales sotanos y escondrijos, q̃ solo quando estan para morir se manifiestan para recibir los santos sacramentos, q̃ no es poca felicidad; pues estan tan escondidos en algunos trascorrales, y retiros de dhas cassas, donde no es façil el descubrirlos, habitando estos indios, mezclados con los meztizos, y la gente ociossa, comunicandose secretamente, y maquinando tanta fiereza de maldades, como las q̃ han executado estos dias. [where there are basements and hiding places, so that only when they are about to die do they come out to receive the Holy Sacraments, which is no small relief. These Indians are well hidden in the back patios and recesses of these houses, where it is not easy to discover them, mixed together with Mestizos and idle people, secretly planning and plotting such savage wickedness as that which they have carried out in recent days.][30]

In a perverse twist, the very architecture that had originally served, at least in the minds of Spaniards, both to distinguish and to defend the traza from the "hostile natives" had been repurposed and occupied by the natives themselves. From attics to basements, Indians had carved out spaces to shield themselves from the gaze and the grasp of the civil and religious authorities. It was disconcerting enough that they should voluntarily risk the health of their souls in this way, but for Barrera there were also more worldly matters at stake. With their thick walls, winding corridors, and shadowy alcoves, these architectonic spaces seemed not only to enable but also to encourage "secret" meetings of "mixed" groups of Indians and Mestizos (along with other "idle people"), convergences that may have led directly to the riot. It was this political threat that caused Fray Antonio Girón, from the parish of Santa Cruz, to call the Indians "enemigos domesticos" (domestic enemies) and explicitly liken their migration into the city center to a military tactic: "Tenemos dentro de nosotros mismos muchos caballos griegos, que nos arrojen fuego, q̃ ponga en contingençia la permanençia de esta fidelisima ciu.ᵈ" (We have within us many Trojan horses, which rain fire on us, putting at risk the permanence of this most faithful city).[31] Echoing Sigüenza's language, for Girón the Indian has receded from the narrative of salvation and instead merits subjection to the permanent surveillance of a weaponized pastorate.

This profound anxiety about the migration of indigenous people to the city center was not entirely new. Although the laws referenced in the segregation informes date back to the second half of the sixteenth century, these are primarily concerned with residential separation in the countryside. The demographic decline of the indigenous population over the course of the sixteenth century corresponded to the gradual expansion of the perimeter of the traza into areas that originally had been designated as Indian. It is only in the second quarter of the seventeenth century that the opposite effect begins to show up in official statements.[32] In this sense, the informes reflect a change in what it meant to be Indian. Broadly speaking, in the sixteenth century the Indian was generally treated as fixed and tied to the community, at least to the extent that the original violence of congregation could be forgotten or erased. Much of the earlier legislation, for example, treated unregulated circulation (such as that of the vagabond/Mestizo) as a transitive problem, something that happened to Indian communities, but for the most part it treated the members of the communities themselves as immobile. By the late seventeenth century, in contrast, the Indian had become the protagonist of precisely this sort of unregulated circulation, at least in the context of Mexico City. The new set of attributes that the ministers ascribed to their parishioners—criminality, arrogance, insubordination, rebelliousness—were expressions of their increasing tendency to appear out of place.

Invisible or displaced, the Indian's "instability" was framed as a direct threat to the material reproduction of the sovereign order. On one hand, Indian tribute was viewed as critical to sustaining the bureaucracy of the colonial state.[33] Núñez de Páez writes, for example, that it is becoming more difficult to collect "las cossas del seruicio de Su Mag.ᵈ y . . . sus tributos" (the things owed in service to His Majesty and . . . his tribute).[34] On the other hand, Indian labor built and maintained much of the city's infrastructure. Guridi thus observes that it is impossible to carry out critical tasks like "la limpia de las asequias, y otras funciones del bien de la Republica" (the cleaning of the canals, and other tasks in the interest of the Republic) without knowing where the Indians are living.[35]

In addition to the impact on the colonial state, the ministers' informes also highlight the effects of Indian mobility on ecclesiastical institutions. Echoing many of the other ministers, Barrera writes that the "principal daño" (principal harm) of the Indians living in the traza is the "extrabio" (loss) of revenue: "no solo diminucion en los tributos reales . . . mas tambien engaño en sus propias parroquias, baptizandose, enterrandose y lo q̃ mas es, casandose en agena Parroquia, de q̃ resultan muchas nulidades de sacramentos, comulgando en las parroquias de españoles los q̃ son meramente indios" (not only the decline of royal tribute . . . but also fraud in their own parishes, being baptized, buried, and worse yet, married in parishes to which they do not belong, causing many sacraments to be invalid, as when those who are truly Indians take communion in Spanish parishes).[36] According to Barrera, it is not only the state but also the parishes that are losing out on the revenue they rightfully deserve. Revealingly, the language he employs to characterize this loss is infrastructural—it is an *extravío*, a deviation from a path or road, or even from a place of residence or barrio.[37] The indigenous population is moving through urban space in unauthorized ways, abandoning the places to which it has been assigned by the temporal and spiritual authorities. To the ministers describing the situation, then, the social system designed to manage flows of certain kinds of people (Indians), resources (tribute and other fees), and ideas (Christianity and idolatry) seems to have collapsed.

Among the most essential components of Mexico City's spiritual infrastructure—the temporal foundations of spiritual authority—were the parish boundaries inscribed on the urban landscape and religious buildings such as churches, chapels, and convents. Matthew O'Hara calls these buildings the "institutional contact points" that anchored broader structures of administration, extraction, and subjectification in the lives of urban residents. Parishioners were obligated to pass through their church at various moments, including major life events such as baptism and marriage as well as the yearly obligation of confession and communion. As I explain later, these activities served as an important mechanism by which the indigenous flock was documented and thus made legible to the authorities, but they also contributed to the economic stability of the parishes. Priests charged fees called *derechos* in exchange for many of the sacraments they performed for their parishioners, including baptism, marriage, and burial. Since these payments constituted an important source of revenue, tensions could easily materialize along the borders between parishes.[38]

It is in the context of such disputes that the explicitly racialized character of the pastoral system—its mechanisms of resource extraction and techniques of knowledge production—becomes clear. The spiritual geography of the city was organized on the basis of a "bipartite parish structure," such that Indians would attend parishes overseen by the regular clergy, while non-Indian parishes run by the secular clergy would receive everyone else.[39] The maps of Indian and non-Indian parishes did not line up with each other, however, but settled into a grid of uneven and overlapping jurisdictions calibrated by race. By going to Spanish parishes instead of their own, Barrera thus asserts, those who are "meramente," or truly Indians, are committing fraud.

This "meramente" is revealing. I have translated the word as "truly," but it also implies a simplification or reduction, a process that strips its object down to its bare essence or natural state. It marks the point at which truth is revealed. This reading resonates with Barrera's call, at the end of his informe, to "desnudar" (strip) the Indian as a complement to segregation. This is not a metaphor, since he is referring to the perceived role of clothing in facilitating the simultaneously spatial and racial "passing" of the Indian. But his use of this word also suggests a specific reading of the location of racial truth, which would seem to inhere in corporeal surfaces. What the call for segregation underscores, however, is precisely the recognition on the part of ministers like Barrera that, beneath the layers upon layers of deceitful surfaces to which the Indian's disappearance was attributed, the stable markers that might have anchored this identity were always already missing. Segregation's function, in other words, was not only to facilitate certain administrative procedures but also, and perhaps even more importantly, to stand in for this absence, to serve, much like sumptuary laws, not to "strip" but precisely to "clothe" the Indian in the naturalizing folds of an artificial matrix of classification. It was infrastructure that anchored identity, rather than the other way around. The "disappearance" of the Indian, in other words, was, like the floods, a crisis of infrastructural collapse.

## BETWEEN SOVEREIGNTY AND ECONOMY

The dazzling discourse of sovereign power produces its own mirror image, split between the monstrous body of the plebeian horde and the empty frame of the disappeared Indian. But this alone does not explain either migration to the traza or the riot itself. For the most part, the ministers make sense of these phenomena in predictably racialized terms, foregrounding claims of Indian criminality, idolatry, and disobedience. Some even echo Sigüenza's attribution of an "innate malice" against the Spaniards. But this rhetoric of paranoia and disgust does not quite drown out the faint outlines of another force that begins to take shape in the background. As noted earlier, Vetancurt's retrospective account of the riot describes an urban landscape that has effectively immunized Indians from sovereign power. Yet it is not only the built environment's material qualities that are responsible for this effect. He also underscores the fact that Indians are being protected by their patrons, "los dueños de las casas" (the owners of the houses), who, by failing to provide their "consent," are effectively obstructing the efforts of the authorities to search out, identify, and remove their escaped parishioners. What is taking place, in other words, is not so much the collapse of sovereignty as the rise of countersovereigns. The architecture of impunity has an owner, whose *dominium* has come into conflict with the *imperium* of the sovereign.[40]

According to Barrera, the invisibility of the Indian is intimately tied to the formation of these social and material relations:

> Por el respecto, q̃ se debe â algunas personas de autoridad, en cuyas cassas habitan, no podemos los curas conducirlos, â vn buscando-los y sacandolos de dhas cassas, por estar fomentados los indios de se-mejantes personas, q̃ los retienen en sus cassas para seruirse de ellos, contraviniendo â las Leyes, q̃ Vexᵃ cita desta nueba recopilacion . . . amparandolos los españoles en sus cassas, escondiendolos debaxo de sus propios lechos, como lo tenemos experimentado. [Out of respect for certain people of authority, in whose houses (the Indians) live, we

priests are unable guide them ("conducirlos"), even if we try to find
and remove them, because they are encouraged by these people, who
retain them in their houses to take advantage of them ("para seruirse
de ellos"), contravening the laws that Your Excellence cites from the
*Recopilación* . . . protecting them in their houses, hiding them beneath their own beds, as we have seen.][41]

These Spanish property owners, notes Barrera obliquely, are "people of authority," and it is precisely this authority that prevents both
the pastor from "guiding" his flock and the laws of the *Recopilación* from materializing as force. Coterminous with the architectonic folds of the house, however, this authority acts as not only an
obstacle in a negative sense but also a magnetizing force in a positive sense, "encouraging" Indians to enter these apparently autonomous zones that have been carved into the built environment. In
this respect, the question of visibility acquires more clarity, to the
extent that the "disappearance" of the Indian is a direct consequence
of the authority of their patron. Barrera conjures the intimate image
of one of his "people of authority" hiding an Indian servant beneath
his own bed. Here the Indian is not invisible—he is not wearing in-
appropriate (that is, non-Indian) clothing or hairstyles—but invested
with the authority of his patron. Finally, the language Barrera uses
to describe the economic relation between Spanish property owners
and their Indian servants is revealing. The former draw the latter into
their houses and hold them there, he writes, "para seruirse de ellos."
While incorporating the language of service to describe the Indians'
activity, the expression also evokes, much like the sixteenth-century
missionary critique of the *encomienda*, a conflation of relative coercion (the Indians are "retained") and exploitation (they are "taken
advantage of"). For the Franciscan, then, the problem is not labor as
such—recall the ministers' concern over the negative influence of
"gente ociossa" on the Indians—but an emergent set of social relations that directly "contravenes" the sovereign order and the image
of the Indian that had been consolidated since the middle of the sixteenth century.

Echoing the comments of the Franciscans, the Augustinian Núñez
de Páez describes the social relations of this emergent economy in
greater detail. After asserting that those who have most resisted the
clergy's attempts to "rescue" their parishioners are "los mismos españoles sus caseros, o sus mujeres o criados" (the Spaniards them-

selves, or their wives or servants), he zeroes in particularly on the role of Spanish women in consolidating these relations. The magnetizing pull that Barrera characterizes as an abstract or indirect "encouragement" here acquires a direct, material, and gendered force:

> Tambien de los Barrios los sacan los españoles: Porque sucede que las Mujeres, a título de compadrasgo o alquilandolos con el Dinero cada vna se lleva vn muchacho o muchacha para tener, quien les sirva, y alla les van criando a lo español con los criados y demas gente, y a ellos les Ponen medias y zapatos y a ellas sayas y los llevan a cumplir con la Yglessia a la cathedral y se van quedando allá para siempre y despoblandose los barrios. [The Spaniards also take them from their barrios, because it so happens that every Spanish woman, in exchange for *compadrazgo* or by hiring them with money, gets herself a boy or girl to have someone to serve her, and there they raise them in the Spanish manner with the servants and everyone else, and they give the boys leggings and shoes and the girls dresses and they take them for their yearly communion at the cathedral and they end up staying there forever and depopulating their districts.][42]

This passage clarifies two important features of the emergent urban economy and the role of the Indian within it. On one hand, economic relations are not only woven together with but also appear to occupy the same plane as kinship relations that are sacralized by the church. Núñez de Páez thus establishes what must have seemed an unsettling or even perverse parallel between the spiritual kinship of compadrazgo, on one hand, and the cash nexus, on the other.[43] The strength of these almost sacramental bonds underscores the difficulty of removing Indian workers from these situations. On the other hand, these economic relations are also expressed culturally. The force that pushes the Indians to adopt non-Indian clothing and customs is not internal, arising out of what Sigüenza calls the Indians' "innata malicia" against the Spaniards, but external, a product of a growing demand for unskilled labor. Yet these same external forces might also exercise a subjectifying effect and become naturalized on both the body and the embodied practices of the Indian worker.

Thus far, this emergent urban economy has taken a fetishized form, embedded in a specific set of architectonic structures and personified in the bodies of certain members of the propertied Spanish elite. This would seem to make it easier to contest—for example, by

granting priests like Núñez de Páez the right to enter Spanish homes
to remove their parishioners, or for that matter by once again implementing segregation. Yet in the closing lines of his informe, the
Augustinian perhaps unwittingly acknowledges that this economy
extends beyond the walls of these mansions. After voicing his complete support for the viceroy's proposal to remove the Indians from
the traza, he signs off as follows: "Los Yndios Panaderos, me Parece
Señor Sera forcosso en la Ciudad administrarlos, donde estan Situa-
das las Panaderias porque Viuen dentro de ellas, o como Vuexᵃ Dispu-
siere, que siempre estoy muy obediente a sus ordenes Para el servicio
de ambas Magestades" (It seems to me, my Lord, that the Indian bakers will have to remain in the City where the Bakeries are located, because that is where they live, or whatever Your Excellency should decide, as I am always most obedient to your commands in service of
both Majesties).[44] Something had shifted even among those who most
fervently supported segregation. The contradiction between sovereignty and economy even worked its way into the segregation order
itself, which explicitly exempted Indians employed in the bakeries
and in personal service—and these exemptions steadily expanded
from 1692 on, gradually becoming the norm by the middle of the
eighteenth century.[45] Sovereignty was hollowing itself out, codifying
an urban economy that had emerged in the interstices between architecture and law.

### BIOPOLITICS AND LEGIBILITY

We have seen how the ministers' reports begin to capture the contours of an emergent urban economy whose operations put it in contradiction with the sixteenth-century spatial order of sovereignty and
segregation. The 1692 riot seemed to confirm the fact that a material
shift had gradually taken shape since the early seventeenth century.
Viewed in this light, the segregation strategy that is prominently ad-
vocated in the informes written by both Sigüenza and the ministers
seems naive. Yet the ministers' interventions go beyond segregation
alone—they also advance a supplementary technique designed not
only to support segregation but also, and perhaps more importantly,
to resolve the contradiction between sovereignty and economy. This
technique—the padrón or ecclesiastical census—would play an important role in facilitating the reconfiguration of the spatial order of
the city.

As discussed in chapter 1, Foucault argues that the core of modern governmentality can be traced back to early pastoral techniques that were consolidated and institutionalized under Christianity. This process occurred not through secularization—a straightforward transfer of ecclesiastical techniques to the state—but rather through the intensification of the pastoral both within and beyond the spheres where it had traditionally been deployed. Foucault provides only a brief historical sketch of the governmentalization of pastoral power, but he does highlight the centrality of the mendicant orders, particularly the Franciscans and Dominicans, given their primarily urban character (in contrast to the monastic orders) and detachment from the territorial structures of the church (such as parishes).[46] In colonial Mexico, however, the pastorate took on a specialized character. By the time of the conquest, the mendicant orders were viewed in opposition to the official church institutions, and Cortés famously requested Franciscan and Dominican missionaries rather than bureaucratic and corrupt diocesan officials.[47] The mendicants were thus at the center of the "spiritual conquest" of Mexico, not only prior to the 1570s during what is generally regarded as their "golden age" but continuing for another century and a half as well.[48] Moreover, the lack of established ecclesiastical structures and the immensity of the task at hand, as well as the ascription of a racialized vulnerability to the indigenous population, paved the way for papal authorization allowing the mendicants to both administer sacraments and oversee special parishes known as *doctrinas de indios*, activities that in Europe were generally reserved for the diocesan clergy under the authority of a bishop. In this respect, the colonial pastorate emerged as both a territorial and a racial project.

In the colonies, then, the individualizing power of the pastorate was always already totalizing as well to the extent that it was routed through the abstraction of race. This convergence is captured in pastoral instruments like the padrón, which served simultaneously to "know" individual (Indian) parishioners and to render the (Indian) flock legible to the colonial authorities. Let us return to Vetancurt's report. In response to the viceroy's request for a map of his parish, the Franciscan begins with a brief textual description of its "deslindes" (boundaries) in the form of a handful of well-known urban landmarks (the Convento de San Jerónimo, the Salto del Agua, and so on). After sketching out these contours, however, he moves on to define the population that inhabits—or to be more precise, *should* inhabit—

them: "Constan de quatro mil, ocho cientas, y nouenta personas, que tengo en Padronadas, Como consta de mi Padron" (They consist of four thousand, eight hundred, and ninety persons, whom I have recorded in my padrón).[49] Parish priests kept careful accounts in the form of baptismal, marriage, and burial records as well as regular padrones, commonly recorded at the time of the yearly obligation to confess and take communion at the parish church. The practice generated documentation that allowed both religious and civil authorities (to whom the documents were frequently turned over) to calculate such figures as the size of the tributary population and relative increases or decreases in that number.

Until now I have discussed only one type of document that formed part of the segregation papers, the informe. Yet these reports, importantly, were bundled together with a set of six padrones. Moreover, these were not ordinary padrones, like the one Vetancurt describes in his informe. Rather than assessing the parishioners living within the parish, the padrones turned instead to what had become the far more urgent question of tracking those who had left the parish and moved into the traza. As far as I have been able to tell, these are the first documents of their kind—tracking *only* those parishioners who had abandoned the jurisdiction overseen by the *ministros de doctrina*. Carried out by the ministers and later compiled by two officers of the Audiencia, Juan de Aréchaga and Juan de Padilla, each of these padrones takes the form of a sort of table that is further divided into boxes (figure 3.1). Each box, in turn, carries a label denoting a specific location—such as the house of a particular Spaniard, the name of a street, or an identifying landmark—and beneath that a list of names, most often clustered into family units, and sometimes a selection of other information such as occupation, marital status, and age. Scrolling along both sides of every page, furthermore, runs a tabulation of the number of *"familias."* Some of the padrones are more detailed than others, which may be a sign of the differences between the religious orders with regard to pastoral methods—the Franciscans, for example, may have been more attentive to such procedures and meticulous in their implementation than the Augustinians.[50] Taking up the overlapping problems of territory and population in new ways, these padrones explode the insular territory of the parish, tracking the flock even as it begins to wander beyond the edges of the pasture.

Consider one of the more detailed padrones, which corresponds to the San José parish that Vetancurt oversaw—he may very well have

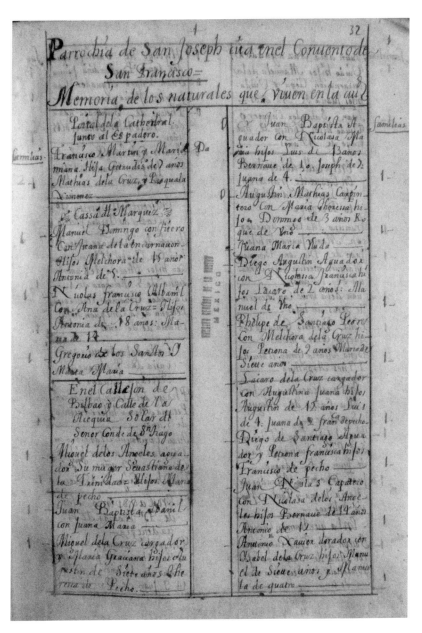

FIGURE 3.1. First page of the padrón of Indians from the parish of San José found living in the traza (1690?). Archivo General de la Nación, Mexico City (*Historia* 413, fol. 32r). Photo by the author.

been the one who walked the streets of the traza, beginning in the central plaza and circling through its southwest quadrant, to record this information. Titled "Memoria de los naturales que viven en la ciu^d" (Account of the natives who live in the city), it unfolds over nine astonishingly detailed folio pages and captures a significant migration from the barrios to the traza—according to Natalia Silva Prada's calculations, nearly one-quarter of San José's total population was at the time living in the center of the city.[51] On the first page, for example, a box labeled "En el Callejon de Bilbao y calle de la ace-quia solar dl Senor Conde de S^ntiago" (On the Callejón de Bilbao and Calle de la Acequia, the yard belonging to the Conde de Santiago) lists thirteen family units. Among them are Miguel de la Cruz, a porter, with his wife María Graciana, and their children, Agustín, age seven, and Theressa, described as "de pecho" (of breast-feeding age); and Juan Baptista, a water carrier, with his wife Nicolasa María, and their children Luis, age thirteen, Bernavé, age ten, Joseph, age seven, and Juana, age four. A small notation in the margin next to each of these units marks their inclusion in the running count of the total number of families. Interestingly, the table also includes the name of a widow, Juana María, who does not figure into this calculation. This detail clarifies at least one of the uses to which the padrón could be put—namely, to calculate the tributary population and secure an important revenue stream for the colonial state. Recall that these padrones were initially recorded by the ministers but later compiled by the Audiencia's officials. Some of the padrones included less detail, but they all generated a set of data about an Indian flock that was no longer contained within the spiritual geography of the parish.[52] The "multiplicity in movement" was once again at the center of the pastoral gaze.[53]

We have seen how, just beneath the surface of their hyperbolic affirmations of criminality and contagion, the informes point to an emerging economic order rooted in the Spanish traza and dominated by Spanish property owners. The padrones capture the heterogeneity of this economy in far greater detail than was possible within the overdetermined generic structure of the informe. To return to the padrón from San José, the men in the thirteen family units are recorded as working in a variety of mostly unskilled vocations: there are five water carriers, two porters, two shoemakers, one carpenter, one gilder, one bricklayer, and one peon. Overall, about 40 percent of the men documented here worked as journeyman artisans, one-third worked in transportation, and the rest were divided between con-struction, food production, and agriculture. Different parishes seem to have specialized in different sectors: most transportation work-ers came from San José, most construction workers from Santa María la Redonda, and most bakers from Santiago Tlatelolco. These work-ers probably received a wage but were also subjected to varying de-grees of coercion—not the least of which was the continued obliga-tion to pay tribute and perform a certain amount of forced labor (such as working on the city's canals).[54]

What is most significant about the padrones, however, is that they were produced in 1690–1691—at least a year *before* the riot took place. As Vetancurt notes in his informe, "Ya deseaban los Mrōs esta justa y zelosa Reducçion, pues el año passado de noventa, hizimos el Padron de los que vivian en la Ciudad" (The Ministers were al-ready desiring this just and zealous concentration, since in the year 1690 we made the padrón of those who were living in the City).[55] Barrera makes a similar point in his informe, noting that at the be-ginning of the previous year all of the ministers had been asked to "empadron[ar] â todos los naturales, q̃ habitan las cassas de Españoles en la ciudad" (make padrones documenting all of the natives who are living in the houses of Spaniards in the city) and had carried out this request.[56] The fact that these records were created before the riot in-dicates that the dual specters of Indian mobility and parish depopu-lation were already a matter of concern for the clergy and for church institutions. Although the riot gave this project new political ur-gency, then its deployment should be understood not (or not only) as a counterinsurgency technique but as an emerging biopolitical modal-ity for managing a racialized population that was no longer contained by the infrastructure of segregation.

A major tension thus runs through the bundle of documents that were tied to the segregation proposal.[57] On one hand, the informes foreground the invisibility and instability of the Indian, emphasizing the administrative and fiscal problems provoked by this disappear-ance for both the colonial state and the ecclesiastical institutions. The padrones, on the other hand, tell a very different story. In them, the Indian continues to be known and legible in spite of the centripe-tal pull of the urban economy and the resulting spatial displacement to the city center. The difference between these documents can be explained partly in terms of genre and timing. As rhetorical state-ments, the informes were intended to persuade the viceroy on policy matters and were written at a moment of shock immediately following the riot. In contrast, the padrones, which were initiated before the riot, were administrative tools designed for the mundane tasks of everyday population management. The informes speak the language of sovereignty; the padrones speak the language of biopolitics. It was the latter that would increasingly characterize the approach to racialized population control in the eighteenth century.

### THE INDIAN AND THE PLEBE

Everyone supported segregation, but segregation, and the "purity" it entailed, meant different things to different people. For Sigüenza, as we have seen, it meant rearticulating "Spanishness" by expelling not only Indians but also non-Indian "others" from the republic of Spaniards. By doing so, the traza would come to ground the formation of an elite bloc defined by Spanish descent. Creoles and Peninsulares— or as he puts it, curiously in the mouths of the Indian rioters, "españoles y Gachupines (Son los Venidos de españa)" (Spaniards and Gachupines [the ones who have come from Spain])—would be united under the banner of racialized counterinsurgency and anchor a new political order in the hands of a Creole administration.[58]

Vetancurt's proposal takes the opposite form. He too calls for the Indians to be returned to their districts and parishes, but adds what is ostensibly the full text of a law containing an early articulation of the system of dual republics, originally issued in 1563 and included in book 6, title 3, law 21 of the *Recopilación*:

> Prohibimos, y defendemos, que en las Reducciones, y Pueblos de los yndios, vivan negros, mulatos y mestizos, porque se ha experimentado son hombres inquietos, de mal vivir, ladrones, jugadores, viciossos y gente perdida, y por huir los yndios de ser agraviados, dejan sus Pueblos y Provin.ᵃˢ, y los negros, mestizos, y mulatos demas de tratarlos mal, se sirven de ellos, enseñan sus malas costumbres y ociosidad y tambien algunos errores y vicios, que podran estragar, y pervertir el fruto que deseamos en orden a su salvacion, augmento, y quietud. [We prohibit and ban Blacks, Mulattoes, and Mestizos from living in the Indian congregations and towns, because experience has shown that they are troubled men, disreputable, thieves, gamblers, depraved and lost, and in fleeing from harm, the Indians abandon their towns and provinces, and the Blacks, Mestizos, and Mulattoes in addition to

treating them poorly, take advantage of them, teach them their evil customs and idleness and also certain errors and vices, which could spoil the result that we desire in the service of their salvation, increase, and peace.][59]

This text conjures up a series of now-familiar tropes, including the figure of the pernicious, unproductive vagabond/Mestizo, now amalgamated with derivatives of blackness, as well as the vulnerable, mimetic Indian. According to this legislation, which was reissued five times between 1563 and 1600, the impure trinity of "Blacks, Mulattoes, and Mestizos" had a uniquely negative effect on the Indian population. Thus, in addition to expelling the Indians from the traza, Vetancurt calls for these "troubled men" to leave the barrios. He concludes his report with the following recommendation: "Sera conveniente, que los dhos negros, y mulatos salgan de los Barrios, y occupen el lugar que en la ciu.d occupan los yndios, y los yndios occupen el que dejan los negros, mulatos, y mestizos, en los Barrios" (It would be opportune for the Blacks and Mulattoes to leave the barrios and occupy the place in the city that the Indians currently occupy, and for the Indians to occupy the place that is left by the Blacks, Mulattoes, and Mestizos in the barrios).[60] Rather than relocating "Blacks, Mulattoes, and Mestizos" to the barrios to establish a zone of Spanish purity in the traza, as Sigüenza proposes, Vetancurt envisions relocating them to the traza to establish a zone of Indian purity in the barrios.

What distinguishes Vetancurt's move from the sixteenth-century precedents from the *Recopilación* is not only the intensification of population management, as the padrones suggest, but also the changing valence of salvation. In the prologue of *Teatro mexicano*, published six years after the riot, the Franciscan took it upon himself to justify writing yet another account of the natural, moral, military, and ecclesiastical history of New Spain. "Mucho se sabe hoy" (Much is known today), he declares, "que se ignoró ayer" (that was ignored yesterday). Here he echoes a common refrain in New World commentary regarding the ignorance of the "ancients" in such fields as geography and the "modern" skepticism according to which textual authority must be modified on the basis of empirical knowledge. Thus, writes Vetancurt, "añadiré en los antiguos lo que despues con la experiencia y curiosidad han investigado los modernos" (I will add to the Ancients what with experience and curiosity the Moderns have investigated since). But the Franciscan also employs this same trope in a very different context. In a revealing passage of the prologue, he reflects on his treatment of the Indian throughout the work and moves from there to consider the state of the missionary project at the end of the seventeenth century:

> En ocasiones volveré por los indios, siguiendo la piedad y deseos de nuestros reyes y supremo consejo de Indias, que cada dia con mas órdenes solicitan su bien, aumento, sosiego, quietud y descanso; y en otras diré lo que sintiere en su contra, porque con los muchos años de administracion he llegado á experimentar sus malicias, y que ya están con el trato de la gente plebeya que comunican muy distintos de lo que estaban en la primitiva de la conversion de las Indias. [At times I will turn to the Indians, following the piety and desires of our kings and supreme Council of the Indies, which each day through more decrees seek their welfare, growth, calm, peace, and relief; and at other times, I will say whatever I might feel against them, because over many years of administration I have come to experience their malice, and they are now, owing to their interactions with the plebeian people, very different than they were in the early years of evangelization in the Indies.][61]

The sixteenth-century crisis of evangelization had by the seventeenth century been normalized, worked into the everyday operations of a colonial project of spiritual and temporal administration. Vetancurt is not especially optimistic about the prospects of evangelization. What is most interesting here is the distinction between this position and the disenchantment of his Franciscan predecessors like Bernardino de Sahagún. Although the passage initially seems to reproduce Sahagún's claim that what the early missionaries had viewed as success was in fact a naive misreading of the situation— a consequence of what I have called the "racial baroque"—Vetancurt instead seems to suggest that these successes may have been real. Something had changed since the early days of apostolic fervor, but it was not at the level of interpretation. Rather, it was something about the nature of the Indians, a shift that was tied to the spatial distribution of the population and triggered specifically by the Indians' contact with these "plebeian people." The collapse of the spatial order of segregation on which colonialism was based had generated new forms of circulation and proximities and by doing so remade the in-

digenous flock, even to the point of taking the possibility of full conversion off the table. What remained was something closer to a permanent regime of spiritual and temporal tutelage, a stopgap measure
that might hold apostasy (not to mention political crisis) at bay. It is
not entirely clear from the passage whether Vetancurt believed that
once again separating the Indians would even be enough to undo the
damage that had already been done.

What is clear, however, is the value of not only separating but
more importantly disarticulating the Indian from the collective
body of the "plebeian people," that is, from the category of the Plebe,
whose meaning, as we have seen, was still unclear in the late seventeenth century. In Europe, Plebe meant "poor," but in Mexico it
signaled "mixture." Sigüenza's much-cited formulation from his account of the riot reflects this disjuncture between the metropole and
the colonies:

> Pregunttarame Vmd como se portó la pleue en aqueste tiempo y res-
> pondo brevemente que bien y mal bien por que, siendo pleue tan en
> extremo pleue q̃ solo ella lo puede sser de la que se reputtare la mas
> infame, y lo es de ttodas las pleues por componerse de indios, de ne-
> gros criollos y vosales de diferentes naciones, de chinos, de mulattos,
> de moriscos, de mestissos, de sambaigos, de lobos y tambien de es-
> pañoles que, en declarandose saramullos (que es lo mismo que píca-
> ros, chulos y arreuata capas) y degenerando de su obligaciones, son los
> peores entre tan ruin canalla. [Your Grace will ask me how the Plebe
> behaved during this time and I will respond briefly: well and poorly.
> Well, because it is such an extremely plebeian Plebe that it and only
> it has come to be reputed as the most infamous of all the Plebes be-
> cause it is composed of Indians, of Creole and African Blacks of dif-
> ferent nations, of Chinos, of Mulattoes, of Moriscos, of Mestizos,
> of Zambaigos, of Lobos, and also of Spaniards who, declaring them-
> selves Zaramullos (which is the same as rogues, rascals, and cape-
> snatchers) and abandoning their obligations, are the worst among
> such a contemptible rabble.][62]

It is important here to clarify that Sigüenza's account was written
not in an administrative document, like the informes, but in a letter to a friend in Spain, Admiral Andrés de Pez. Still, it was intended
for publication—Sigüenza himself suggests as much in the closing
paragraph—and written for a Spanish audience.[63] For this reason, the

text is filled with moments of translation directed toward an audience potentially unfamiliar with the details of everyday life in New Spain. We have already seen Sigüenza parenthetically explain the word *gachupín* for a metropolitan audience; elsewhere he includes another awkwardly unnecessary parenthesis defining the word *tortilla*—"ya sabe Vmd que asi se nombra el pan de mais por aquestas parttes" (Your Grace already knows that this is what the bread made from corn is called in these parts).[64] I would suggest that the description of the Plebe serves a similar function. The Mexican Plebe is irreducible to its European counterpart, and this excess, which makes it the most "plebeian" of all possible Plebes, is precisely its doubly racialized mixture—it contains both many different "races" and many "mixed-race" bodies. This Plebe, moreover, cannot be redeemed and serves only to fill out the ranks of the insurrection or ruin the natural innocence of the Indian.

Colonial elites would continue to draw on this emergent discourse of surplus population, which linked notions of impurity to infrastructural breakdown, well into the next century. In the instructions left for his successor in 1755, for example, the Viceroy Conde de Revillagigedo notes the dangers of the "impure" masses and, echoing the language Sigüenza had applied to the Indian in his informe, describes them as an "abultado cuerpo" (enormous body) that, overcoming its natural fear of the authorities, "pudo sacar la cabeza en el tumulto del año de 1692, clamando contra el gobierno por la escasez y carestía del maíz" (showed its face during the riot of 1692, clamoring against the government because of the scarcity and shortage of corn).[65] The location of the threat to the social order had shifted from the Indian to the Plebe.

Sigüenza places Indians first on the list of the members of the "contemptible rabble" that made up the Plebe, but their inclusion was to some extent an open question. The statement by the Real Acuerdo that set the segregation project in motion signals a different view of the relation between the Indian and the Plebe. As we have seen, it begins by citing a juridical precedent for congregation from the *Recopilación* and goes on to affirm that enforcing this law is now an urgent matter, owing to "el deplorable estrago que cometieron los yndios unidos a la ynfima plebe su semejante" (the deplorable destruction committed by the Indians united with the vile Plebe, its likeness).[66] Here the Indians are like and near, but not quite of, the Plebe.

This is where Vetancurt comes in. His segregation proposal constitutes an attempt to cut short this budding "union" by grounding it in the built environment—race continues to be conceptualized primarily in infrastructural terms. But beyond this major strategy of segregation elaborated in the *informes*, Vetancurt and the other ministers also lay out a minor strategy of population management in the *padrones*. Against the "disappearing Indian" in the former, the latter generates a detailed and highly individualized image of the Indian body as both detached from its traditional ecclesiastical jurisdiction—uprooted from the space that previously served to render it legible as Indian—and at the same time distinguished from the human masses of the *traza*. Population data seemed to offer the possibility of concentration without segregation, racialization and extraction without separation. For Vetancurt, writing at the end of the seventeenth century, salvation was no longer strictly a spiritual question but also an intensely temporal one, deeply interwoven with the conditions of possibility for the everyday operations of key colonial institutions—from the flows of tribute that supported the colonial bureaucracy and the forced labor that was supposed to enable proper flood control to the "spiritual capital" on which the religious orders depended.[67]

## CONCLUSION

On July 10, the viceroy issued an order to move forward with the segregation of the city. All Indians inhabiting the zone circumscribed by Sigüenza's path—except for those working in the bakeries or in personal service, as noted earlier—would be given twenty days to move back to their districts, after which time any transgressor would be sentenced to 200 lashes and six years' hard labor in the *obrajes* (textile factories). Any person offering living quarters within the Spanish *traza* to an Indian would be punished with a fine of 100 pesos and two years of exile from Mexico City. The new law would be publicized by the enthusiastic parish priests and officials of the republic of Indians, using the "lengua Bulgar" (common language) to ensure that no one could feign ignorance of the new requirement.[68] The policy had a rapid impact, and colonial administrators scrambled to figure out how best to reallocate housing and property to those returning to the barrios. Work done primarily by Indian laborers in the city center came to a temporary halt. Yet the urban economy had not been dismantled, and the contradiction that had generated the centripetal flow from the districts to the center remained unresolved.[69]

For many historians, it has become something of an article of faith that what best explains the failure of segregation is the process of mestizaje. An early and influential article published in 1938 by a young Edmundo O'Gorman set out a path that has for the most part been followed by scholars ever since. Based largely on a collection of documents he had located at the Archivo General de la Nación, and of which he had published a selection earlier that same year—precisely the informes I have examined in this chapter—the Mexican historian argues that the Spanish colonial project was predicated on a Hegelian dialectic: namely, that the foundational "principle of separation" designed to facilitate the integration of the indigenous population into Christianity and Western culture would, if successful, end up canceling out its raison d'être, leaving behind the hard, empty shell of the built environment that no longer reflected the social order that had emerged. O'Gorman thus explains the results of the segregation order given in the wake of the 1692 riot:

> No he podido averiguar la observancia que se dió a esta disposición: es probable que en un principio se ejecutara, pero lo importante para nosotros es llamar la atención a que, como todas las leyes que contrarían las costumbres y necesidades vitales, pronto debió caer en desuso como lo demuestran hechos posteriores. Fué una ilusión creer que una simple línea más imaginaria que real, fuera suficiente para evitar la unión de dos pueblos vecinos de una misma ciudad. [I have not been able to figure out the degree to which this disposition was observed: it is probable that it was followed at first, but what is important here is to call attention to the fact that, like all laws that contradict customs and vital needs, it must have quickly fallen into disuse, as later events demonstrate. It was an illusion to believe that a simple line, more imaginary than real, would be sufficient to prevent the union of two peoples living together in a single city.][70]

In spite (or perhaps because) of the acknowledged lack of evidence, O'Gorman's thesis has proved to be highly influential over the years.[71] In it we perceive the demographic narrative of salvation that would be codified—right around the time O'Gorman was writing—by the postrevolutionary Mexican state. But there is also a striking parallel between the figure of the Mestizo in the official ideology of the Mexican state and the corresponding figure of the Plebe for its colonial predecessor. Both represent collective bodies racially defined by "mixture"

and therefore in opposition to "purity"; both elaborate a notion of ho-
mogeneity based on and encompassing radical heterogeneity; and both
are ideological projects that serve to affirm the state apparatus as the
key mediator of this product of a demographic drive internal to the
population. Equally analogous is the place of the Indian with regard
to both the late colonial Plebe and the post-revolutionary Mestizo. On
one hand, both bodies are constituted through the absorption of the
Indian; on the other, neither is capable of entirely assimilating the Indian. No doubt, there is an important difference with regard to the
moral valence ascribed to either object—the Mestizo stands for progress and hope, the Plebe for degeneration and ruin—but in structural
terms the two categories are analogous. We might say that the first
systematic theory of mestizaje was forged in the colonial state's response to the 1692 riot.

Ultimately, mestizaje as such cannot explain the collapse of the
infrastructure of segregation, since the urban economy that drew peripheral workers into the traza continued to be organized along racial lines. But mestizaje also fails to account for the architectures
and techniques that replaced the segregated spatial order. By firmly
establishing at the center of the political imaginary the notion that
the sixteenth-century infrastructure of racial segregation was, much
like the city's hydraulic systems, crumbling and ineffective, the segregation proposals, and especially the ministers' interventions, set
in motion a spatial reordering that would unfold over the course of
the next century. As a result, the city's segregated grid would be replaced without abandoning concentration as a governing technique—
a sort of concentration without segregation. On one hand, plans to in-
stall a new policing structure on the basis of administrative districts
known as *cuarteles* or wards began to appear as early as 1696, as a direct response to the riot. Ward officials would monitor residents extensively, borrowing the ministers' techniques and meticulously re-
cording the name, racial classification, marital status, employment,
assets, address, and gender of each resident in account book–like registers. Policing became significantly more active and aggressive, and
the number of arrests skyrocketed. This reformed repressive apparatus reflected Bourbon notions of governance, above all "the impera-
tive to attack the vices of the populace not simply on moral grounds,
but primarily for economic and utilitarian reasons."[72]

On the other hand, the ministers' complaints about the migration
of their parishioners to the traza and their ongoing disputes over ju-

risdiction served as one of the major justifications for the so-called secularization of parishes in the mid-eighteenth century. The city's complicated and racially segregated "bipartite parish structure" was replaced with a single grid according to which all residents would belong to the parish in which they lived, regardless of race. By no means did this shift signify an overcoming of racial hierarchy or differentiation, as priests were still required to keep separate baptismal, marriage, and burial records for Indians and non-Indians.[73] With the replication and expansion of the techniques that were deployed in the ministers' padrones, the Indian remained legible even within the plebeian multitude.

It was yet another Creole intellectual who drafted the plan for parish secularization. Following in the footsteps of Sigüenza and the Indian ministers three-quarters of a century earlier, José Antonio Alzate examined topographical images and took to the streets himself in order to rationalize the spiritual terrain of the city. Beyond the clear analogy, it seems that Alzate specifically drew on the reports that had been prepared for the segregation project, including, as the art historian Barbara Mundy notes, a map of the city made by Sigüenza. The influence of Sigüenza's maps of the valley of Mexico and New Spain on Alzate's work is well known, but it is not clear how those images would have helped him craft a detailed city plan. Mundy speculates that Sigüenza may have produced a map of Mexico City to accompany his segregation proposal, and that this was the map that had come into Alzate's hands: "Sigüenza's means for achieving social order in the city was diametrically opposed to those of Alzate's 1769 plan: instead of integrating the different castes of [the] city through their geographic location, he aimed to separate them completely. The end goal was the same, however, in that correct assignment of people and arrangement of places was seen as key to achieving greater urban harmony, and perhaps Sigüenza used a city plan to show his proposal, which Alzate then inherited."[74] Whether the map to which Alzate referred was a graphic image, as Mundy proposes, or the textual itinerary that formed part of the segregation proposal itself, the details are less important than the genealogy. The rationalization of urban space and the dispersion of pastoral techniques may have indicated that segregation had entered into decline, but concentration was now reconfigured on the basis of a police regime that would continue to view and manage the social order through the spatial order.

# CHAPTER 4

# COLLECTION: IMPERIAL BOTANY
# AND RACIALIZED LIFE

*It was not that curiosity had diminished . . . or that knowledge had regressed, but rather that the fundamental arrangement of the visible and the expressible no longer passed through the thickness of the body. Hence the epistemological precedence enjoyed by botany. . . . At the institutional level, the inevitable correlatives of this patterning were botanical gardens and natural history collections.*
MICHEL FOUCAULT, *THE ORDER OF THINGS*

TWO DECADES AFTER PLAYING his instrumental role in the reorganization of the social geography of Mexico City, the Creole intellectual José Antonio Alzate found himself entangled in a heated dispute with the Spanish botanist Vicente Cervantes, who had been sent to the capital of New Spain in 1787 with orders to establish a new botanical garden there. In the course of the debate, which centered on the value and validity of Linnaean taxonomy, Alzate made a casual yet nevertheless significant observation about the relation between plants and (certain kinds of) people:

Porque las plantas en las tierras que conocemos aqui por calientes son de un verde mas obscuro, y las mismas transportadas à temperamentos templados lo son menos: vaya de analogía: ¿puede de esta observacion deducirse alguna cosa útil respecto al color de los negros? [Given that plants in the lands that we consider here to be hot are of a darker green, and the same plants transported to temperate climates are less so, by analogy, might something useful be deduced from this observation about the color of Blacks?][1]

Alzate here posits an analogy between "las plantas" (plants) and "los negros" (Blacks) and suggests that both may be subject to the same set of external determinants that were factored into the eighteenth-century understanding of climate. But the analogy also implies a "program of research" that would investigate these forces, the extent of their effects, and the mechanisms by which they might or might not be reversed. If environmental pressures act in relatively simultaneous and equivalent ways on each of these objects, it should be possible to test this effect through the scientific study of one or the other. In this sense, the study of plants was not easily separable from the study of race.[2]

The backdrop for Alzate's analogy is the general epistemic shift that Foucault describes in the epigraph to this chapter, characterized for my purposes here by the rise, in the late eighteenth century, of Spanish imperial botany and the emergence of a network of botanical gardens on which this project depended. Indeed, while many scholars have treated this dispute as a confrontation between European and Creole knowledges, the gardens themselves were not especially controversial, since both Alzate and Cervantes participated in and materially supported their operations and expansion.[3] As central nodes in a global network of organic flows, plants from the farthest reaches of the empire were collected within their walls. Alzate's description of the movement of plants from "tierras . . . calientes" to "temperamentos templados" captures the dominant directionality of these transfers. The artificial space of the gardens, moreover, translated contemporary botanical theories into architectonic form while at the same time enabling the application of these theories within a relatively controlled environment.

Like natural history more generally, then, Spanish imperial botany was in many ways a concentration project. In the prologue of his 1785 Spanish translation of the influential, multivolume *Histoire naturelle, générale et particulière* by the French naturalist Georges-Louis Leclerc, Comte de Buffon, José Clavijo y Fajardo writes that "el estudio de la Naturaleza . . . pide precisamente tener presentes todas las producciones, ó á lo menos gran número de ellas: de otro modo no podríamos ver la Naturaleza sino desmembrada" (the study of Nature necessarily requires that all of its products, or at least a great number of them, are present: otherwise we would only be able to see Nature in a dismembered state). It was critical not only to secure the immediate, physical presence of this multiplicity of objects but also to deposit them within a single, architectonic site—an operation Clavijo y Fajardo describes as one of "reduci[endo] en cierto modo el orbe al breve recinto" (reducing the globe, in a certain sense, to a small enclosure). Forming a general collection would also enable experimentation and thereby generate new knowledge. Reading about natural history in books is one thing, he goes on, but true understanding comes from a direct engagement with things themselves, from handling and working with them "mediante ciertos experimentos fáciles y manuales" (through certain simple and manual experiments). After all, "el buen Anatómico y el buen Piloto se forman, el uno disecando cadáveres, y el otro surcando los mares" (the skilled Anatomist and the skilled Pilot are trained, on one hand, by dissecting cadavers and, on the other, by sailing the seas). Such an enormous task would be impossible for a single man, finally, so Clavijo y Fajardo argues that the Enlightened state, with its substantial bureaucratic and fiscal capacities, must step in. The state project of concentration in the form of the general collection (*colección*) thus appeared as the condition of possibility for posing and resolving scientific questions about the natural world.[4]

These eighteenth-century intellectuals illustrate a shift in (or perhaps an expansion of) the logic of concentration, by which it increasingly came to be conceptualized in scientific terms. This shift had a dual character in the sense that it gave rise, on one hand, to a *science of concentration* by which the architectures and techniques of concentration were subsumed by and mediated through precise calculation and experimentation and, on the other hand, to a view of *concentration as science*, part of the laboratory arsenal, a technique for controlling for variables, a method for generating new and productive knowledge about the nature of things. The general collection became the paradigmatic form of concentration during the Enlightenment precisely because in it these twinned scientific functions were most effectively combined. While personal collections of "exotic" and "curious" objects continued to serve, as they had since the Renaissance, as a means of accumulating and displaying prestige, state-sponsored, institutional collections of a "general" or totalizing character were now being assembled for scientific, political, and economic purposes.[5]

At first glance, the general collection appears to diverge significantly from the other forms of concentration that I have traced in this book. An initial doubt—whether people and plants are the same sort of objects—is certainly justified, but Alzate's analogy suggests that in the late eighteenth century their commonalities resonated at least as much as their differences. Indeed, given what Foucault calls botany's "epistemological precedence" during this period, we might expect to find not only that plants became a privileged object of study but also that this particular object may have appeared to "speak" for others.[6] A more substantive objection is that congregation, enclosure, and segregation are techniques of population management, while the collection seems to address a different set of problems—of information rather than control, of investigation rather than governance. But this too is a tenuous distinction. On one hand, we have seen that earlier concentration projects both facilitated and were facilitated by the production of knowledge about colonial territories, bodies, and populations. On the other hand, Spanish imperial botany in fact constituted an intensification and expansion of the techniques of biopolitical governance, which, as Antonio Lafuente and Nuria Valverde suggest, aimed to convert "diversity, local variation, and qualia into data" that could be easily systematized, compared, and managed at a distance.[7] Although the botanical garden encloses plants instead of people, then, my claim is that it is better viewed as continuous with rather than radically distinct from the centralized town, disciplinary institution, and segregated neighborhood.

Infrastructures of concentration are central in Foucault's account of the emergence of the concept of life in late Enlightenment thought. Natural history, he argues, aimed to classify "things themselves" by scrutinizing their visible elements, a practice that made plants, whose organs cluster across their surfaces, the privileged object of taxonomic inquiry. But only a small set of elements were defined as relevant. Everything else, from the remaining physical characteristics of the plant to the external conditions essential to its survival, was filtered out. A multiplicity of physical elements was thus reduced to an artificial order. The fetishization of "things themselves" and the erasure of context made possible the rise of institutional collections like botanical gardens, which served as "unencumbered spaces in which things are juxtaposed."[8] In both theory and practice, however, these spaces were anything but "unencumbered." Especially in the context of empire, which entailed the global circulation of plant life across significant geographical and climatic difference, the botanical garden was always subject to external forces that continuously exerted material effects on everything it contained. Central to late-eighteenth-century botanical practice, then, was the drive to quantify and classify not only these "things themselves" but also the global spaces and environments that enabled and sustained their existence.[9] The rise of the botanical garden under the aegis of Spanish imperial botany generated global infrastructures of calculation and experimentation in an effort to define and mediate these environmental limits.

Like so many aspects of Foucault's work, many critics have argued that this omission—much like the absence of race in *The Order of Things*—is largely a result of his Eurocentric frame and desire to craft "universal" history. The Brazilian race theorist Denise Ferreira da Silva traces an alternative trajectory of the emergence of what she calls "the racial" in late Enlightenment thought. Her rereading of the Western philosophical and scientific canon locates race at the core of the modern subject as well as the modern concept of life. In the late eighteenth century, the Cartesian split between the interiority of the mind and the exteriority of the body was reconfigured and mapped onto a global terrain that rendered the European (White) subject "transparent," or self-determining, in contrast to the (non-White) "others of Europe," defined by what Silva calls "affectability," a quality similar to what I have described here as vulnerability. These "affectable others" were subject both to the forces of nature (such as climate) and to the forces of self-determined human subjects (such as colonization). For Silva, the racial is precisely this irreducible and unsublatable split between transparency and affectability.[10]

Silva's suggestive rereading of Foucault's corpus excavates the racial from these inaugural moments in the production of Western reason. Nevertheless, by largely detaching these thinkers from the material forms and practices in which they were embedded and through which they were activated, it can be difficult at times to perceive the limits of each articulation as well as the blockages that had to be overcome, and therefore to explain historical transitions.[11] Furthermore, attending to the material conditions of possibility for the philosophical developments analyzed by Silva forces us to acknowledge the imperial terrain out of which they emerged. Building on the work of Foucault as well as his critics, this chapter traces a "circuitous, imperial route" for the late-eighteenth-century transition from the classical to the modern episteme and the emergence of the concept of life.[12] By attending to the global infrastructures of concentration and circulation that enabled late Enlightenment botany, this history places race at the center of this shift. Specifically, I am interested in the way in which the concentration of plants at specific infrastructural locations—namely, the Royal Botanical Gardens in Madrid and Mexico City—enabled the mathematization of environment and led as a result to the development of not only a new science of plant geography but also new techniques of biopolitical governance. Both turned on the emergent concept of life, formulated in the context of empire and always already racialized from its earliest appearance.

## ABSTRACTION AND IMPERIAL BOTANY

If Spanish colonialism had entered into crisis by the end of the seventeenth century, as we saw in chapter 3, the eighteenth century is generally viewed as a period of reform. The rationalization of empire known as the Bourbon reforms touched on many aspects of imperial rule, among them the organization of commerce. Historians emphasize the Crown's efforts, for example, to restructure trade between Spain and the Americas in such a way as to ensure the colonies' role as an exporter of raw materials and to stimulate manufacturing on the Iberian Peninsula. Imperial economics was thus coupled from the start to the encoding of nature as "natural resources" characteristic of Enlightenment science. In the field of botany, for example, the Linnaean system emerged in Sweden as part of a largely economic project known as "cameralism," organized around the promotion of self-sufficiency through the acclimatization of foreign plants.[13] More generally, "plant mercantilists" throughout Europe sought "to multiply their own resources and diminish their tribute to foreigners."[14] In Bourbon Spain, imperial botany seemed to offer an escape from the high costs of expanded conquest and the fetishization of precious metals. As Casimiro Gómez Ortega, director and primary instructor at the Royal Botanical Garden of Madrid, wrote in a 1777 letter to José de Gálvez, then minister of the Indies,

Doce naturalistas con otros tantos chymicos o mineralogistas esparcidos por sus estados, producirían por medios de sus peregrinaciones una utilidad incomparablemente mayor, que cien mil hombres combatiendo por añadir al Imperio Español algunas provincias, cuyos productos hayan de sepultarse en el olvido, como lo están por la mayor parte los que cría la Naturaleza en las que ya se poseen. [Twelve naturalists along with a handful of chemists or mineralogists dispersed throughout its territories would, by means of their travels, produce a benefit that is incomparably greater than a hundred thousand men fighting to add a few provinces to the Spanish Empire, the products of which would be buried in obscurity much like the majority of Nature's products in the lands already under her control.][15]

In Gómez Ortega's vision, conquest is replaced by a sort of "green" capitalism, a lean and enlightened empire administered by scientists instead of conquistadors. The commercialization of colonial plant life would be even more valuable than the precious metals that had defined Spanish colonial extraction for centuries. Unlike gold and silver, moreover, plants offered the advantage of being renewable— "tienen sobre las minerales la ventaja de poderse propagar y multiplicar al infinito una vez poseídas y connaturalizadas" (they have the advantage over minerals of being able to be propagated and multiplied infinitely once possessed and naturalized).[16] Botany offered a fantasy of limitless wealth.

Mercantilism required certain forms of quantification, standardization, and abstraction to serve as the basis of exchange—how else to calculate a balance of trade, for example—and imperial botany in many ways mirrored these same procedures. Foucault writes that the taxonomic system developed and deployed by Enlightenment botanists sought to reduce the diversity of the natural world to a small cluster of variables that could in turn be easily identified, counted, and compared.[17] Linnaeus believed that all plants could be classified on the basis of their morphology, that is, the elements visible on their surface. All that had to be accounted for, as Gómez Ortega wrote in his textbook on the Linnaean method, was the *"Número, Figura, Proporcion, y Situacion"* of the plant's fructification (the generative parts of the plant, namely the fruit and flower).[18] Classification would proceed, for example, by counting up the number of stamens, or male organs, in order to discern the relevant class, and then the number of pistils, or female organs, in order to identify its order. Out of a multiplicity of physical features and sensory inputs, a privileged set was extracted and entered into discourse. By linking morphology to nomenclature, this system converted botanical specimens into a standardized matrix of precise measurements and descriptors that facilitated the global circulation of plant life. It was precisely the tendency of plants to present their organs to the gaze of the observer that made botany the privileged site of scientific knowledge during this period.

According to Foucault, it was not only the remaining elements of

the plant that were deemed extraneous and filtered out but other inputs as well. Significantly, external factors that sustained and enabled the growth and development of particular plants were likewise
stripped away. "The description thus obtained . . . leaves each being its strict individuality and expresses neither the table to which
it belongs, nor the area surrounding it, nor the site it occupies. It is
designation pure and simple."[19] Lafuente and Valverde similarly ex-
plore the deployment of Linnaean botany as a form of what they call
Spanish imperial biopolitics. They suggest that the metropolitan
botanists' intense focus on morphology isolated plants from the local conditions in which they were found, to the frustration of Creole intellectuals.[20] This erasure manifests visually in the thousands
of images produced under the aegis of the Spanish botanical expeditions in which the specimen, depicted in great detail, is foregrounded
against the blank white space of the page (figure 4.1). "This pictorial
approach," writes the art historian Daniela Bleichmar, "deracinates
naturalia, removing local plants . . . from their surroundings through
a process of visual erasure that transforms them into decontextual-
ized products that can circulate globally."[21]

But imperial botany never entirely ignored external determinants—
temperature, atmospheric pressure, humidity, latitude, and so on—in
either theory or practice. On the contrary, these factors too were ab-
stracted and quantified, converted into precise measurements alongside those of the plants to which they were linked. In his *Explicación
de la filosofía y fundamentos botánicos de Linneo* (1778), for example, Gómez Ortega's colleague at the Royal Botanical Garden of Madrid, Antonio Palau y Verdera, translates and glosses Linnaeus's aph-
orism regarding the factors governing the relation between plants and
place: "Los Lugares en que nacen por su naturaleza las plantas son re-
spectivos à las Regiones, Clima, Suelo, y Tierra" (The Locations where
plants are naturally born relate to Region, Climate, Soil, and Ground).
He goes on to define each of these elements, noting, for example, that
climate can be broken down into the three measurable dimensions
of latitude, longitude, and altitude. The first is measured from the
equator up to 90 degrees in either direction; the second is measured
from El Hierro, the westernmost of the Canary Islands, and adds up to
360 degrees; and the third is the vertical distance from sea level, measured with a barometer by translating atmospheric pressure into
height.[22] An array of scientific instruments capable of taking these
readings—microscopes, thermometers, barometers, compasses, and
so on—thus accompanied botanical expeditions in the Americas.

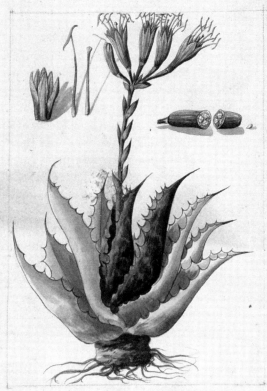

Agave Americana Linn.
Metl seu Maguei *Hrz. 27o.*

Vix ulla planta nec in medicina nec in oeconomia utilior, licet hodie vinum quem Pulque vocant tantum conficiant.

Agave vinifera

FIGURE 4.1. Illustration of "Agave Americana Linn." Painted as part of the Royal Botanical Expedition of New Spain under the direction of Martín de Sessé and José Mariano Mociño (ca. 1787–1803). Courtesy of Hunt Institute for Botanical Documentation, Carnegie Mellon University, Pittsburgh, PA, Torner Collection of Sessé and Mociño Biological Illustrations.

The mathematization of climate generated new methods for mapping and imagining geographies of equivalence. Until the middle of the eighteenth century, one of Linnaeus's basic assumptions was that plants had a natural range of temperatures that they could tolerate, and that as a result similar plants would grow within the same latitudinal zone. As he writes in *Oeconomia Naturae* (1749), "Plants impatient of cold live within the torrid zones; hence both the Indies tho' at such a distance from one another have plants in common."[23] Later, altitude became equally important as a measure capable of bringing distant locations into natural proximity. Palau thus affirms that "en la misma altura produce unas mismas especies" (at the same altitude the same species are produced). Aquatic plants in the Americas, he argues, are generally the same as their European counterparts, and the same is true for high altitudes: "Las plantas de los alpes de Lapponia, Siberia, Cantones, Pyreneos, Brasil, y otros, aunque muy distantes las unas de las otras, suelen ser tambien de unas propias especies, por estar en igual elevacion" (The plants of the mountains of Lapland, Siberia, Switzerland, the Pyrenees, Brazil, and others, though very distant from one another, tend to be of the same species, due to being at the same elevation).[24] Imperial botany thus transformed geographical incommensurability into a patchwork of spatial analogues, a global restructuring that necessarily underwrote the project of botanical extraction and capture through acclimatization on the Iberian Peninsula.

The reduction of both plants and their environments to a set of standardized variables that could be measured, mapped, compared, and operationalized produced a new vision of both nature and geography. Distance and difference were no longer synonymous, for example, but neither was analogy sufficient. These new techniques of representation, furthermore, gave rise to specialized infrastructures designed to mediate geographies of equivalence, facilitate acclimatization, and operationalize imperial botany.

### INFRASTRUCTURE, COLLECTION, AND GLOBAL CIRCULATION

In his *General y natural historia de las Indias* (1537–1548), the early naturalist of the Americas Gonzalo Fernández de Oviedo describes the pineapple as the most wonderful fruit he has ever seen. "A lo menos en España, ni en Francia, ni Inglaterra, Alemania, ni en Italia, ni en Secilia, ni en los otros Estados de la Cesárea Majestad, así como

Borgoña, Flandes, Tirol, Artués, ni Holanda, ni Gelanda, y los demás, no hay tan linda fructa" (At least in Spain, France, England, Germany, Italy, Sicily, or any of the other States of Your Caesarian Majesty, such as Burgundy, Flanders, Tyrol, Artois, or Holland, or Zeeland, and the rest, there is no fruit so fine). But the inhabitants of those European kingdoms would have to do without its incomparable taste. "Yo las he probado a llevar" (I have attempted to transport them), writes Oviedo, "e por no se haber acertado la navegación, e tardar muchos días, se me perdieron e pudrieron todas, e probé a llevar los cogollos y también se perdieron. No es fructa sino para esta tierra u otra que, a lo menos, no sea tan fría como España" (and due to navigational error and a delay of many days, all of them were lost and went bad, and I attempted to transport shoots and they too were lost. It is a fruit but for this land or another that, at least, is not so cold as Spain).[25]

Oviedo's description reflects both a belief in geographical incommensurability and a recognition of the logistical problems involved in the global circulation of botanical specimens in the sixteenth century. It is for these reasons that the main botanical materials that did circulate at that time were largely (though not entirely) textual or graphic representations of plants rather than plants themselves.[26] By the eighteenth century, however, these limits no longer seemed quite so impossible to overcome. From 1745 to 1819, 345 separate shipments of live specimens, 299 (89 percent) of which were composed of plants, were made to metropolitan Spain.[27] As important as the development of new techniques for stabilizing and mobilizing plant materials over time and space was the gradual emergence and codification of new ways of thinking about, quantifying, and comparing the continental differences that Oviedo had seen as so formidable two and a half centuries before. Spanish imperial botany thus led not only to new methods of calculation and standardization but also to efforts to design, build, and calibrate infrastructures of equivalence and circulation capable of facilitating the safe transfer of botanical materials across vast geographical distance and climatic difference.[28]

Initially established in 1755 but relocated and reorganized under Gómez Ortega's direction in 1781, the Royal Botanical Garden of Madrid was a central node in this global infrastructure. The vegetable riches of the empire flowed into this "center of calculation," where they were carefully guarded, studied, classified, and propagated. The order of the garden was disciplinary and hierarchical, even milita-

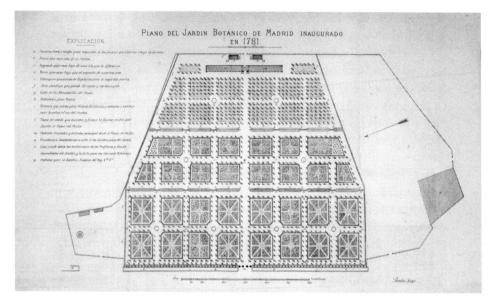

FIGURE 4.2. Map of the Botanical Garden of Madrid inaugurated in 1781. From Colmeiro, *Bosquejo histórico y estadístico del Jardín Botánico de Madrid.* Courtesy of Dumbarton Oaks Research Library and Collection, Rare Book Collection, Washington, DC.

ristic. Regulations regarding its administration and maintenance were rigid and detailed. Likewise, a map of the garden in 1781 highlights the regularized spatial order of the grounds and the plants they contained—segmented into three levels of descending height, each level was cut into squares and arranged in distinct geometric patterns in accordance with the Linnaean system (figure 4.2).[29] The two-dimensional grid was thought to facilitate comparison, bringing similarities and differences into relief through the production of proximity, distance, and juxtaposition. "The locus of this history," writes Foucault, "is a non-temporal rectangle in which, stripped of all commentary, of all enveloping language, creatures present themselves one beside another, their surfaces visible, grouped according to their common features, and thus already virtually analysed, and bearers of nothing but their own individual names. . . . The garden . . . replace[s] the circular procession of the 'show' with the arrangement of things in a 'table.'"[30]

But the garden was not merely an endpoint, a vegetable hoard of sorts where specimens would drop out of circulation. To identify the components and track the flows of the global infrastructural network into which it was inserted, I turn to Gómez Ortega's *Instrucción sobre el modo más seguro y económico de transportar plantas vivas por mar y tierra á los paises mas distantes* (1779). As the title indicates, the book was intended as a manual for administering the long-distance transportation of plants, a set of "best practices" for the project of Spanish imperial botany. The enormous distances between colonies and metropole posed a series of complex logistical questions about the shipment of live plants, the same questions to which Oviedo had alluded two and a half centuries before. The availability of fresh water, fertilizers, and capable attendants; changing climatic conditions, storms, and the salty sea breeze; infestations of animal and insect pests—all of these factors had to be carefully managed during the long sea voyages. Gómez Ortega's manual sought to address these and other challenges with a detailed set of instructions as well as plans for the construction of special crates in which to transport live plants. These designs too corresponded to the climatic specificity of the plants that each type of crate was made to carry; plants accustomed to different climates, he writes, require "caxones de diferente construccion, y de mayor resguardo" (crates of different construction and greater protection).[31]

Gómez Ortega's book thus served as a guide for global circulation and imperial extraction. Britain and France had saved money and improved their balance of trade, he argues, through the strategic implementation of imperial botany. In 1727, for example, a number of coffee plants that had been propagated in the Royal Botanical Garden of Paris were shipped to Martinique and transplanted. They grew so well there that the French colonies were soon able to meet the immense demand for coffee in the metropole and to sell "considerables porciones de él por el comercio en otros Reynos de Europa" (considerable portions of it through commerce in other Kingdoms of Europe).[32] The French example, for Gómez Ortega, demonstrated the mercantile utility of botanical science. Spain could likewise cultivate coffee in its American colonies—the coffee produced in Puerto Rico, Cuba, and Caracas is just as good, he asserts, as that grown in French Martinique. But the project goes beyond relegating production to the colonies:

Yo presumo que en las costas de las Provincias meridionales de España prosperaria tambien esta cosecha con la ventaja de que en ellas no se experimentaria el inconveniente que en algunas Colonias Americanas, donde la continua humedad del ambiente no permite que se sazone y seque bien el fruto lo qual perjudica mucho á su buena calidad y reposicion. [I presume that along the coast of the southern Provinces of Spain this harvest will also prosper, with the advantage that they do not experience the problem faced in some American Colonies, where the constant humidity of the environment does not allow the fruit to season and dry well, which greatly prejudices its good quality and recovery.][33]

In Gómez Ortega's vision, the Spanish colonies do not necessarily operate only as a site of slave-based commodity production by which to supply the metropole, as in the case of French Martinique. Rather, their contribution is the raw, cellular material itself that is to be extracted and studied, manipulated, propagated, and produced—that is to say, not merely consumed—in the metropole as well. In fact, he suggests, the climate of southern Spain is actually more propitious to the cultivation of coffee than the Caribbean region. By relocating foreign species to less humid Iberian territories, Spanish imperial botany could presume to surpass colonial production and effectively improve on the global distribution of plant life given by nature.

This was the case not only for cash crops like coffee but also for staples such as grains. As an example, Gómez Ortega identifies a variety of Chinese rice that was capable of growing on non-irrigated land. Acquired by the Royal Society of London and distributed among the British botanical gardens, the seeds sprouted but did not bear fruit. In Spain, on the other hand, a similar process generated more favorable results. Gómez Ortega had gotten his hands on a small number of seeds, which he redirected to his contact at the Botanical Garden of Puzol in Valencia. Owing to the favorable climate, the experiment yielded a significant quantity of seed, which, as a consequence, "no solo podrá multiplicarse en aquel Reyno con inmensa utilidad de sus habitantes, sino tambien en otras Provincias y climas de Europa, donde poco á poco será ya mas facil connaturalizarle" (will not only be able to multiply in that Kingdom with immense utility for its inhabitants, but also in other Provinces and climates of Europe, where little by little it will be easier to acclimatize it).[34] In other words, the project of acclimatization would loop into an ever-expanding cycle of propagation and adaptation, each climatic step laying the groundwork for the next. Little by little, over time, useful plants from abroad would be made to grow in the varied climates of Europe.

Gómez Ortega's account of the Chinese rice is exceptional only to the extent that it constitutes a sort of by-product of British imperialism, of "enlightened" competition between imperial rivals. Lettered correspondence was certainly important for the blossoming of botanical science in Spain, but the primary interest of the Spanish Crown and its botanical agents was the management of its own mercantile empire. For this reason, the principal site of extraction was its own colonial possessions. As with the rice, in turn, the aim was to transfer these plants—and their acclimatized descendants—to metropolitan territory. Such a process would require, in the first place, a sort of botanical mapping that, with the bureaucratic and financial backing of the state, would take possession of "las riquezas vegetables esparcidas por los vastos dominios del Rey . . . especialmente las de la América Española" (the vegetable riches distributed across the vast domains of the King . . . especially those of Spanish America).[35] But it would also require, in addition to botanical expeditions to the farthest reaches of the empire, major capital investment on the part of the imperial state to develop new infrastructural forms.

One such form was the stove-heated greenhouse, which appears as two thin gray rectangles marked with the letter "a" and labeled "Ynvernaderos, ó estufas" at the top of the map of the garden in figure 4.2. For Gómez Ortega, who learned about the use of greenhouses during his stay at the Jardin du Roy in Paris, these technologies offered new opportunities for managing and transforming botanical specimens recovered from colonial territories:

Los *Guayabos*, y los *Papayos*, frutales de América, que nunca se habian visto en nuestra Península, nos han nacido últimamente en el Invernadero del Real Jardin Botánico de Madrid, y desde él los hemos comunicado á los Correspondientes, que residen en territorios mas templados, donde no hay duda que prosperarán. De esta forma viene á ser un Jardin Botánico el centro de las correspondencias de su clase, de los experimentos útiles en punto de la Botánica y Agricultura, y de la propagacion de las plantas dignas de multiplicarse. [We have recently been able to grow *Guava* and *Papaya trees*, fruit trees from America that had never been seen on our Peninsula, in the Greenhouse of the Royal Botanical Garden of Madrid, and from there we have sent them to Corresponding (Gardens), which are located in more temperate territories, where there is no doubt that they will prosper. In this way, a Botanical Garden becomes the center of correspondences of its class, for useful experiments regarding Botany and Agriculture, and the propagation of those plants worthy of being multiplied.][36]

The greenhouse enabled Peninsular botanists to cultivate fruit trees that arrived from distant colonies—and more importantly from distinct climates—and thereby begin the process of adapting them to new environmental conditions. Frames of iron, glass, and coal thus radically expanded the limits of the botanical collection by enabling, for the first time, "the mobilization not only of specimens but of *entire environments.*"[37] This capacity fundamentally transformed the relation between location and climate. Until this point these categories had been so intertwined that it was impossible to treat them as independent variables, but the introduction of the greenhouse helped to untangle this knot, materially and conceptually detaching one from the other. Artifice thus made possible a reconfiguration of the contours of equivalence and transformed the environment into an object of scientific knowledge and experimentation.[38]

Still, this technology was imperfect, capable perhaps of smoothing out small climatic intervals between spatial or temporal moments but not entirely—let alone permanently—remaking environments. Its small capacity and intensive resource cost precluded the Madrid greenhouse as a final destination; it could serve only as a point of passage on a circuit toward a set of subordinate or peripheral "gardens of acclimatization" that, Gómez Ortega hoped, would provide more favorable natural conditions for cultivation and gradual adaptation. In this respect, the botanical garden in Madrid was doubly a center—of both "useful experimentation" in the greenhouse, for example, and of "correspondences" across a constellation of dispersed sites linked through the continuous circulation of knowledge and things. In addition to the greenhouses in Barcelona and Valencia to which the botanist refers in his book, then, state agents sought to develop a network of gardens in strategic locations of Spain—Córdoba, Granada, Málaga, Cartagena (Murcia), and Orotava on the Canary Island of Tenerife.[39]

In practice, however, this infrastructure of acclimatization remained more a dream than a reality. Many of these gardens were small and privately owned, and their existence depended more on personal friendships and patronage than on institutional support. When the owners moved on or died, the gardens likewise disappeared. Moreover, bitter disputes between high-ranking officials like Gómez

Ortega and the minister of the Indies, Antonio Porlier, about which gardens to promote further contributed to institutional fracture.[40] As a result, this infrastructural network never came together as a systematized project of acclimatization. On the contrary, it made up a relatively piecemeal series that was sustained and motivated more by clientelism than by the quantification and abstraction of climatic variables and the delineation of clear and systematic procedures for circulating American plants progressively through the stages necessary to adapt them to their new conditions.

These examples are illustrative of the failure of Spanish imperial botany, which ended up being less an economic boon than what the Spanish historian Francisco Javier Puerto Sarmiento calls a "broken illusion."[41] The project may not have yielded significant economic benefits, but it nevertheless produced changes at both the material and epistemic levels. Spanish imperial botany recognized the structural conditions of geography and environment and developed complex, multilayered infrastructural forms in an effort to manage these challenges. From the greenhouse and the "gardens of acclimatization" to the detailed instructions to colonial officials and naval personnel charged with collecting, preparing, and transporting specimens back to the Iberian Peninsula, this assemblage of botanical sites and practices reflects a recognition of the need for both measuring and mediating spatial incommensurabilities.

## THE MANY CLIMATES OF CHAPULTEPEC

Spanish botanical infrastructure failed on the Iberian Peninsula because it could not systematically address the relation between living beings and their environments. I turn now to the botanical garden established at Chapultepec Hill in Mexico City toward the end of the eighteenth century. The colonial garden faced similar challenges to the successful concentration of plant life and was integrated into the global network of Spanish imperial botany whose "center of calculation" was Madrid.[42] Yet its administrators adopted a different approach, one that both acknowledged and at the same time operationalized the geographical specificity of the Americas through increasingly sophisticated forms of measurement. Rather than adopt the two-dimensional grid favored by Gómez Ortega in Madrid, his counterparts in Mexico City fashioned a three-dimensional microcosm by transforming a centralized landscape of diverse environmental conditions into a rationalized topography that would ideally be capable of concentrating, sustaining, and managing the totality of plant life in New Spain.

The totalizing character of the Royal Botanical Garden of Mexico reflects the archival project out of which it emerged. Elsewhere I have charted the rise of a new archival logic in late-eighteenth-century Spain in relation to the establishment, protagonized by the historian Juan Bautista Muñoz, of the Archivo General de Indias (AGI) in 1785. The aim of this archive was to collect at a single location all of the historical documents related to Spanish colonial rule, which at the time were dispersed throughout the empire. It both shaped and was shaped by the emergence of a new mode of historical reason, according to which authority was rooted in archival documents rather than published accounts.[43] Soon after, the viceroy of New Spain proposed the foundation of an "Archivo general de Papeles" (General Archive of Papers) in Mexico City, explicitly taking the AGI as his model. To save on expenses, the unfinished palace on top of Chapultepec Hill was selected as an ideal site for this newly centralized archive.

But this archival project extended beyond papers. In a 1791 letter to the king, the viceroy explicitly links the concentration of historical documents with the concentration of plant life. Combining the two would make fiscal sense, since employees of the archive might be able to work at the garden as well: "con un sueldo se satisface a ambas atenciones" (with one salary both duties are satisfied). But in a more general sense, the projects also seemed to express a similar objective. The viceroy articulates this sentiment in its negative form: "No siendo opuestos entre si estos dos establecimientos, ningún inconvenien.te ofrece su reunión en Chapultepeque" (Not being opposed in themselves, there is no obstacle to uniting both establishments in Chapultepec). For his part, Vicente Cervantes, the director of the garden who had studied under Gómez Ortega in Madrid, frames this association in more positive terms. Like the General Archive, he declares, the botanical garden would serve as a "deposito general" (general deposit) where it would be possible not only to organize but also to "propagar abundantemente todas las diferentes especies de Vegetales" (abundantly propagate all the different species of Plants) from across New Spain. Archive and garden were both conceived, then, as "generalizing" projects that would concentrate dispersed objects into a systematic and ordered whole.[44]

The spatial transformation of Chapultepec was conditioned on two moments of enclosure, simultaneously material and epistemic.[45] The first took place soon after the conquest and transformed what had once been the gardens of the Mexica nobility into a controlled terrain that was stripped of indigenous pasts and inserted instead into a Western regime of natural history. Francisco Cervantes de Salazar's Latin dialogues, published in the mid-sixteenth century, are clear on this point. As explained in chapter 2, the text was written as a tool for Latin instruction at the University of Mexico and takes the form of a walking tour in which two locals, Zamora and Zuazo, show a Spaniard, Alfaro, the most impressive sights of Mexico City and its surroundings. Most prominent among the latter is Chapultepec Hill, which is "indorum annalibus & aquae multitudine praestātissimo" (noted in the chronicles of the Indians and also for its abundant water supply).[46]

As the characters of the dialogue traverse the city limits, proceeding along the main road through a bucolic scene of irrigated fields and pastures, the local guides point out the forested "altitudine magna promontorium" (promontory of great height) rising in the distance. Arriving at the base of the hill, Alfaro notices the walls that encircle the garden and leave only a single point of entry. What is the reason, he asks, for this enclosure that limits access to so few? The walls, Zuazo responds, serve to keep out the crowds of Indians and thereby prevent them from defiling the fresh, clean water from the spring. This physical and symbolic barrier thus excludes the indigenous population from the garden while at the same time severing the textual links between the hill and the preconquest histories rooted there. Upon reaching the summit of this now racially purified and culturally unmoored Chapultepec, the three look out over the vast expanse below them, exclaiming that from this viewpoint "sunt subiecta oculos latere nequeant" (nothing below may escape the eyes). The "subjected" position of the object of the gaze—in both senses of the term, that is, both spatial (below) and political (subordinated)—highlights the colonizing operation of this action, and in this regard it comes as no surprise that this speech is coupled to a call for the conquest of Florida.[47] These "voyeurs" take in the entirety of the city as well as the surrounding countryside through which they had passed earlier.[48] Awed by the sight, the Spaniard Alfaro declares,

O Deum immortalē quā bellum, quam gratum & oculis & animo, quantāq varietate iucundum, se hinc spectaculum exhibet, vt summa cum ratione affirmare ausim, orbem vtruq̄ hoc loco circunscriptum & circumductum esse: & quod de homine Greci tradunt, Microcosmon id est paruum mundum ipsum appellantes: idem de Mexico dici posse, loco plano & latissimo tota posita est, & omnis vndequaq̄ visui obiecta. [O immortal God! What a spectacle is displayed from here! How beautiful, how pleasing to eyes and mind, how delightful in variety! I should dare assert on excellent reasoning that both worlds have been joined and encompassed in this place; and the term *microcosmos* that the Greeks employ for man, that is, a small universe, can likewise be said of the City of Mexico. The whole is situated on an extensive, level plain completely exposed to our gaze on all sides.][49]

At this point, things bleed into words. Alfaro goes on to request a brief introduction to the natural (and moral) history of New Spain: "Quod tamen cognoscendum mihi supremum & vltimum restat . . . de Nouae Hispaniae, cuius primatum tenet Mexicus, tēperie & ingenio, deq̄ Indorū moribus & vita . . . me docete" (Please instruct me about the last and final things left for me to learn, that is, about the climate and nature of New Spain, whose head is Mexico City, and about the life and customs of the Indians).[50] In response, the locals reference the work of a natural historian named Juanote Durán, who had apparently written a geography of the New World in the 1530s that was unpublished at the time and has since been lost. Citing Durán, they narrate at length the dimensions of the territory, its various regions and climes, the fertility of the soil, and the products it yields, as well as the customs of the native population. Totalizing gaze and textual description thus go hand in hand.

It is precisely the act of enclosure that allows Cervantes de Salazar to reinscribe Chapultepec into a colonial regime of knowledge. On one hand, the walls secure the garden and its contents from the threat of contamination posed by the indigenous population; on the other hand, this material expulsion subtends the insertion of the site—and the territory at large—into the epistemic frame of natural history. The view from the top of Chapultepec transforms the city below, as a symbol of colonial rule and a crossroads of global circulation, into a microcosm. In the context of late-eighteenth-century botany, however, this microcosmic capacity will be reversed and displaced onto Chapultepec itself.

If the sixteenth-century natural histories of Cervantes de Salazar and Juanote Durán are made possible by the material and epistemic enclosure of Chapultepec, the installation of the botanical garden at the site is inaugurated through a second act of enclosure. The microcosm of Mexico City celebrated by Cervantes de Salazar, where the urban fabric encompasses the universe and the garden serves as the point from which it can be seen, yielded to the microcosm of the garden, subjected to the rationalizing spirit of the late Enlightenment. This project, conceived and implemented by Peninsular and Creole figures, including the botanist Vicente Cervantes, the architect and engineer Miguel Constanzó, and the physician Martín de Sessé, sought to represent hyperlocalized environmental conditions, or microclimates, on the three-dimensional landscape of Chapultepec Hill. An incipient form of plant geography, the botanical garden thus not only resonated with but also lay the groundwork for the emergence of Humboldtian science just over a decade later.

Chapultepec came to serve as the location of the garden as a result of the failure of its initial site, known as the Potrero de Atlampa. Beginning in May 1789, a variety of seeds and plants from other parts of New Spain, the Americas, and even Europe were acquired and sown at this four-acre plot. But a problem quickly arose. Atlampa was a lowland subject to frequent flooding that ruined the plants and at times made it impossible for students to attend class. In addition, the soil was so "tepetatoso, axido, y salitrovo" (clayey, arid, and nitrous) that not even maize would grow there.[51] These obstacles led to a search for a more suitable location.

By the end of 1791 the botanical garden had been reorganized and relocated to a more permanent form, divided between two sites: a small teaching garden at the viceroy's palace and a larger agricultural garden at Chapultepec Hill. While the former has received a great deal of attention from scholars, the latter has been largely ignored or overlooked. I suspect there are two reasons for this: first, the symbolic importance of the palace, along with the corresponding prevalence of documentation about it; and second, the dominant disciplinary approach to botanical history, which tends to read the garden through the intellectual lineage of the *letrados* who studied there. I do not mean to discount the pedagogical influence of the garden on the intellectual culture of New Spain—by training the next generation of doctors, scientists, and pharmacists in Enlightenment botany, it shaped the way nature was seen and understood well into the nineteenth century.[52] But the grounds of Chapultepec served an equally if not more important task. It was there that the agricultural side of botanical science would be carried out, where species identified and collected in the course of ongoing botanical expeditions across New Spain would be transplanted and cultivated. The two sites were designed to operate in tandem, and a constant flow of people and plants circulated between them. Cervantes and Constanzó agreed that it would be easy enough, on one hand, to simply bring plants from Chapultepec to the palace to be used for instructional purposes; on the other hand, Chapultepec was close enough that no one would complain about having to walk a few miles in order to reach "un paraje donde pueden juntarse en mayor numero que en otra parte las producciones vejetales de todos los Climas" (a location in which, more than anywhere else, the vegetable products of every Climate may be gathered).[53] All the plant species from the many climates of New Spain could be concentrated there.

Whereas the palace had to be radically altered in order to serve the desired purpose, what made Chapultepec so ideal were its "natural" virtues. As Cervantes affirms, the site offered "un basto terreno de varias calidades, y temperamentos" (an expansive plot of varied qualities and temperatures), which as a result would be able to accommodate any plants sent back by the botanical expedition, led by Sessé, or by botanical aficionados and correspondents elsewhere.[54] In his own report, Constanzó lays out the utility of the site in more explicit detail:

> Chapultepeque goza de quantas circunstancias pueden apetecerse: un cerro elevado ciento y cincuenta pies sobre el terreno en que tiene asiento: ofrece una situacion amena, y deliciosa con variedad de aspectos, y está expuesto á todos vientos, en donde las plantas según su naturaleza, y habito, hallaran oportuno abrigo: por esta razon las faldas del Cerro las produce mui varias, y particulares: en las que miran al sur, y al Poniente se ven muchas, propias unicamente de climas calientes, y en las que miran al Norte, y oriente, las de Climas frios: al pie del mismo Cerro hay competente terreno, en que *una ves acotado* se pueden acomodar perfectamente las plantas q^e nacen en sitios mas, o menos altos, mas, o menos humedos. [Chapultepec enjoys all of the conditions that could be hoped for: a hill elevated 150 feet above ground level, it offers a pleasant and delightful location with a variety of qualities, and exposed to all the winds, where plants will find appropriate shelter according to their nature and habitat. For this reason, the slopes of the Hill have varied and particular characters: in

those which face south and west, there are many that resemble warm climates, and in those that face north and east, cool climates. At the base of the Hill there is sufficient land that, *once enclosed*, plants that grow in more or less elevated and more or less humid places will be perfectly accommodated.][55]

Where Cervantes de Salazar rhetorically extols the "great height" of the "promontory" of Chapultepec, Constanzó reinscribes the hill scientifically as a series of planes, each subject to a set of measurable and rationalizable variables. These planes, furthermore, were constructed through a relation of equivalence that was intended to operate in substitution for the native habitat of the plants. Owing to a specific combination of sun, wind, and altitude, the south- and west-facing slopes took on the characteristics of hot climates, while those that faced north and east matched cold climates. Meanwhile, the base of the hill was capable of hosting plants adapted to either wet or dry zones. (This last characteristic in particular must have come as a great relief after the regular flooding at Atlampa.) The varied climates of Chapultepec, wrote Sessé several years later, made it possible, under the direction of Cervantes, to "connaturalizar por mayor y a menos costo que en ningun otro [terreno] de las inmediaciones, las plantas de los diversos climas que componen esta America" (naturalize the plants from the diverse climates that make up this America in great numbers and at less cost than at any other nearby site).[56]

These comments reveal that the construction of the garden required more than passive observation—it also required a second act of enclosure. When Constanzó states that Chapultepec will be able to serve as an ideal garden only after it has been "acotado," he is describing, on one hand, a demarcation or division, a literal fencing in, that is, by erecting *cotos* (boundaries; from the Latin *cautus*, or "defended"); and, on the other, an epistemic inscription of the meaning of each of these divisions, on the basis of the proper authorities (a sort of metaphorical defense). Thus, the gardens of Chapultepec described on one hand by Cervantes de Salazar and on the other by Cervantes, Constanzó, and Sessé all depended on some form of enclosure. The first round actualized the racial exclusion through which colonial rule often worked, while the second built on this foundation by further fragmenting the space through demarcation and inscription. In one sense, this is precisely what Foucault is talking about when he describes the classical garden, in which, by instituting order, things are made to signify without words. But the reorganization of Chapultepec went an important step further: it classified things as well as the space that enveloped, bound, and sustained them. It was not only the items laid out on the table that were subjected to the classifying and quantifying gaze, but also the table itself.

The establishment of the Royal Botanical Garden of Mexico thus gave rise to both a more sophisticated theory of climate and a more effective infrastructure of acclimatization than the botanists in Madrid had produced. Instead of a patchwork archipelago of "gardens of acclimatization," organized more by patronage than calculation, the transformation of Chapultepec into a rationalized spectrum of microclimates placed external determination at the center of the botanical project. To the two-dimensional theory of climate that was dominant in Spain, botanical practice in New Spain added a third dimension. From the abstract plane of the cartographic projection, a topographical imprint became necessary.

## PLANT GEOGRAPHY AND RACIAL AFFECTABILITY

The proposed rationalization of Chapultepec also dovetailed with and laid the groundwork for the elaboration of a new mode of scientific thought, namely plant geography. Mountains had been important in the study of plant diversity since the mid-eighteenth century. Jorge Cañizares-Esguerra has traced this argument from Linnaeus to Andean botanists like Francisco José de Caldas, who was an important influence on the Prussian scientist Alexander von Humboldt.[57] In his famous *Tableau physique*, for example, Humboldt weaves together cartography with the careful measurement of environmental phenomena to illustrate topographically the zones of habitability of Andean plants (figure 4.3). Cañizares-Esguerra suggests that mountains offered a "natural laboratory" for studying the relation between living beings and their environments. But while the unparalleled verticality of the Andes certainly made it exemplary, Chapultepec was being discussed in similar terms more than a decade earlier. Moreover, the botanical garden was even more of a laboratory than the Andes, in the true etymological sense of the word, as a site of human labor. The operationalization of Chapultepec articulated by Cervantes, Constanzó, and Sessé demonstrated a new imperial capacity to order nature through infrastructures of equivalence that transformed the way space and the living beings that inhabited and circulated through it were seen and mobilized for particular ends.

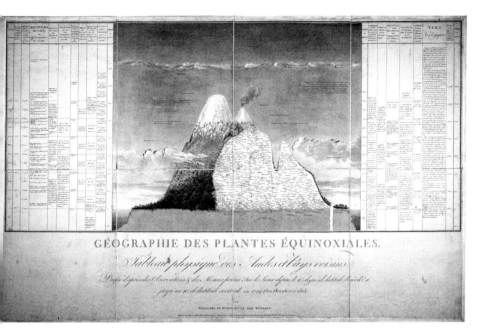

FIGURE 4.3. *Tableau physique des Andes et Pays voisins* (Physical tableau of the Andes and neighboring countries). From Humboldt and Bonpland, *Essay on the Geography of Plants.*

With the approval of Charles IV, Humboldt traveled with his companion Aimé Bonpland though Spanish America between 1799 and 1804, the final year of which he spent in New Spain. In his *Political Essay on the Kingdom of New Spain* (1811), Humboldt praises the state of the natural sciences in Mexico as well as the "distinguished botanists" with whom he worked during his stay, Cervantes and Sessé among them. "The city of Mexico," he adds, "exhibits a very interesting botanical garden."[58] Humboldt did not travel extensively in New Spain, opting instead to base his work on statistical data provided to him by the Spanish authorities. This suggests that he depended even more heavily on his local counterparts and that his botanical observations would have been carried out in and around Mexico City, more likely than not at the garden.[59]

Humboldt's work can be seen as moving beyond the traditional botany I have examined here but also as building directly on precisely the kind of work that was happening at Chapultepec in order to fashion a new method and object of scientific knowledge. At the opening of his *Essay on the Geography of Plants* (1807), he distinguishes his own work from that of the Linnaean botanists who preceded him, who were "concerned almost exclusively with the discovery of new species of plants, the study of their external structure, their distinguishing characteristics, and the analogies that group them together into classes and families." However valuable this work may have been, argues Humboldt, "it is no less important to understand the Geography of Plants, a science that up to now exists in name only, and yet is an essential part of general physics."[60] Already apparent here is a shift away from the classifying logic of taxonomy and toward a "general physics" that attempts to grasp the laws that determine the unfolding of nature over space and time. I want to emphasize two key characteristics of this new approach. The first is methodological, namely the mathematization of the natural and social worlds through precise measurement. Humboldt and Bonpland carried an array of state-of-the-art scientific instruments with them in their travels, including sextants for calculating latitude, chronometers for calculating longitude, Ramsden barometers for calculating air pressure and elevation, a repeating circle and theodolite for calculating the elevation of distant points, numerous thermometers to gauge temperature, and an electrometer and an electroscope for measuring electrical charge.[61] And these instruments were put to good use, their readings inscribed in journals, published in books, and engraved in images. As he writes in the *Essay*, "Mr. Bonpland and I brought back collections containing over 6,000 species of tropical plants that we gathered ourselves during the course of our botanizing. Since we were also carrying out at the same time astronomical observations as well as geodetic and barometric measurements, our manuscripts contain materials that can determine exactly the position and elevation of these plants. We can show the breadth of the latitudinal zone occupied by these plants, their maximum and minimum elevation, the nature of the soil in which they grow, and the temperature of the plants' native soil."[62] Certainly, measurement formed part of the toolkit by which Chapultepec had been operationalized at the hands of Cervantes, Sessé, and Constanzó, but it was Humboldt who intensified and formalized these procedures, fully incorporating them into and thereby transforming the practice of botanical collection. The resulting data are integrated into topographical renderings that aim to make visible the implicit and explicit limits written into the laws of nature. Such "botanical maps" would depict "long bands, whose irresistible extension causes the population of states to decrease, the nations to be separated, and creates stronger obstacles to communication than do mountains and seas."[63] As noted earlier, the *Tableau physique*, published with the *Essay*, famously joins this wealth of data capturing a multiplicity of natural variables (temperature, altitude, air pressure, humidity, electricity, and so on) with a topographical representation of South America and the Andes. In a sense, this image could be seen as an extension of the project that began at Chapultepec.

Along with precise measurement, a second characteristic of Humboldt's plant geography is a broadening of its scope, a change in the object of knowledge. The shift away from "things themselves" to complex assemblages—*vegetation* rather than *plants*, for example— also led Humboldt, at the same time as Georges Cuvier was developing his approach to comparative anatomy in Paris, to think more in terms of function than form. "In living nature," he writes in the *Essay*, "many causes contribute to the modification of vital functions, and none can be neglected to explain the phenomena of the organization of matter."[64] The "general deposit" of the Royal Botanical Garden of Mexico had aimed to collect the totality of the plant life of New Spain within the rationalized planes of Chapultepec Hill, but Humboldt's "general physics" redirected this gaze back onto the elements that composed the natural and social world. His method thus represents an attempt to tease out the emergent divide between organic beings and inorganic matter, but also the deeply material relations that nevertheless link them together within a general ecology.[65] For example, Humboldt sees a "very analogous" relation between plants and animals with regard to the action of external forces on bodily function, or as he puts it, "the irritability of their fibers and the stimuli that excite them."[66] But this analogy operates differentially—certain global regions, defined by an array of climatic variables, are more adequate to the social and biological development of certain living organisms: "These results comprise in one view the climate and its influence on organized beings, the aspect of the country, varied according to the nature of the soil and its vegetable covering, the direction of the mountains and rivers which separate races of men as well as tribes of plants; and finally, the modifications observable in the condition of people living in different latitudes, and in circumstances more or less favourable to the development of their faculties."[67] Life appears, and must be thought, within a specific context.

By exploring the impact of external forces on the development of "organized beings" including both plants and humans, Humboldt's

approach thus goes beyond Alzate's analogy between "las plantas" and "los negros," with its emphasis on surface appearance, and
makes possible a new theory of the human body and specifically of
racialized life framed in a global register. Where plant life is "mo-
notonous and hopelessly dull," as in Europe, agricultural productiv-
ity and population growth are maximized. In the tropics, conversely,
the forces of nature simply overpower those of culture. "In the lands
near the equator, man is too weak to tame a vegetation that hides the
ground from view and leaves only the ocean and the rivers to be free.
There nature demonstrates its savage and majestic character (carac-
tère sauvage et majestueux) that render impossible all efforts of cultivation." The power of nature overcomes the efforts of the human
populations inhabiting these regions to transform and appropriate it.
As a result, he continues, "the character of the savage (sauvage) is
modified everywhere by the nature of the climate and the soil where
he lives."[68] Linguistically and climatically linked to tropical vegetation, the savage is defined by what Silva calls "affectability."

Humboldt's theory of race is thus doubly spatial, framed in terms
of geography as well as of subjectivity. He conceptualizes the question of external determination in relation to a reconfigured locus of
autonomy, and it is through imperial botany that the knowing subject is constituted. In this respect, plant geography develops a curious
relation to imperial appropriation:

The frail plants that people, out of love of science or refined luxury,
grow in their hothouses are mere shadows of the majestic equinoctial plants; many of these shapes will remain forever unknown to
the Europeans. . . . In Europe, a man isolated on an arid coast can enjoy in thought the picture of faraway regions: if his soul is sensitive to
works of art, if he is educated enough in spirit to embrace the broad
concepts of general physics, he can, in his utter solitude and without
leaving his home, appropriate everything that the intrepid naturalist has discovered in the heavens and the oceans, in the subterranean
grottos, or on the highest icy peaks. This is no doubt how enlightenment and civilization have the greatest impact on our individual
happiness, by allowing us to live in the past as well as the present,
by bringing to us everything produced by nature in its various climates, and by allowing us to communicate with all the peoples of the
earth. Sustained by previous discoveries, we can go forth into the future, and by foreseeing the consequences of phenomena, we can understand once and for all the laws to which nature subjected itself. In

the midst of this research, we can achieve an intellectual pleasure, a moral freedom that fortifies us against the blows of fate and which no external power can ever reach.[69]

At first glance, the project of imperial botany as articulated from the metropolitan center appears to be entirely exhausted. The greenhouses that glistened with Gómez Ortega's desire are once again inserted back into the overdetermined global space in which they were originally rooted. Technological mastery and the artificial production of "environment" are written as a tragic narrative of impossibility. And yet, it is worth considering in what specific way the project has failed. After all, Humboldt is referring specifically to the European gardens that relied on the greenhouse, rather than sites like Chapultepec that aimed instead to take advantage of their "natural" characteristics. Indeed, Humboldt would later write glowingly of the "garden of acclimatization" at Orotava, which he and Bonpland had visited en route to the Americas: "The establishment of a botanical garden at Teneriffe," he affirms in his *Personal Narrative of Travels to the Equinoctial Regions of the New Continent* (1814), "is a very happy idea, on account of the double influence, which it may have on the progress of botany, and on the introduction of useful plants into Europe. . . . The Canary Islands, from the mildness of their climate and geographical position, afforded the most suitable place for naturalising the productions of the two Indies, and serving as a repository to habituate the plants gradually to the colder temperature of the south of Europe."[70]

How to reconcile these apparently contradictory statements regarding the potential of the botanical garden and more generally of the project of imperial botany? In my view, something different is at stake in each case. With regard to Orotava, Humboldt remains focused on the same project that occupied Spanish botanists under the direction of Gómez Ortega, one that was limited to the mechanics and presumed mercantile benefits of acclimatization. This is, in other words, a primarily economic project. But the critique of the garden laid out in the earlier *Essay on the Geography of Plants* operates on a very different level. What marks the greenhouse as a failure is not so much that its products have no utility but rather that they do not evoke the *aesthetic experience* of tropical nature. The greenhouse produces little more than "shadows of the majestic equinoctial plants," the very same plants that overpower the feeble efforts of the savage indigenous inhabitants of a global region written in affectability. The failure of the greenhouse paradoxically reaffirms the self-determination of the European (White) knowing subject.

Even as the project of imperial botany begins to drop away, then, it leaves behind a newly consolidated scientific apparatus that writes the racial as woven into the fabric of a global space that, for its part, serves as the stage of appearance of the category of life itself. Plant geography and general physics are thus the clearest expression in Humboldt's work of the procedure through which late Enlightenment science produced a global distribution of affectability. Humboldt's imperial botany underwrites both the infrastructural systems that enable the global circulation and concentration of natural products, as at Orotava, and the production of scientific knowledge that captures the unfolding of nature over time and space, as in the *Essay on the Geography of Plants*. Both are part of a civilizing project of colonial extraction and transformation. But imperial botany also operates as a sort of insulation that shields the self-determined character of the European (White) subject from the continuous threat of external determination. At the same time, this subject's mastery over colonial nature slips easily into a parallel mastery over colonized humanity, defined by its analogous relation to "savage" vegetation. Racialized bodies and social configurations are written as differential exteriorizations of the productive law of life and of the particular mental capacities produced within distinct global regions.[71]

## CONCLUSION

Race does not enter into Foucault's archaeology of the human sciences in *The Order of Things* because he never abandons Europe as the domain of his inquiry—only in his later work, as I have suggested, does the question of colonization make even a brief appearance. This is especially true of his analysis of the emergence of the modern concept of life at the beginning of the nineteenth century. For Foucault, it is Cuvier, bent over the dissection table of his Parisian laboratory, who embodies this transition. In contrast, I have suggested an alternative, imperial trajectory that highlights not only the centrality but also the inscription or embeddedness of race within the very concept of "life itself." In this account, Alexander von Humboldt's early work on plant geography constitutes a "crucial link" between the practice of natural history characteristic of late-eighteenth-century Spanish imperial botany and the "science of man" at the beginning of the nineteenth century.[72]

Foucault's analysis of biopolitics picks up where his excavation of the modern concept of "life itself" leaves off. In the first volume of *The History of Sexuality*, published in French in 1976 (the same year he delivered his "Society Must Be Defended" lectures at the Collège de France), he traces the consolidation of a new political modality that takes life as its object. It is here that the question of race, glaringly absent in *The Order of Things*, finally enters the picture. Importantly, Foucault does not treat the rise of what he calls "modern, 'biologizing,' statist" racism in the nineteenth century as an entirely new phenomenon.[73] In this way he avoids the trap encountered by scholars who cannot see beyond the conceptual boundaries of "scientific racism" and who thus dismiss claims about racism prior to the nineteenth century as anachronistic. Yet Foucault's description of this nineteenth-century shift to "a new racism modeled on war" ends up problematically reifying the category of race itself. "You can see that, here, we are far removed from the ordinary racism that takes the traditional form of mutual contempt or hatred between the races."[74] What Foucault refers to as "ordinary racism" is thus grounded in a racial economy that has been fully naturalized. It presumes the prior existence of a real object ("the races") that only later enters into a system of representation or becomes synchronized with a new modality of power. Furthermore, he encodes a theory of "race relations" that naturalizes not only racial belonging but also racist conduct.[75] Rather than some biological substrate over which an ideological fabric is later draped or around which "natural" enmities inevitably coalesce, however, race is best understood as the product of a series of racializing procedures. What I have argued in this chapter, moreover, is that the modern concept of "life," assembled on the basis of an array of infrastructures and material practices that were inseparable from European colonialism, is itself inseparable from racialization. There is no pure or transcendent concept of life, ontologically prior to some racial ideology or veil—rather, "life itself" is always already racialized from the moment of its historical emergence.

This account of the emergence of racialized life also challenges the conventional reading of racial thinking in the late Enlightenment. During the eighteenth century, this story goes, racial difference was seen strictly as a result of environment, which meant that identity was relatively fluid. It was only in the nineteenth century that the location of race shifted to the body, making it fixed and immutable. This transition gave rise to the "scientific racism" that many historians of the nineteenth century privilege as racism's one "true" form.[76]

By focusing on the split between transparency and affectability, however, my analysis shows that the concept of race is never entirely fluid or entirely fixed, but rather is expressed differentially through particular kinds of bodies. Even in the nineteenth century, race operated as an analytic capable of defining the extent to which a body was autonomous and self-determined, on one hand, or always already subject to external forces, on the other. The racial, in other words, is precisely that which determines which bodies are fixed and which are fluid.[77]

Cañizares-Esguerra has argued that, faced with European theories of climate that threatened their superior position in the colonial hierarchy, seventeenth-century Creoles outlined a new theory of race. Using the early modern discourse of astrology, they distinguished their own bodies, defined as we saw in chapter 3 by the purity of Spanish descent, from indigenous ones and argued that only the latter were subject to the negative influence of New World stars. This allowed them simultaneously to accept and to insulate themselves from dominant European theories of degeneration. For Cañizares-Esguerra, this is a notable case because it shows that "the first modern views of the racialized body" emerged in Spanish America, but he acknowledges that Creole patriotic astrology did not catch on in Europe and therefore cannot be seen as the "origin" of scientific racism.[78] Cañizares-Esguerra's analysis of this aborted theory of race conjugates the relation between fixity and fluidity, between body and environment.

Although the white supremacist astrology of the seventeenth century proved a dead end, this chapter shows that the same logic reappeared in the late Enlightenment debates about botany and plant geography that were channeled through the American colonies generally and New Spain specifically.[79] Once again we find the racializing caesura that splits humanity into two types of bodies—one self-determining, the other externally determined. By the nineteenth century, however, the pressures of external determination were provided not by what had become an obsolete theory of astrology, but primarily by an environment subjected to increasingly intense forms of statistical rationalization. This scientific approach to climate had emerged as a supplement to Spanish imperial botany and manifested in the array of infrastructural forms, from greenhouses and "gardens of acclimatization" to the transformation of landscape into microclimates, that were developed under the auspices of this project. In this way, Spanish imperial botany and the botanical collections on which it depended gave rise to a new science not only of concentration but also of race at the turn of the nineteenth century.

# PRIMITIVE RACIALIZATION

*The broader social contradictions of neoliberal capitalism in which the Rural City is embedded ensure that those returning to their lands are faced with continued marginalisation while Nuevo Juan de Grijalva itself is transformed into little more than a space of cramped housing, high unemployment, and persistent poverty. Furthermore, as the raw memory of alienation fades and the routines of an administered everydayness congeal around them, the day may come when the inhabitants . . . announce that they are satisfied.*
JAPHY WILSON, "NOTES ON THE RURAL CITY"

*Hegemony is always the forgetting of primitive accumulation, the original sin of political economy.*
ALBERTO MOREIRAS, "TEN NOTES ON PRIMITIVE IMPERIAL ACCUMULATION"

ON SEPTEMBER 17, 2009, the Mexican president Felipe Calderón made an unusual appearance in a remote corner of the southernmost state of Chiapas, in order to inaugurate a newly built city called Nuevo Juan de Grijalva. Accompanied by the governor of Chiapas, Juan Sabines, and wearing a wreath of pink flowers, Calderón told the crowd that this, the first of a series of so-called sustainable rural cities (*ciudades rurales sustentables*), would be the solution to the problems of rural Mexico. "Estoy convencido, amigos" (I am convinced, my friends), he declared, "que una de las causas estructurales de la pobreza en México es la dispersión de la gente" (that one of the structural causes of poverty in Mexico is the dispersion of the people). Seemingly going off script for a moment, he continued: "Yo no sé por qué los poblados se regaron tanto. Quizá es por la costumbre, la tradición" (I don't know why the communities were so scattered. Maybe it's because of custom or tradition). Regardless of the original cause, he said, it would be far more expensive to deliver water and other services to three houses thirty kilometers apart than to do so for four hundred houses "reunidas en un perímetro como éste" (grouped together in a perimeter like this one). The key to addressing poverty and marginalization in the poorest states of Mexico, then, would be to have "una política pública que estimule la concentración en centros de desarrollo, en ciudades rurales, como ésta" (a public policy that stimulates concentration in centers of development, in rural cities like this one).[1]

Against dispersion, concentration. The resonance between this project and the array of colonial techniques of population management examined in this book should be immediately clear. Since the introduction of the *campo de reconcentración* by the Spanish military in Cuba at the end of the nineteenth century, these forms and practices of concentration have proliferated in Latin America and throughout the world. Indeed, the link between many of these sites goes beyond mere resemblance. One might easily sketch out, for example, a genealogy linking Spanish camps in Cuba to American camps in the Philippines, and from there to "strategic hamlets" during the US war in Vietnam, passing into the *aldeas vietnamitas* in Guerrero, Mexico during the "dirty war" of the 1970s and the *aldeas modelo* or *polos de desarrollo* in Guatemala during the genocidal military campaigns of the 1980s. This would be both accurate and at the same time somewhat misleading, if only because concentration-based strategies of counterinsurgency have proliferated to such an extent that the directionality of these borrowings may at times be too diffuse to trace.[2]

The state of Chiapas is well known because of the Zapatista movement, which rose up against the Mexican government in 1994 and since then has sought to build autonomy in recuperated territory and defend itself from the state's ongoing campaign of low-intensity war. For this reason, many critics have interpreted the rural cities project as part of a broad strategy of counterinsurgency. Yet only one site, Santiago El Pinar, is located anywhere near Zapatista territory, and in any case the project is currently expanding to other states like Puebla. Beyond the logic of counterinsurgency, then, the rural cities in many ways appear as a classic mechanism of "primitive accumulation," as described by Marx, by which peasants are violently separated from the land and converted from subsistence farmers into wage laborers. On one hand, the process serves to facilitate the enclosure and concentration of collectively held resources in the hands of the state or transnational capital. Some of these lands will be used to build megadams and hydroelectric plants, for example, while others have been granted as concessions to North American mining companies. On the other hand, the project aims to transform indigenous peasants once and for all into neoliberal subjects, "freed" from their ties to the land and the collective and inserted as individuals and family units into labor markets and global commodity flows.[3]

Designed to remake indigenous subjectivity through the reconfiguration of space, the rural cities "are laid out in a rigid grid formation, within which diverse communities are thrown together, fragmented into individual families, and reconstituted in homogeneous rows of identical houses."[4] Infrastructural integration and the provision of services can be read as mechanisms for making people live "better," though (as with their colonial predecessors) these programs are always ideological and seek not merely to sustain but to radically transform the lives to which they are directed. As the geographer Japhy Wilson notes, these cities are urbanistically and architecturally organized to encourage the atomization of individuals and families by minimizing public space and orienting inhabitants away from the little that remains. In Nuevo Juan de Grijalva, for example, there are no parks and no central plaza. Houses are built with their backs facing the street and their porches opening inward. Meanwhile, patios are too small and hot to grow crops or raise animals for consumption, and as a result residents are induced, often for the first time in their lives, to purchase all or nearly all of the food they consume. This process of subjectification, moreover, is framed in racializing terms. Calderón speculates that indigenous "dispersion" may be the result of a naturalized tendency embedded within an indigenous culture that is ancient, static, and obsolete. Culture is thus mobilized to do the work of race. Framed as a project of "modernization," concentration represents not only the delivery of infrastructural services but also the production of coevalness between the "backward" indigenous population and the "modern" Mestizo population of Mexico. As one high-ranking state official explained, the establishment of rural cities should not be seen as "a single act of relocation in a housing estate" but rather as *a project that implies a change of life in its inhabitants.*[5]

This comparison highlights two important distinctions between the counterinsurgency model of concentration and the colonial (and postcolonial) projects I have focused on in this book. First, while the former appear in a context of nominal war, the latter are deployed in a context of nominal peace. We have to be careful about these terms, of course, since they are closer than is conventionally assumed—as Foucault reminds us, a war is always raging beneath the surface of every peace.[6] Especially in the colonial context, then, the difference is one of degrees, but this does not mean that we should not attend to it. Agamben's reading of the concentration camp, for example, turns precisely on this distinction. The camp is born, he argues, out of a temporal state of emergency linked to a colonial war.[7] My claim, in contrast, is that concentration initially emerges through the construction of a colonial "peace." Concentration constitutes, rather than suspends, the social order.

The second difference concerns the question of race. Laleh Khalili observes that "the racialization of the enemy" plays a crucial role in the practice of counterinsurgency, especially when it is carried out in colonial space, since "ultimately a racial hierarchy resolves the tensions between illiberal methods and liberal discourse, between bloody hands and honeyed tongues, between weapons of war and emancipatory hyperbole." By rendering certain populations disposable, the logic of race indexes the uneven deployment of violence and care. Khalili argues, for example, that the purported "whiteness" of the Boers shaped their treatment by the British. Although they too were confined in concentration camps, compared to "Black" internees they enjoyed double the rations, exemption from heavy manual labor, and the support of pro-Boer activists in Britain.[8] Generally speaking, the "caesura" of racialization defines the contours of concentration, especially once the camp has "boomeranged" from the colony back to the metropole—from the World War II–era death camps in Nazi Germany and Japanese internment camps in the United States to the detention center at Guantánamo Bay today.[9]

The temporality of racialization is somewhat different, however, in the concentration projects I have examined here. If racialization has already taken place and forms the enabling ground for concentration as counterinsurgency, then congregation, enclosure, segregation, and collection reverse this process, with concentration operating as the enabling ground for racialization. Race is not the starting point, in other words, but the end product of concentration, which for its part is conceptualized as a racializing procedure.[10] In reality, of course, the distinction is not so clear. Racialization has to be constantly reproduced through a multiplicity of projects operating across various levels of scale, often in conflict with each other, and concentration can be used to shore up or undermine existing racial projects. Nevertheless, as Calderón's discussion of indigenous "dispersion" suggests, certain categories that emerged through colonial concentration projects have endured to the present day. Much like physical infrastructures that stubbornly persist in the landscape, race may operate infrastructurally by facilitating certain forms of circulation and accumulation that remain relatively consistent over time.

This book has laid out a framework for racialization that is both *historically* linked and *formally* identical to Marx's concept of primitive accumulation. On one hand, as Marx himself recognized, primitive accumulation was routed through European colonialism and as a consequence was bound up with racialized forms of expropriation and extraction, including "the extirpation, enslavement and entombment in mines of the indigenous population" of the Americas and "the conversion of Africa into a preserve for the commercial hunting of blackskins."[11] This is an important claim, but it treats race as always already constituted, a "natural" category that seems to offer itself up to be harnessed in more or less brutal ways. Building on the work of Silvia Federici, I have suggested instead that primitive accumulation should be read in part as a process of racialization, as *"an accumulation of differences and divisions within the working class,* whereby hierarchies built upon gender, as well as 'race' and age, became constitutive of class rule and the formation of the modern proletariat."[12] For Federici, primitive accumulation actively *produces* race (note her use of quotation marks) as both a condition of possibility for and an integral component of ongoing capital accumulation.

On the other hand, both capitalism and race have histories, operate as modalities of domination, and most importantly are easily naturalized. After laying out the process of capital accumulation in exhaustive detail, Marx observes that each step in the circuit presupposes the step that precedes it. "The whole movement, therefore, seems to turn around in a never-ending circle, which we can only get out of by assuming a primitive accumulation (the 'previous accumulation' of Adam Smith) which precedes capitalist accumulation; an accumulation which is not the result of the capitalist mode of production but its point of departure."[13] For political economists like Smith, this problem was solved by resorting to a morality tale: once upon a time, some people worked hard and saved their earnings while others were lazy and squandered them. This story serves both to explain and to justify the emergence of capitalists, on one hand, and workers, on the other. Less a history than a theology of original sin, it constructs a homogeneous and empty time in which the systemic logic of capital has been transformed into a set of natural "laws." Capitalism has no history—it is simply the way things are. This claim conveniently erases the foundational violence and expropriation that jumpstarted the capital-relation.

In contrast, Marx sought to excavate the "actual history" of largely colonial violence required to create the conditions in which capitalist accumulation could proceed under its own momentum. The introduction of history shatters the illusion of capitalism as the necessary consequence of an array of "propensities" embedded in human nature and thus constant over the *longue durée* of human existence. For Marx, capitalism has a history—it begins to emerge at a particular historical moment out of something else, a different and noncapitalist set of social relations. Primitive accumulation thus "appears as 'primitive' because it forms the pre-history of capital, and of the mode of production corresponding to capital." Although critics like David Harvey have read primitive accumulation (or as he calls it, "accumulation by dispossession") as an ongoing mechanism of accumulation, especially following the shift in the global economy since 1973, what is most interesting and at the same time most difficult about the concept is precisely its inseparability from the problem of disjuncture and transition.[14]

Just as it is difficult for the political economists whom Marx sets out to critique to conceive of the violent processes of primitive accumulation that set capitalism into motion—thus, Adam Smith's theology of original sin—it can be equally difficult to conceptualize the violent processes of racialization that constitute race itself. The "natural laws" of the capitalist economy run parallel to the "natural" disposition toward certain forms of exploitation and extraction that is attributed to racialized populations. As familiar as we are with the argument that race is a social construction, likewise, it is easy for critics today to fall into the trap of taking for granted the "natural" character of the objects to which racial meanings are applied. To do so is to erase the violent yet productive processes that constituted these objects in the first place. Hegemony always depends on the forgetting of primitive accumulation, as Alberto Moreiras suggests, but this is equally true of what we might call "primitive racialization."

This is where infrastructure becomes important. By concentrating human and nonhuman objects within specific architectonic structures, the centralized towns, disciplinary institutions, segregated districts, and general collections I have examined here create the conditions in which racializable groups may emerge. But infrastructure also tends toward invisibility as the practices it enables become familiar and routine. Even disgruntled residents of Nuevo Juan de Grijalva, Wilson observes, may eventually find that the memory of dispossession fades into the background of everyday life in the rural city. Only by engaging carefully with infrastructure—those sociotechnical materials that function as systems and by doing so enable other objects and systems to operate—can we begin to unsettle these well-sedimented social relations and unforget the foundational violence that made them possible.

President Calderón finished his speech in Nuevo Juan de Grijalva with an "inspirational" parable that is perhaps not surprisingly quite popular in management literature.[15] Once upon a time, "cuando se hicieron las que ahora son grandes ciudades en Europa, en el viejo continente" (when what are now the great cities of Europe, on the old continent, were built), a traveler was walking along and came across three men working in a quarry. What are you doing? he asked the first man. "Estoy puliendo una piedra" (I'm polishing this stone), he replied. And what are you doing? he asked the second. "Estoy ganando un jornal" (I'm earning a day's wage), the man replied. Finally, he asked the third man the same question. In response, the man lifted his gaze to the heavens and said, "Estoy construyendo una catedral" (I'm building a cathedral). With this, Calderón wrapped up his speech:

> Y los tres eran canteros, los tres ganaban un jornal, pero uno tenía la vista imaginaria en lo que serían esas torres mágicas del Gótico europeo, que construyeron esas ciudades, que son ahora precisamente orgullo de la humanidad. Yo creo, chiapanecos, que con adobe mexicano, y con mucho esfuerzo, y con mucha entrega, y con mucha unidad, no sólo construiremos muchos Juan de Grijalva. Vamos a construir el México que queremos y algún día lo verán orgullosos nuestros hijos. Felicidades a todos y que disfruten esta nueva ciudad rural. [And all three were stonecutters, all three were earning a day's

wage, but only one was imagining what would be those magical towers of the gothic Europe that built the cities that are now the pride of humanity. I believe, *chiapanecos*, that with Mexican adobe, and with a great deal of effort, dedication, and unity, we will build not only many Juan de Grijalvas . . . but also the Mexico we want, so that one day our children will see it with pride. Congratulations to everyone and enjoy this new rural city.]

Calderón's story does not quite make sense in context, and the metaphor linking rural city to gothic cathedral is awkward, but in any case the moral of the story seems relatively clear. The Mexican state has replaced the church as the transcendent object of adoration and sacrifice. It is through daily work in the market economy and, crucially, the proliferation of infrastructures of concentration that the state's subjects realize this vision of the future.

If the rural cities have generally succeeded at dispossessing resettled residents, however, this process of subject formation has not gone according to plan. Some of the inhabitants of Nuevo Juan de Grijalva have abandoned the new homes and returned to their *milpas*, while others have organized demonstrations and even land occupations against what they perceive as an attempt to privatize their *ejido* property.[16] Calderón's promise of "trabajo digno" (dignified work) has proved largely empty—unemployment is high, and what jobs are available pay low wages and depend heavily on state subsidy.[17] This failure could be read as epiphenomenonal, resulting from certain contingencies such as political corruption or unexpected shifts in regional and global markets, but it also may suggest a broader shift in terms of the dynamics of racialization linked to concentration projects in postcolonial peripheries. I have argued here that it is the production of spatial proximity among human and nonhuman objects that creates the conditions in which specific forms of vulnerability may be materially mapped onto bodies and collectivities and retroactively naturalized. Whereas in the sixteenth century indigenous communities were racialized primarily as objects of extraction, obligated to pay tribute and perform forced labor, today the mostly indigenous peasant communities of Chiapas are being racialized once again. This time, however, concentration serves less to constitute objects of extraction than to tenuously warehouse what is becoming a surplus population, increasingly superfluous to the needs of capital.

## INTRODUCTION

1. Tone, *War and Genocide in Cuba*, 204. For Weyler's comment in the original Spanish, see Tone, *Guerra y genocidio en Cuba*, 269.

2. Tone, *War and Genocide in Cuba*, 194–224.

3. See, for example, ibid., xiii; Mühlhahn, "The Concentration Camp in Global Historical Perspective," 545; Hyslop, "The Invention of the Concentration Camp"; Khalili, *Time in the Shadows*, 174–176; and Everdell, *The First Moderns*, 117.

4. Weyler, *Mi mando en Cuba*, I, 11.

5. Agamben, *Homo Sacer*, 166.

6. Lund, *The Mestizo State*, xiv.

7. Throughout this book, I have chosen to capitalize the names of all racial/racializing categories (except when quoting others) as a stylistic means of signaling that "Indian" and even "Spaniard," for example, occupy the same conceptual register as "Mestizo" and "Black." As I explain later, these names should be understood not as more or less accurate descriptions of bodies or populations but as the products of historically and geographically situated processes of racialization. It may be helpful for the reader, then, to imagine that these words have been placed in quotation marks wherever they appear, although for the sake of readability I have omitted them.

8. Simone, "People as Infrastructure."

9. I borrow this formulation from Holt, *The Problem of Race in the Twenty-First Century*, 27–28.

10. Marx, *Capital*, I, 874–875. See also Federici, *Caliban and the Witch*, 63–64.

11. Quijano, "Coloniality of Power, Eurocentrism, and Latin America," 533–540. See also Mignolo, *The Darker Side of Western Modernity*.

12. Quijano, "Coloniality of Power," 533–540.

13. Ibid., 536, 537.

14. "Imagine the sistema de castas as dual ladders, one for race and one for class, that parallel and reinforce each other, so that a specific racial label becomes naturally associated with a specific economic status. Now, how did capitalino conditions fail to meet these requirements? The problem was that the 'economic' ladder lacked sufficient rungs, or put another way, that the socioeconomic structure of Mexico City more closely approximated a pyramid, with the vast majority of people languishing at the bottom. In short, most castas were poor: many faced permanent or frequent unemployment; the fortunate ones worked as laborers, servants, or, at best, artisans. Any advantage that, for instance, a mestizo had over a mulatto in clambering up to the next level was so minor, I suggest, that few would allow their lives to be dominated by a desire for racial improvement." Cope, *The Limits of Racial Domination*, 162. For a related critique of the underlying schema of world-systems theory, the source of many of the claims about the

global division of labor, see Stern, "Feudalism, Capitalism, and the World-System," though note the important caveats on pages 865–871.

15. Quijano cites, among other works, Mariátegui, *Siete ensayos de interpretación de la realidad peruana*; González Casanova, "Internal Colonialism and National Development"; Prebisch, *The Economic Development of Latin America and Its Principal Problems*; and Wallerstein, *Historical Capitalism*.

16. "The enactment of the decolonial option in the twenty-first century starts from epistemic delinking: from acts of epistemic disobedience." Mignolo, *The Darker Side of Western Modernity*, 139.

17. Important works in the "caste versus class" debate include Chance and Taylor, "Estate and Class in a Colonial City"; and McCaa, Schwartz, and Grubessich, "Race and Class in Colonial Latin America." For a contemporary critique of this debate, see Seed, "Social Dimensions of Race," 602–604.

18. This large and growing body of literature includes, but is by no means limited to, Cope, *The Limits of Racial Domination*; Carrera, *Imagining Identity in New Spain*; Lewis, *Hall of Mirrors*; Katzew, *Casta Painting*; Silverblatt, *Modern Inquisitions*; Hill, *Hierarchy, Commerce, and Fraud in Bourbon Spanish America*; Martínez, *Genealogical Fictions*; O'Toole, *Bound Lives*; Rappaport, *The Disappearing Mestizo*; and Twinam, *Purchasing Whiteness*.

19. See, for example, Hill, *Hierarchy, Commerce, and Fraud*, 201–202; Carrera, *Imagining Identity in New Spain*, 10–11; Rappaport, *The Disappearing Mestizo*, 3–7, 37–42; and Twinam, *Purchasing Whiteness*, 42–45. Hill is equally suspicious of the term "colonial," which she regards as specific to the sort of European domination characteristic of the nineteenth and twentieth centuries. "Where a concept or category did not exist, it is not helpful . . . to pretend that it did." Hill, *Hierarchy, Commerce, and Fraud*, 5.

20. Nirenberg, "Race and the Middle Ages," 75. Nirenberg insightfully insists that "any history of race will be at best limited, strategic, and polemical and at worst a reproduction of racial logic itself"; consequently, such studies should be read "not as prescriptive but as provocations to comparison." Although his intervention focuses primarily on the medieval/modern divide, I have found it helpful for grappling with the theoretical difficulties posed by periodization more generally. Ibid., 86–87. For a valuable analysis of racial discourse that locates its efficacy in the embrace of both fixity and fluidity, see Stoler, "Racial Histories and Their Regimes of Truth."

21. Stepan, *"The Hour of Eugenics,"* chap. 3. I discuss the relation between race and environment in more detail in chapter 4.

22. While Silverblatt accepts the periodizing distinction between "traditional" caste (a "legal or social" category) and "modern" race (a "biological" category), she nevertheless aims to foreground continuities over disjunctions by employing Hannah Arendt's language of "race thinking": "Race thinking does not negate the colonial caste system nor does it deny that caste and race systems represent two different modes of organizing and explaining inequality. Race thinking, however, does help us see what the race vs. caste division hides: that race and caste were not separate systems, but interpenetrating." In a sense, my intervention extends this framework to its limit by asking how the methodological centering of continuity may call into question the very distinction on which it is

based. See Silverblatt, *Modern Inquisitions*, 17. For a thoughtful reflection on the value of race as an analytical category for colonial Latin America, see O'Toole, "The Work of Race in Colonial Peru."

23. "Based on the available data, we know that blacks and Indians throughout [Latin America] continue to disproportionately suffer from poverty and underdevelopment. Although the most egregious systems of labor exploitation have mostly ended, the available evidence consistently demonstrates that these groups continue to be more likely to live in poverty, be illiterate, die at a younger age, reside in substandard housing and bear the greatest burden of police abuse." Telles, "Race and Ethnicity and Latin America's United Nations Millennium Development Goals," 189. On the rise of liberal and neoliberal multiculturalism, see Winant, *The World Is a Ghetto*; and Melamed, *Represent and Destroy*, 1–17. On racial multiculturalism in Mexico, see Chorba, *Mexico, from Mestizo to Multicultural*; Overmyer-Velázquez, *Folkloric Poverty*; and Saldívar, "It's Not Race, It's Culture."

24. On "neo-racism," see Balibar, "Is There a Neo-Racism?" On "color-blind racism," see Bonilla-Silva, *Racism without Racists*.

25. Balibar, "Is There a Neo-Racism?," 18. Balibar further notes that nonbiological forms of racism have existed at least since the consolidation of anti-Semitism in late medieval and early modern Spain. See also Stoler, "Racial Histories and Their Regimes of Truth," 197–201.

26. For Omi and Winant, moreover, these projects begin with the conquest and colonization of the Americas. Omi and Winant, *Racial Formation in the United States*, 56, 61–62 (emphasis in original). Importantly, even some scholars of the colonial period who are careful about anachronism have found the racial formation framework helpful. See, for example, Hill, "Between Black and White," 270–271; and O'Hara, *A Flock Divided*, 255–256n87.

27. Singh, *Black Is a Country*, 223; Gilmore, *Golden Gulag*, 18. I have also found Chris Chen's work indispensable for clarifying the relation between capitalism, racialization, and the production and management of surplus populations. See Chen, "The Limit Point of Capitalist Equality."

28. My discussion of racialized premature death is informed by Rob Nixon's analysis of "slow violence" and Lauren Berlant's discussion of "slow death." See Nixon, *Slow Violence and the Environmentalism of the Poor*; and Berlant, *Cruel Optimism*, chap. 3, especially 113–114.

29. Rabasa, *Writing Violence on the Northern Frontier*, 6.

30. Foucault, *"Society Must Be Defended,"* 241; Foucault, *The History of Sexuality*, 143, 139.

31. Foucault, *The History of Sexuality*, 149, 137; Foucault, *"Society Must Be Defended,"* 254; Foucault, "Nietzsche, Genealogy, History," 154. On the "enigma" of biopolitics, see Esposito, *Bíos*, 13–44.

32. Foucault, *"Society Must Be Defended,"* 257, 103. It is important to note that Aimé Césaire had outlined the "boomerang effect of colonization" over two decades earlier. See his *Discourse on Colonialism*, 41.

33. In an analysis of hydraulic infrastructure and urban planning in Mexico City, Ivonne del Valle suggests that "the state racism [Foucault] sees as characterizing the form of power in nineteenth-century Europe in fact had been operating

since the early sixteenth century in European colonies." Del Valle, "On Shaky Ground," 210. For an early and influential analysis of Foucault, colonialism, and race (written, significantly, prior to the publication of his lectures), see Stoler, *Race and the Education of Desire*.

34. Foucault, *"Society Must Be Defended,"* 254.

35. Foucault, *Security, Territory, Population*, 88, 96. Stuart Elden calls this move "not a shift of accent, but, rather, a substitution." Elden, "Government, Calculation, Territory," 563.

36. Schmitt, *Political Theology*; Schmitt, *The Nomos of the Earth*, 92–99. I develop this analysis in more detail in Nemser, "Primitive Spiritual Accumulation and the Colonial Extraction Economy."

37. Agamben, *Homo Sacer*, 36.

38. Mbembe, "Necropolitics," 24.

39. Ibid., 25–26.

40. Ibid., 27–30. Though interested in the historical specificity of "late modern occupation," Mbembe recognizes earlier modes of conquest and colonization as certainly technical if not infrastructural as well: "Each stage of imperialism also involved certain key technologies (the gunboat, quinine, steamship lines, submarine telegraph cables, and colonial railroads)." Ibid., 25. The infrastructures examined in this book suggest that such an analysis might be usefully extended to prior colonial projects, especially because, as I suggest later, new infrastructures often build on the foundations laid by their predecessors.

41. For an excellent review of recent scholarship on infrastructure, see Larkin, "The Politics and Poetics of Infrastructure."

42. It is important to acknowledge here that this scholarship tends to be rooted in an experience of infrastructure that is specific to the global North, where the density and consistency of infrastructural space congeal into what Kathryn Furlong has called the "modern infrastructure ideal." Assumptions about smooth and unbroken flows may not correspond to the experience of infrastructure in the global South, where failure and collapse often register not as exceptional events but simply the conditions of everyday life. See Furlong, "STS Beyond the 'Modern Infrastructure Ideal'"; Edwards, "Infrastructure and Modernity," 188; and Larkin, *Signal and Noise*, 242–243.

43. Star, "The Ethnography of Infrastructure," 380–381.

44. Olsen, *In Defense of Things*, 140–141. I am less interested in the ontological questions that have been posed by actor-network theory and the so-called new materialism than in the way the concept of infrastructure might contribute to a historical analysis of racialization, colonial governance, and continuity/disjuncture. For this reason, I appreciate Olsen's "bricoleur" approach to "thing theory." Olsen, *In Defense of Things*, 12–14.

45. For a helpful reading of these debates, see Williams, *Marxism and Literature*, 75–89.

46. In Spanish, too, the word *infraestructura* is commonly given as the translation of "base." Rankin, "Infrastructure and the International Governance of Economic Development," 62n1.

47. On infrastructure and disposition as "a propensity within a context," see Easterling, *Extrastatecraft*, 71–73.

48. Lefebvre, *The Production of Space*, 31, 39, 53, 151. See also Lefebvre, *The Urban Revolution*, 15; and Lefebvre, "An Interview with Henri Lefebvre," 27–38.

49. Larkin, "The Politics and Poetics of Infrastructure," 329.

50. For an extensive analysis of the development of transportation infrastructure in colonial Mexico, see Hassig, *Trade, Tribute, and Transportation*, 160–219. It is interesting to note that infrastructures like these are often barely visible in descriptions of extraction and transportation in colonial Latin America, despite their critical importance. See, for example, Elliott, *Spain and Its World*, 19–21.

51. Star, "The Ethnography of Infrastructure," 382.

52. Marx, *The Eighteenth Brumaire of Louis Bonaparte*, 15.

## CHAPTER 1: CONGREGATION

1. Cuevas, *Documentos inéditos del siglo XVI para la historia de México*, 166. Unless otherwise noted, all translations are my own.

2. Verdesio, "Invisible at a Glance," 339–353.

3. See, for example, Sepúlveda, *Tratado de las justas causas de la guerra contra los indios*, 106–109.

4. Federici, *Caliban and the Witch*, 63–64 (emphasis in original).

5. The period in question roughly corresponds to James Lockhart's second stage of cultural change among the Nahuas. See Lockhart, *The Nahuas after the Conquest*, 429–432. On the politics of ethnogenesis in colonial South America, see Schwartz and Salomon, "New Peoples and New Kinds of People," 443–501.

6. Torre Villar, *Las congregaciones de los pueblos de indios*, 32–33; Gerhard, "Congregaciones de indios en la Nueva España antes de 1570," 388.

7. See, for example, older scholarship such as Cline, "Civil Congregations of the Indians in New Spain," 349; as well as more recent scholarship, including Lockhart, *The Nahuas after the Conquest*, 44–45; and García Martínez, *Los pueblos de la sierra*, 165–166.

8. See Torre Villar, *Las congregaciones de los pueblos de indios*, 57; and Ramírez Ruiz and Fernández Christlieb, "La policía de los indios y la urbanización del altepetl," 142.

9. "Discurso de la reducción general de los indios y estado de ella, que se le dejó al Virrey por su antecesor el Conde de Monterrey," AGI *México* 25, núm. 480, fol. 20r; see also fol. 2r. On the *reducción general* in Peru, see Mumford, *Vertical Empire*.

10. As I suggest in the epilogue, contemporary examples of spatial intervention in Mexico, such as the "sustainable rural cities" *(ciudades rurales sustentables)* currently under development in the states of Chiapas and Puebla, are part of a long genealogy of concentration that extends back to the colonial period.

11. The best example of late mendicant criticism comes from the Franciscan Juan de Torquemada's *Monarquía indiana* (1615). In book 5, chapter 43, he argued that congregation had been a disaster for the indigenous population, contributing to abuses by Spanish landowners and population decline. Paradoxically, he further asserted that congregation had made the indigenous population *more* dispersed because now, when the inhabitants of the new communities ran away, they chose to disappear in the remote countryside rather than return to their old

villages, with which the priests were familiar. What is notable about Torquemada's critique, then, is that he does not dispute the underlying logic of congregation—that dispersion is bad and concentration good. The only question is one of effective implementation. See Torquemada, *Primera parte de los veinte i un libros rituales i monarchia indiana*, I, 686–690. Early mendicant criticisms of congregation include Pedro de la Peña, Francisco de Bustamante, and Agustín de Coruña to Philip II, February 25, 1561, in *Cartas de Indias*, I, 150; and Jacinto de San Francisco to Philip II, in *Códice Franciscano*, ed. García Icazbalceta, II, 242.

12. "Carta de Fray Pedro de Gante al Emperador D. Carlos, exponiéndole el sensible estado á que tenia reducido á los indios el servicio personal," February 15, 1552, in *Cartas de Indias*, I, 101.

13. Foucault, *Security, Territory, Population*, 165, 227.

14. Ibid., 229–231, 126.

15. Foucault, "The Subject and Power," 334.

16. The Italian philosopher Carlo Galli argues that the political space of modernity emerged as a philosophical response to the crisis provoked by the so-called discovery of the New World. "In Galli's account, modern political geometry originates in a principle that is not itself geometrical; it comes into being through the 'geometrization,' we might say, of a prior colonial space." Building on these reflections, my reading of congregation aims to provide a material account of the "geometrization" of colonial space. On what sorts of colonial infrastructures, we might ask, does this shift at the level of political thought depend? See Sitze, "Editor's Introduction," lvi; and Galli, *Political Spaces and Global War*, 26–33.

17. See Rama, *La ciudad letrada*, 17–29; Merrim, *The Spectacular City*, 61–65; and Kagan, *Urban Images of the Hispanic World*, 28–39.

18. We know, for example, that the first viceroy of New Spain, Antonio de Mendoza, brought with him a personally annotated copy of the 1512 Paris edition of Alberti's book, and Francisco Cervantes de Salazar, one of the first professors at the University of Mexico, specifically names Vitruvius in his 1554 Latin dialogues, which were intended to be used as teaching tools. See Edgerton, *Theaters of Conversion*, 114; Cervantes de Salazar, *Life in the Imperial and Loyal City of Mexico in New Spain*, 42.

19. Rama, *La ciudad letrada*, 17; see also Merrim, *The Spectacular City*, 63; Kubler, *Mexican Architecture of the Sixteenth Century*, 99.

20. Descartes, *Discourse on the Method for Conducting One's Reason Well*, 7–8. Enrique Dussel argues that modern philosophy, from Descartes on, is structured by the conquest. "Before the *ego cogito* there is an *ego conquiro*; 'I conquer' is the practical foundation of 'I think.'" By proposing an alternative *ego aedifico* ("I build"), I want to insist on the value of a materialist approach that attends to colonial infrastructures for thinking historically about the specific mechanisms through which colonial relations of domination are produced and endure over time. See Dussel, *Philosophy of Liberation*, 3.

21. Toussaint, *Información de méritos y servicios de Alonso García Bravo*, 9–10.

22. On the *relaciones geográficas*, see Mundy, *The Mapping of New Spain*.

23. Terraciano, *The Mixtecs of Colonial Oaxaca*, 27.

24. Gibson, *The Aztecs under Spanish Rule*, 198–202.

25. Bentancor, "Matter, Form, and the Generation of Metals"; Bentancor, "La disposición de la materia en la *Información en derecho* de Vasco de Quiroga."

26. On Quiroga's work, see Bentancor, "La disposición de la materia en la *Información en derecho* de Vasco de Quiroga"; and Gómez, *Good Places and Non-Places in Colonial Mexico*.

27. Quiroga specifically cited More's influence and marveled at the ability of this "varon prudentísimo" (most prudent man) to design a republic so appropriate to the "disposicion, sitio, y manera y condicion y secretos de esta tierra y naturales de ella" (disposition, location, manner, condition, and secrets of this land and its natives) without ever having seen it in person. Quiroga, "Informacion en derecho del licenciado Quiroga," 511.

28. Ibid., 368.

29. Ibid., 368–369.

30. For Quiroga, gathering the indigenous people together would help them "llevar las cargas que se han de llevar, de necesidad está y consiste el servicio de Dios y de su Magestad en esta tierra, y el pró é bien comun de ella y de los conquistadores y pobladores y naturales" (bear the burdens that they must bear, which of necessity consists of the service of God and his Majesty in this land, and in favor of the common good, as well as [the good] of the conquistadors and settlers and natives). Ibid., 499.

31. Ibid., 466.

32. A transcription of the "Instrucción" is available in Torre Villar, *Las congregaciones de los pueblos de indios*, 313–327.

33. Ibid., 315.

34. Ibid., 316. The *Diccionario de autoridades* (1732) offers various definitions of the verb *formar*, including "juntar y congregar diferentes cosas, uniendolas entre si para que hagan un cuerpo" and "poner en orden." Real Academia Española, *Diccionario de la lengua castellana*, III, 780.

35. García Martínez, *Los pueblos de la sierra*, 153.

36. Torre Villar, *Las congregaciones de los pueblos de indios*, 317–318.

37. Ibid.

38. "Id quoque quod diu efflagitatum et non ita dudum institutum est de reductione indorum ad certos populos, ut non sparsim more ferarum sed communiter oppida inhabitent, dici non potest quantae sit utilitatis futurum ad omnem barbarorum informationem" (Additionally, regarding the concentration of Indians in fixed settlements, which for so long has been desired and only recently has been undertaken, so that they are no longer dispersed like wild beasts but live together in towns, it cannot be expressed how useful it will be for the instruction of the barbarians). Acosta, *De procuranda indorum salute*, I, 166–167. Unless otherwise noted, all translations from Latin are my own, although I have consulted and benefited from the Spanish translation on the cited page.

39. Ibid., I, 538–539.

40. Ibid., I, 540–541.

41. Torre Villar, *Las congregaciones de los pueblos de indios*, 320.

42. Gerhard, *A Guide to the Historical Geography of New Spain*, 27; Gerhard, "Congregaciones de indios," 347–48.

180 NOTES TO PAGES 42–57

43. Terraciano, *The Mixtecs of Colonial Oaxaca*, 24–27.

44. Torre Villar, *Las congregaciones de los pueblos de indios*, 323–324.

45. Pedro de la Peña, Francisco de Bustamente, and Agustín de Coruña to Philip II, February 25, 1561, in *Cartas de Indias*, I, 150. A similar argument is made in the letter by Jacinto de San Francisco to Philip II, *Códice Franciscano*, ed. García Icazbalceta, 242.

46. Foucault, *Security, Territory, Population*, 341.

47. Valadés, *Retórica cristiana*, 209 (misprinted as 109 in facsimile).

48. "Copia de la Instrucción que se dio a los jueces de la demarcación," AGI *México* 25, núm. 48e, fol. 1v.

49. "Discurso de la reducción general de los indios y estado de ella, que se le dejó al Virrey por su antecesor el Conde de Monterrey," AGI *México* 25, núm. 48o, fol. 3v.

50. Federici, *Caliban and the Witch*, 86, 103.

51. "Discurso de la reducción general de los indios y estado de ella, que se le dejó al Virrey por su antecesor el Conde de Monterrey," AGI *México* 25, núm. 48o, fol. 19v.

52. Foucault, *The History of Sexuality*, 145.

53. Lomnitz, *Death and the Idea of Mexico*, 67–72.

54. Foucault, "The Incorporation of the Hospital into Modern Technology," 143. More recently, historians have challenged Foucault's analysis, showing, for example, that mortality rates in European hospitals were relatively low and discharge rates relatively high. See Henderson, *The Renaissance Hospital*, chap. 8.

55. Guerra, "The Role of Religion in Spanish American Medicine," 185.

56. On the "highly individualist" character of the Galenic medicine that was imposed in colonial Mexico, see Fields, *Pestilence and Headcolds*, 109–110.

57. Gómez, *Good Places and Non-Places*, 81–82.

58. See Phelan, *The Millennial Kingdom of the Franciscans in the New World*.

59. Motolinía, *Memoriales de Fray Toribio de Motolinía*, 18.

60. García Icazbalceta, *Códice Mendieta*, II, 80–81, 79.

61. Ibid., II, 90.

62. Ibid.

63. Ibid., II, 93.

64. Lomnitz, *Death and the Idea of Mexico*, 73–80.

65. Newson, "Medical Practice in Early Colonial Spanish America," 376–377.

66. García Icazbalceta, *Códice Mendieta*, II, 90.

67. For an example of the ease with which communication slips into commerce (and conquest, for that matter), see Vitoria, *Political Writings*, 278–280.

68. Torre Villar, *Las congregaciones de los pueblos de indios*, 316.

69. Foucault, *Security, Territory, Population*, 19.

70. Lockhart, *The Nahuas after the Conquest*, 14–20.

71. Schroeder, *Chimalpahin and the Kingdoms of Chalco*, 126–131.

72. Lockhart, *The Nahuas after the Conquest*, 17.

73. See Bernal García and García Zambrano, "El altepetl colonial y sus antecedentes prehispánicos," 52–55; and Leibsohn, "Primers for Memory," 161–187.

74. Lockhart, *The Nahuas after the Conquest*, 28–29; Horn, *Postconquest Coyoacan*, 90.

75. Gibson, *The Aztecs under Spanish Rule*, 197; Horn, *Postconquest Coyoacan*, 91.

76. Ibid., 77–78.

77. Ibid., 198–200; Horn, *Postconquest Coyoacan*, 86–87.

78. Gibson, *The Aztecs under Spanish Rule*, 226.

79. Ibid., 224; for percentages, see ibid., 231–232.

80. "En ocasiones, los nuevos pueblos fueron formados con gente procedente de altepeme distintos, lo que implicaba concertar diferentes linajes gobernantes, estructuras familiares y hasta lenguas." Ramírez Ruiz and Fernández Christlieb, "La policía de los indios y la urbanización del altepetl," 148; see also Gibson, *The Aztecs under Spanish Rule*, 284.

81. Gerhard, "Congregaciones de indios," 358; AGI *Indiferente* 1529, núm. 37.

82. Gibson, *The Aztecs under Spanish Rule*, 44; Horn, *Postconquest Coyoacan*, 31.

83. See Terraciano, *The Mixtecs of Colonial Oaxaca*, 124; Horn, *Postconquest Coyoacan*, 30–38; Lockhart, *The Nahuas after the Conquest*, 53–56; Gerhard, "La evolución del pueblo rural mexicano," 574–575. For the changing meaning of the term "altepetl," see Horn, *Postconquest Coyoacan*, 33.

84. Lockhart, *The Nahuas after the Conquest*, 115.

85. Ibid., 115–116.

86. Chimalpahin, *Annals of His Time*, 89. Because the translators opted to use "commoners" for *macehualtin*, I have altered the translation by reinserting the original Nahuatl in this passage.

87. Marx, *Capital*, I, 873–874.

88. Read, *The Micro-Politics of Capital*, 19–36.

89. Marx, *Capital*, I, 899.

90. Read, *The Micro-Politics of Capital*, 25. "Primitive accumulation is not simply the accumulation of wealth, or a transfer of the means of production from the hands of the artisans and peasantry to the hands of the nascent capitalists, it is also the accumulation of subjectivity." Ibid., 153.

91. See, for example, Nemser, "Primitive Spiritual Accumulation and the Colonial Extraction Economy."

92. Rabasa, *Writing Violence on the Northern Frontier*, 6.

## CHAPTER 2: ENCLOSURE

1. I quote the Latin passages from the facsimile edition of Francisco Cervantes de Salazar's *Francisci Ceruantis Salazari Toletāi, ad Ludouici Viuis Valentini exercitationem, aliquot Dialogi* (1554), 271r–v, included in Cervantes de Salazar, *Life in the Imperial and Loyal City of Mexico*, with English translation, 55–57.

2. Cervantes de Salazar, *Dialogi*, 271v; Cervantes de Salazar, *Life in the Imperial and Loyal City of Mexico*, 56.

3. The Colegio has received only passing scholarly attention since the 1980s. The most detailed studies of the institution include Castañeda Delgado, "El Colegio de San Juan de Letrán de México"; Gómez Canedo, *La educación de los marginados durante la época colonial*, 219–283; and Greenleaf, "San Juan de Letrán." More recently, scholars have considered the parallel project of *recogimiento*

aimed at Mestiza girls in both New Spain and Peru. See Burns, *Colonial Habits;* van Deusen, *Between the Sacred and the Worldly;* and Holler, *Escogidas Plantas.*

4. Bernand, "Los nuevos cuerpos mestizos de la América colonial," 89. I use the gendered pronoun here both because of my focus on the male Mestizo and because tributary obligations were applied to men.

5. See Gómez Canedo, *La educación de los marginados,* 281; Greenleaf, "San Juan de Letrán," 136.

6. On the "racial baroque," see Nemser, "Primitive Spiritual Accumulation and the Colonial Extraction Economy."

7. Martínez, *Genealogical Fictions,* 152, 143–152.

8. Burns, *Colonial Habits,* 40.

9. Rappaport, *The Disappearing Mestizo,* 4. Consider the following formulation: "A biological *mestizo* whom the Crown made a member of the *casta* of Spaniards was a Spaniard, not a *mestizo.*" Here the social construction framework proposes the social reality of classification that nevertheless encodes a real, biological foundation over which it is laid. See Hill, *Hierarchy, Commerce, and Fraud,* 223.

10. Marx, *Capital,* I, 896.

11. Lewis, *Hall of Mirrors,* 78–80. Although Lewis does not use the language of "intersectionality," her argument resonates strongly with the concept formulated by Black feminist scholars in the United States. See, for example, Crenshaw, "Mapping the Margins."

12. Van Deusen, *Between the Sacred and the Worldly,* chap. 2.

13. As a royal *cédula* from 1558 put it, "Porq̃ somos informados q̃ son muchos los q̃ assi ay vagamundos, *especialmente mestizos,* ha parescido q̃ conuiene q̃ se de ordẽ cómo essa gẽte ociosa tome assiento y manera de biuir" (As we are informed that there are many such vagabonds, *especially Mestizos,* it has seemed useful to order that these idle people be settled and cultured). Puga, *Prouisiones, cedulas, instrucciones de Su Magestad,* fol. 205r (emphasis added).

14. Marx, *Capital,* I, 899.

15. See book 7, title 4, law 4, in *Recopilación de leyes de los reynos de las Indias,* II, 284v.

16. Juan de Zumárraga to Philip II, December 4, 1547, in Cuevas, *Documentos inéditos,* 152–153.

17. According to Tamar Herzog, the emergence of anti-Gypsy legislation in early modern Spain was based on the assumption that "there was no Gypsy nation" and that the category was instead "taken on voluntarily by people who sought out a bad life (*mal vivir*)." Herzog, *Defining Nations,* 128–133.

18. "The facility with which mestizos 'disappear' owes to the fact that there was no sociological group for mestizos to belong to, just a category to which they were assigned." Rappaport, *The Disappearing Mestizo,* 11.

19. *Instrucciones que los virreyes de Nueva España dejaron a sus sucesores,* I, 14.

20. Gómez Canedo, *La educación de los marginados,* 282; van Deusen, *Between the Sacred and the Worldly,* 34–35.

21. On the life of Pesquera, see Gómez Canedo, *La educación de los margina-*

*dos*, 243–249. Gómez Canedo speculates that the memorial was written by Pesquera himself, while Greenleaf suggests that the author may have been the Franciscan Pedro de Gante. See Gómez Canedo, *La educación de los marginados*, 235; and Greenleaf, "San Juan de Letrán," 117. The Council's letter to the king as well as two copies of the memorial, titled "La orden q̃ se tiene en el colegio de los niños de la doctrina de mex^co donde estan recogidas dozientas personas pocas mas o menos," each written in a different hand, are held at the Archivo General de Indias in Seville, AGI *Indiferente* 737, núms. 90 and 90a-b, respectively. Although there are several published transcriptions of the memorial, I prefer to use the first manuscript copy here (núm. 90a, no pagination), since the printed versions either modernize the spelling or differ from the source. However, where the source text is damaged or unreadable, I have used Gómez Canedo's transcription, which does not modernize the spelling, to fill in the gaps. See Gómez Canedo, *La educación de los marginados*, 337–345.

22. See van Deusen, *Between the Sacred and the Worldly*, 18–20. As van Deusen shows, the word *recogimiento* also has a set of gendered meanings that have to do with virtue and behavioral norms, which, not surprisingly, were applied especially to women.

23. Foucault, "'*Omnes et Singulatim*,'" 308–310.

24. Compare Burns, *Colonial Habits*; van Deusen, *Between the Sacred and the Worldly*; and Holler, *Escogidas Plantas*.

25. Mendieta, *Historia eclesiástica indiana*, 226.

26. On Sahagún's ethnography of the Nahuas, see Klor de Alva, "Sahagún and the Birth of Modern Ethnography," 31–52.

27. Gómez Canedo, *La educación de los marginados*, 352.

28. Ricard, *The Spiritual Conquest of Mexico*, 224–226.

29. Council of the Indies to Charles V, October 23, 1552, AGI *Indiferente* 737, núm. 90.

30. Moya de Contreras to the Audiencia of Mexico City, April 24, 1579, AGI *México* 70, ramo 2, núm. 18.

31. Martín Enríquez to Philip II, April 12, 1579, AGI *México* 20, núm. 19, fol. 3v.

32. "Es verguenza vella porqs de adobes y todo sesta cayendo" (It is an embarrassment to see because it is made of adobe bricks and the whole thing is falling down). Martín Enríquez to Philip II, March 18, 1575, AHN, *Documentos de Indias* 25, núm. 31, fol. 3v.

33. Castañeda Delgado, "El Colegio de San Juan de Letrán de México," 86.

34. On the association of Mestizos with specific kinds of occupations, see Seed, "Social Dimensions of Race," 581; and Cope, *The Limits of Racial Domination*, 14–17.

35. Juan de la Plaza, "Sobre el seminario," in Zubillaga, "Tercer Concilio Mexicano," 192–196. For a helpful reading and contextualization of the memoriales, see Poole, *Pedro Moya de Contreras*, 160–164.

36. Plaza, "Sobre el seminario," 195.

37. Quoted in Acosta, *De procuranda*, II, 67n147, 68n151.

38. Prieto, *Missionary Scientists*, 17–19. For a sketch of Plaza's life, see Zubi-

llaga, "Tercer Concilio Mexicano," 180–190. Plaza also composed a catechism for the Third Mexican Council that drew heavily on Acosta's thinking. See Burkhart, "The 'Little Doctrine' and Indigenous Catechesis in New Spain," 172.

39. My reading of Acosta in this section has benefited from Larissa Brewer-García's analysis of the prohibition of Mestizo ordination within the Jesuit order in Peru. Importantly, she shows how, in the wake of this prohibition, Mestizo translators were drafted to produce textual materials that would facilitate ongoing missionary efforts as well as language instruction for Spanish priests. The exclusion of Mestizo bodies thus went hand in hand with the appropriation of their linguistic skills. See Brewer-García, "Bodies, Texts, and Translators."

40. Acosta, *De procuranda*, II, 52–53. On Acosta's views of the importance—and limits—of the use of indigenous languages for the project of evangelization, see del Valle, "José de Acosta," 309–315.

41. Acosta, *De procuranda*, II, 48–49.

42. Ibid., I, 198–199.

43. Nemser, "Primitive Spiritual Accumulation and the Colonial Extraction Economy."

44. Acosta, *De procuranda*, II, 56–57.

45. Ibid., II, 54–55 (emphasis added).

46. Martínez, *Genealogical Fictions*, 151.

47. Acosta, *De procuranda*, II, 254–255.

48. Pineda, *Diálogos familiares de agricultura cristiana*, I, 321.

49. Martínez, *Genealogical Fictions*, 47. This confusion has led some scholars to differentiate "blood" from "milk," with the former referring to "inheritance or inborn quality" and the latter to what "would today be called nurture or socialization." Since breast milk was viewed as a form of blood, however, such a distinction is untenable. See Schwartz and Salomon, "New Peoples and New Kinds of People," 478; and Saignes and Bouysse-Cassagne, "Dos confundidas identidades," 18.

50. Acosta, *De procuranda*, II, 62–67. On the construction of "pastoral Quechua" as a "lengua general" in Peru, see Durston, *Pastoral Quechua*. On the use of Nahuatl as the "lengua general" of New Spain, see Ricard, *The Spiritual Conquest of Mexico*, chap. 2.

51. Acosta, *De procuranda*, II, 66–67.

52. Ibid., II, 68–69. While the term *indigenarum* would logically include Creoles, the emphasis on indigenous languages here and "Indian" nature and customs later in the chapter suggests that Acosta's primary focus is the figure of the Mestizo.

53. Burns, *Colonial Habits*, 35–36.

54. Acosta, *De procuranda*, II, 68–69.

55. Ibid., II, 70–71.

56. "For Acosta, it is the imbibing of a corrupt, indigenous milk supply which permanently stains the mestizo body." Brewer-García, "Bodies, Texts, and Translators," 371.

57. The significance of the absent father is compounded by common gendered assumptions about inheritability and the relative strength of male over female inputs. Most early modern commentators believed that semen was the "key agent"

in reproduction. Because of the loss of blood during menstruation, the female body was deemed too weak and too cool to generate reproductive fluids as potent as those of the male. As a result, inheritance, even in the most straightforward physical terms, was generally thought to come primarily from the father. By dedicating the realm of the pedagogical to the father and, in the case of the Mestizo, eliminating him entirely, Acosta thus offers a significant reformulation of the gendered relations of reproduction. See Martínez, *Genealogical Fictions*, 48–49.

58. Mörner, "La afortunada gestión de un misionero del Perú en Madrid en 1578," 270. The article contains a brief description of Loaysa's life as well as an analysis and transcription of the *relación*.

59. Loaysa "cit[ed] the authority of Father José de Acosta and his work *De Procuranda Indorum Salute*." Lodares, "Languages, Catholicism, and Power in the Hispanic Empire," 20.

60. Gómez Canedo, *La educación de los marginados*, 282; van Deusen, *Between the Sacred and the Worldly*, 34–35.

61. Philip II to Moya de Contreras, December 2, 1578, Hans P. Kraus Collection, Library of Congress, http://hdl.loc.gov/loc.mss/mespk.k09500. This cédula, along with those sent elsewhere, are transcribed in Konetzke, *Colección de documentos para la historia de la formación social de Hispanoamérica*, I, 514.

62. Sabine Hyland suggests that this exclusion was enforced primarily through a discourse of illegitimacy, and she contrasts the relatively open situation in Peru with the far more exclusionary conditions in New Spain. See Hyland, "Illegitimacy and Racial Hierarchy in the Peruvian Priesthood," 434–436.

63. Poole, "Church Law on the Ordination of Indians and *Castas* in New Spain." See also Morales, *Ethnic and Social Background of the Franciscan Friars in Seventeenth-Century Mexico*, 34–37. For an example of a possible exception, see the case of Antonio del Rincón in McDonough, *The Learned Ones*, 44–46.

64. Brewer-García, "Bodies, Texts, and Translators," 375.

CHAPTER 3: SEGREGATION

1. Recent historiography of the riot includes Cope, *The Limits of Racial Domination*, chap. 6; and Silva Prada, *La política de una rebelión*. Although many scholars (including myself) have used the word "uprising" or "rebellion" to describe the event in an effort to make its political character explicit, the political conjuncture in which I find myself writing leads me to foreground the term "riot" as a political form in itself. For a valuable analysis of the riot as a struggle in the sphere of circulation, which tracks the continuities (and differences) between the "golden age of riot" in the early modern period and the racialized "surplus rebellions" of the present day, see Clover, *Riot. Strike. Riot.*

2. Various printed editions of this text exist, but in most cases the text has been modernized and even edited. For this reason, I have used Irving Leonard's edition, published as Sigüenza y Góngora, *Alboroto y motín de México del 8 de junio de 1692*. Translations are my own, though I have consulted and borrowed from Leonard's translation, published as "Letter of Don Carlos de Sigüenza to Admiral Pez Recounting the Incidents of the Corn Riot in Mexico City, June 8, 1692," in Leonard, *Don Carlos de Sigüenza y Góngora*, 210–277. Following Anna

More, I use "Creole" to describe "colonial subjects of Spanish descent who identify with an American rather than European homeland." More, *Baroque Sovereignty*, 264n10.

3. More, *Baroque Sovereignty*, especially chap. 4 on Sigüenza's account of the riot.

4. Sigüenza, *Alboroto y motín*, 35, 43.

5. In Francisco Cervantes de Salazar's 1554 dialogues, the peninsular visitor Alfaro comments that every house in the city center is so well built that it should be called "non aedes . . . sed arces" (not a house . . . but a fortress). The local guide responds, "Tales oportuit principio fieri, in tanta hostium multitudine, cum cingi muris & turribus muniri ciuitas non posset" (Because of the large, hostile population, they had to be built like this at first, since it was impossible to surround the city with walls and defend it with towers). Cervantes de Salazar, *Dialogi*, 258v; Cervantes de Salazar, *Life in the Imperial and Loyal City of Mexico*, 39 (translation altered).

6. On the trials and punishments of the supposed rioters, see Cope, *The Limits of Racial Domination*, 150–160. On the discourse of mixture and purity in the pulque prohibition, see Nemser, "'To Avoid This Mixture.'"

7. Sigüenza to Conde de Galve, July 5, 1692, AGN *Historia* 413, fol. 5r.

8. The informes and padrones are bundled together and held today at the Archivo General de la Nación (AGN), *Historia* 413. Edmundo O'Gorman published a transcription of the informes in 1938, but it modernizes the spelling and contains a number of minor errors. Additionally, as I discuss later, the published version excludes the padrones entirely. For these reasons, I cite the archival documents here. See O'Gorman, "Sobre los inconvenientes de vivir los indios en el centro de la ciudad."

9. Cope, *The Limits of Racial Domination*, chap. 1.

10. Ibid., 22.

11. Silva Prada, *La política de una rebelión*, 288–291. Similarly, Martínez argues that it was only in the late seventeenth century that an official discourse regarding the "purity" of Indians and the "impurity" of people of African descent was codified. See Martínez, *Genealogical Fictions*, chap. 8.

12. See Nemser, "Archaeology in the Lettered City."

13. More, *Baroque Sovereignty*, 164–169.

14. Sigüenza to Conde de Galve, July 5, 1692, AGN *Historia* 413, fol. 5r. These militarized patrols were specifically framed in the language of citizenship, calling up "todos los vezinos de dicha Ciudad." Conde de Santiago to Conde de Galve, AGN *Patronato* 226, núm. 1, ramo 19, fol. 11r.

15. More, *Baroque Sovereignty*, 163–164. Similarly, Anthony Pagden observes that the term "español," first used in relation to the two republics, had by the end of the seventeenth century acquired a "narrowly racial definition." Pagden, "Identity Formation in Spanish America," 79–80.

16. More, *Baroque Sovereignty*, 164, 169.

17. Foucault, "The Subject and Power," 314.

18. Foucault, *Security, Territory, Population*, 98–99.

19. Conde de Galve, June 21, 1692, AGN *Historia* 413, fol. 1r.

20. Real Acuerdo, June 26, 1692, AGN *Historia* 413, fol. 1v.

21. More, *Baroque Sovereignty*, 10–11.

22. Real Acuerdo, June 26, 1692, AGN *Historia* 413, fol. 2r.

23. Vetancurt, *Teatro mexicano*, II, 265–266.

24. By likening the Indians to Moors, Vetancurt's descriptive metaphor— "como moros sin señor"—could be read as a rhetorical technique that blurs the distinction between gentile (like the Indians) and infidel ("enemies of the Christian faith," like Jews or Muslims) that had been used by voluntarist theologians like Bartolomé de Las Casas during the sixteenth century. See, for example, Martínez, *Genealogical Fictions*, 96.

25. Antonio Girón to Conde de Galve, July 9, 1692, AGN *Historia* 413, fol. 18r.

26. José de la Barrera to Conde de Galve, July 1, 1692, AGN *Historia* 413, fol. 14v.

27. Bernabé Núñez de Páez to Conde de Galve, July 4, 1692, AGN *Historia* 413, fol. 13r.

28. Antonio de Guridi to Conde de Galve, n.d., AGN *Historia* 413, fol. 17r.

29. Núñez de Páez to Conde de Galve, July 4, 1692, AGN *Historia* 413, fol. 10r.

30. Barrera to Conde de Galve, July 1, 1692, AGN *Historia* 413, fol. 14v.

31. Girón to Conde de Galve, July 9, 1692, AGN *Historia* 413, fols. 18v, 19r. The burning of Troy was a commonplace among these authors. See, for example, Sigüenza, *Alboroto y motín*, 71; and Thomas de la Fuente Salazar, *Relación breve, narración verdadera e histórica sucinta de la erección fundación sucitación de la venerable Tercera Orden de penitencia de N.P. Santo Domingo* (1693), cited in Muriel, "Una nueva versión del motín del 8 de junio de 1692," 112.

32. Estrada Torres, "Fronteras imaginarias en la ciudad de México."

33. "In the region surrounding Mexico City alone, tribute revenues peaked at over 450,000 pesos per year during the sixteenth century, while eighteenth century revenues consistently averaged over 200,000 pesos. These were considerable sums. Although the income could not begin to keep pace with the millions generated in mining, it was still sufficient to pay large portions of Mexico's colonial administrative salaries in the late seventeenth century." Milton and Vinson, "Counting Heads," paragraph 5.

34. Núñez de Páez to Conde de Galve, July 4, 1692, AGN *Historia* 413, fol. 10v.

35. Guridi to Conde de Galve, n.d., AGN *Historia* 413, fol. 17v.

36. Barrera to Conde de Galve, July 1, 1692, AGN *Historia* 413, fol. 14r.

37. The *Diccionario de autoridades* (1732) includes the following definition for the reflexive form of the verb *extraviar*: "alejarse del sitio y bárrio donde antes vivia" (to distance oneself from the place and district where one previously lived). Real Academia Española, *Diccionario de la lengua castellana*, III, 699.

38. O'Hara, *A Flock Divided*, 26, 47–48.

39. Ibid., 48. For a helpful account of the transformation of Mexico City's parishes from the colonial period to the twentieth century, see Moreno de los Arcos, "Los territorios parroquiales de la ciudad arzobispal."

40. A parallel process seemed to occur in the *pulquerías*, which priests were similarly prohibited from entering. Vetancurt notes the dangerous convergence of "negros, y mulatos, y mestizos, y muchos españoles: los indios que eran de los negros enemigos, se han hecho con la bebida camaradas con tanta inmunidad de iglesia, porque ningún ministro real puede entrar á aprehender ni á sacar de la

pulquería delincuente (que esa es una de las condiciones del asentista)" (Blacks, and Mulattoes, and Mestizos, and many Spaniards: the Indians who used to be enemies of the Blacks have become comrades with this drink, with great immunity from the church, since no royal minister may enter to apprehend or remove a delinquent from the pulquería [this is one of the conditions of the pulque vendor]). Vetancurt, Teatro mexicano, I, 499. On the ministers' views of the pulquería in the aftermath of the riot, see Nemser, "'To Avoid This Mixture,'" 105–107.

41. Barrera to Conde de Galve, July 1, 1692, AGN Historia 413, fol. 14r.

42. Núñez de Páez to Conde de Galve, July 4, 1692, AGN Historia 413, fols. 10v, 11v.

43. Girón echoes these complaints, insisting on the need to ensure that "indios encompadren con indios y no con otros" (Indians become the godparents of Indians and not of others). Girón to Conde de Galve, July 9, 1692, AGN Historia 413, fol. 18v.

44. Núñez de Páez to Conde de Galve, July 4, 1692, AGN Historia 413, fol. 13r.

45. Conde de Galve, July 10, 1692, AGN Historia 413, fol. 23r. On the expansion of exemptions, see Sánchez Santiró, "El nuevo orden parroquial de la ciudad de México," 75.

46. Foucault, "'Omnes et Singulatim,'" 312–313.

47. Cortés, Letters from Mexico, 333–334.

48. The classic study on the role of the mendicants in the colonization of Mexico is Ricard, The Spiritual Conquest of Mexico. For Ricard, the arrival of the Jesuits marks the beginning of the end for the mendicants. As Karen Melvin has recently shown, however, the religious orders in fact successfully expanded and developed after the 1570s, although they shifted their focus to the cities. See Melvin, Building Colonial Cities of God.

49. Vetancurt to Conde de Galve, July 1, 1692, AGN Historia 413, fol. 16r.

50. Silva Prada, La política de una rebelión, 169.

51. AGN Historia 413, fols. 32r–40v; Silva Prada, La política de una rebelión, 173–174.

52. Curious details occasionally bring this landscape to life, such as the following example from the padrón of Santa Cruz: "en cassa de El Lizenciado Guerrero donde mataron a vn hombre de vn pelotaso ay seis familias." AGN Historia 413, fol. 43r.

53. Foucault, Security, Territory, Population, 125.

54. Silva Prada, La política de una rebelión, 570–574; Cope, The Limits of Racial Domination, 94–97.

55. Vetancurt to Conde de Galve, July 1, 1692, AGN Historia 413, fol. 16r. Under Archbishop Francisco Aguiar y Seijas, the Mexican church made significant efforts to document the total population of the archdiocese. See Silva Prada, La política de una rebelión, 167–168; Bravo Rubio and Pérez Iturbe, "Tiempos y espacios religiosos novohispanos."

56. The padrón for his parish carries the date January 27, 1691. AGN Historia 413, fols. 14r, 55r.

57. This tension is imperceptible in the published version of the segregation documents, which does not include the padrones. Since relatively few scholars have consulted the archival documents themselves, the padrones have been

largely overlooked. Important exceptions are Cope, *The Limits of Racial Domination*, 89–90; and Silva Prada, *La política de una rebelión*, 165–170.

58. Sigüenza, *Alboroto y motín*, 65.

59. Vetancurt to Conde de Galve, July 1, 1692, AGN *Historia* 413, fol. 16r. It is worth noting that Vetancurt explicitly modifies the text of the law, removing any mention of Spaniards as an object of prohibition. Compare the cited text to the 1563 original in the *Recopilación de leyes*, II, 200v.

60. Vetancurt to Conde de Galve, July 1, 1692, AGN *Historia* 413, fol. 16r. Note the slippage here: the Mestizo "disappears" from one clause to the next.

61. Vetancurt, *Teatro mexicano*, I, xv–xvii. On the "quarrel between the Ancients and the Moderns," see Pagden, *European Encounters with the New World*, chap. 3.

62. Sigüenza, *Alboroto y motín*, 51.

63. Escamilla González, "El siglo de oro vindicado," 194–195.

64. Sigüenza, *Alboroto y motín*, 47.

65. *Instrucciones que los virreyes de Nueva España dejaron a sus sucesores*, I, 289–290.

66. Real Acuerdo, June 26, 1692, AGN *Historia* 413, fol. 1v.

67. On the production and uses of "spiritual capital," see O'Hara, *A Flock Divided*, chap. 5.

68. Conde de Galve, July 10, 1692, AGN *Historia* 413, fols. 22r-23v.

69. Robles, *Diario de sucesos notables*, II, 263–264; Muriel, "Una nueva versión del motín del 8 de junio de 1692," 113; Silva Prada, *La política de una rebelión*, 247.

70. O'Gorman, "Reflexiones sobre la distribución urbana colonial de la ciudad de México," 812–813. See also O'Gorman, "Sobre los inconvenientes de vivir los indios en el centro de la ciudad."

71. Some recent examples include Viqueira, *Propriety and Permissiveness in Bourbon Mexico*, 6–8; and Gonzalbo Aizpuru, "El nacimiento del miedo, 1692," 31.

72. Carrera, *Imagining Identity in New Spain*, 110–111; Scardaville, "(Hapsburg) Law and (Bourbon) Order," 5.

73. Moreno de los Arcos, "Los territorios parroquiales de la ciudad arzobispal," 14; O'Hara, *A Flock Divided*, 96–100.

74. Mundy, "The Images of Eighteenth-Century Urban Reform in Mexico City," 67.

## CHAPTER 4: COLLECTION

1. José Antonio Alzate, "Respuesta de Pedro el Observador á los que, con título de consejos saludables, le remitió D. Ingenuo en el Suplemento à la *Gaceta de México* del 3 de Febrero de 1789," in *Gacetas de literatura de México*, I, 133.

2. The entirety of the dispute between Alzate and Cervantes has been published in Moreno de los Arcos, *Linneo en México*. On analogy as a constitutive element of scientific discourse, see Stepan, "Race and Gender." Alzate also saw "Indian" bodies in much the same terms. In an essay written two years later, he argues forcefully that the moral and physical "caracteres" (characteristics) of the

indigenous population of Mexico must likewise be attributed to the influence of climate. Alzate, "Un indio de la Nueva España," 162.

3. Despite his criticism of Cervantes, Alzate made frequent shipments of Mexican seeds to the garden in Madrid and was named as an official correspondent of the institution by its director—and Cervantes's teacher—Casimiro Gómez Ortega. See Clark, "'Read All About It,'" 153.

4. Clavijo y Fajardo, "Prólogo del traductor," xiii–xviii.

5. On collecting and collections in the eighteenth-century Hispanic world, see Deans-Smith, "Creating the Colonial Subject," 175–182; De Vos, "Natural History and the Pursuit of Empire in Eighteenth-Century Spain"; and Cabello Carro, "Spanish Collections of Americana in the Late Eighteenth Century."

6. Consider the following experiment proposed by Buffon: A number of "Blacks" would be taken from Senegal and transported to Denmark, where "the difference in the blood and the opposition of color is the greatest." There they would be permanently locked away (from the French verb cloîtrer, which Clavijo y Fajardo gives as "tener reclusos" [to imprison them] in his Spanish translation) with "their women" and "scrupulously" prevented from interbreeding. In this way, Buffon thought, it would be possible to determine the amount of time necessary for the northern climate to "whiten" the subjects' skin color. If this experiment exemplifies the increasingly scientific mode of concentration characteristic of the Enlightenment—filtered of course through the logic of the Atlantic slave trade—it also presented two significant obstacles. On one hand, there was the spatial problem posed by active resistance and escape (as we have seen, the history of concentration can also be told as a history of flight); on the other hand, there was a temporal problem of duration, since it would take, in Buffon's own estimation, "a rather great number of centuries" for any effects, such as they were, to become visible. Given that plants are unlikely to run away and that their acclimatization was thought to proceed far more rapidly, Alzate's analogy could be read as a counterproposal by which to circumvent these limitations, by making "las plantas" speak for "los negros." It is hard to say whether the Creole knew specifically of Buffon's proposal, but he was very familiar with the French naturalist's work in general, citing him approvingly in his dispute with Cervantes. Buffon, Histoire naturelle, XIV, 313–314. For the English translation, I have followed Spary, Utopia's Garden, 107; for Clavijo y Fajardo's Spanish translation, see Buffon, Historia natural, general y particular, XVI, 47. On Buffon's theory of climate and the limits of external determination, see Eddy, "Buffon, Organic Alterations, and Man."

7. Lafuente and Valverde, "Linnaean Botany and Spanish Imperial Biopolitics," 141.

8. Foucault, The Order of Things, 143.

9. On the importance of geography and spatial thought in the Enlightenment, see Withers, Placing the Enlightenment. On the quantification of climate during this period, see Bourguet, "Measurable Difference."

10. Silva, Toward a Global Idea of Race, 116–117.

11. Although she does not follow this trajectory, Silva gestures toward such a reading, as when she distinguishes between Cuvier, who remained in his laboratory, and Darwin, who traveled extensively in the Americas—inspired, it is worth

mentioning, by the example of Alexander von Humboldt, to whom I turn later in this chapter. See Silva, *Toward a Global Idea of Race*, 109.

12. Here I am drawing on Ann Stoler's colonial reading of Foucault in *Carnal Knowledge and Imperial Power*, 143–144.

13. See Koerner, *Linnaeus: Nature and Nation*. In contrast to the colonial or mercantile models implemented by other European powers, botanical autarky proposed a sort of "import substitution" that would, through scientific knowledge and practices, "create a miniaturized mercantile empire within the borders of the European state." Ibid., 188.

14. Schiebinger, *Plants and Empire*, 5–6.

15. Puerto Sarmiento, *Ciencia de cámara*, 155–156.

16. Gómez Ortega, *Instrucción*, 22.

17. Foucault, *The Order of Things*, 144–158.

18. Gómez Ortega, *Curso elemental de botánica*, x.

19. It was only with Cuvier, argues Foucault, that geography became significant as part of the conditions of existence for "life itself." Foucault, *The Order of Things*, 150–151, 298–299.

20. Lafuente and Valverde, "Linnean Botany and Spanish Imperial Biopolitics."

21. Bleichmar, *Visible Empire*, 151.

22. Palau y Verdera, *Explicación de la filosofía, y fundamentos botanicos de Linneo*, 220–221. Compare Linnaeus, *Linnaeus' Philosophia Botanica*, 284.

23. Linnaeus, "The Oeconomy of Nature," 69–70. The text is credited to Isaac J. Biberg, who was a student of Linnaeus, but was written by Linnaeus himself. See also Koerner, *Linnaeus: Nature and Nation*, 119–120.

24. Palau, *Explicación de la filosofía*, 221; compare Linnaeus, "On the Increase of the Habitable Earth," 90–91.

25. Oviedo, *General y natural historia de las Indias*, 239, 242–243.

26. De Vos, "Natural History and the Pursuit of Empire," 225. The sixteenth-century naturalist Francisco Hernández tried to bring plants back with him from New Spain. The few that survived the journey were transplanted in Seville but quickly died. See González Bueno, "La aclimatación de plantas americanas en los jardines peninsulares," 40.

27. Of the remaining shipments, eighteen (5 percent) contained animals and sixteen (4 percent) minerals. Not surprisingly, most took place in the late 1770s and 1780s, the period in question here. See De Vos, "Natural History and the Pursuit of Empire," 215–216, 219.

28. On the formation of "centers of calculation," which are able to dominate at a distance by using techniques of mobility (the capacity to transport objects back to the center), stability (so they are not distorted in the process), and combinability (to translate them into a common register, as in the procedure I have called abstraction), see Latour, *Science in Action*, 223, and chap. 6 more generally.

29. On the order of the garden, see Puerto Sarmiento, *Ciencia de cámara*, 78–93. Some Spanish gardens, including Cartagena and Málaga on the Mediterranean coast, were run by military institutions and served not only as sites for acclimatization but also as producers of medical supplies for military operations. But this character was generalized, shaping even the Royal Botanical Garden of Madrid. In other ways, too, the military was deeply enmeshed in Spanish imperial botany.

192 NOTES TO PAGES 144-153

Naval forces, for example, were charged with most of the transatlantic transportation of plants. See Puerto Sarmiento, *La ilusión quebrada*, 10, 223, 82; and González Bueno, "La aclimatación de plantas americanas en los jardines peninsulares," 44.

30. Foucault, *The Order of Things*, 143.

31. Gómez Ortega, *Instrucción*, 29. On the related question of institutional logistics, see Figueroa, "Packing Techniques and Political Obedience as Scientific Issues."

32. Gómez Ortega, *Instrucción*, 5-6.

33. Ibid., 6-7.

34. Ibid., 8-9.

35. Ibid., 11.

36. Ibid., 9-10. Gómez Ortega saw the Tabasco pepper (*malagueta*) as another valuable opportunity for imperial botany and laid out a similar proposal for using the greenhouse at the Madrid garden and the network of corresponding gardens to introduce it into the Iberian Peninsula. See Bleichmar, *Visible Empire*, 127-131.

37. Parry, *Trading the Genome*, 23.

38. Ibid., 23-27.

39. Puerto Sarmiento, *La ilusión quebrada*, 198-225.

40. Ibid., 199-201.

41. Ibid., 7; the quotation comes from the title of the book. See also Puerto Sarmiento, *Ciencia de cámara*, 91-93.

42. Cervantes made clear that "uno de los principales fines" (one of the principal goals) of the botanical garden at Chapultepec would be to channel plant specimens to its counterpart in Madrid. AGI *México* 1430, núm. 308, fol. 5v.

43. Nemser, "Eviction and the Archive"; see also Cañizares-Esguerra, *How to Write the History of the New World*, chap. 3.

44. Revillagigedo to Porlier, September 26, 1791, AGI *México* 1430, núm. 307; "Testimonio del expediente formado sobre establecer en Chapultepec el Jardin Botanico," AGI *México* 1430, núm. 308, fol. 5v.

45. For a detailed analysis of the centrality of enclosure practices to the project of British imperial botany, see Drayton, *Nature's Government*.

46. Cervantes de Salazar, *Dialogi*, 268v; Cervantes de Salazar, *Life in the Imperial and Loyal City of Mexico*, 52.

47. Cervantes de Salazar, *Dialogi*, 281v, 283v; Cervantes de Salazar, *Life in the Imperial and Loyal City of Mexico*, 71, 74. See also del Valle, "On Shaky Ground," 212; and Merrim, *The Spectacular City*, 78-80.

48. On the gaze of the "voyeur," see de Certeau, *The Practice of Everyday Life*, 91-110.

49. Cervantes de Salazar, *Dialogi*, 284r-v; Cervantes de Salazar, *Life in the Imperial and Loyal City of Mexico*, 74-75.

50. Cervantes de Salazar, *Dialogi*, 286r-v; Cervantes de Salazar, *Life in the Imperial and Loyal City of Mexico*, 77.

51. "Testimonio del expediente formado sobre establecer en Chapultepec el Jardin Botanico," AGI *México* 1430, núm. 308, fol. 2v; Rickett, *The Royal Botanical Expedition to New Spain*, 9, 15-16.

52. López, "Nature as Subject and Citizen," 80.

53. "Testimonio del expediente formado sobre establecer en Chapultepec el Jardin Botanico," AGI *México* 1430, núm. 308, fols. 2r, 6r. For concrete examples of circulation between the two gardens, see Rickett, *The Royal Botanical Expedition*, 19–20, 58. See also López, "Nature as Subject and Citizen"; and González Bueno, "Plantas y luces," 114–115.

54. AGI *México* 1430, núm. 308, fol. 5v.

55. AGI *México* 1430, núm. 308, fols. 1v–2r (emphasis added). Sessé made a similar set of arguments several years later in a 1794 report to the king on the state of the project. See Rickett, *The Royal Botanical Expedition*, 18–19.

56. Sessé to Charles IV, March 28, 1794, quoted in Moziño, *Tratado del xiquilite y añil de Guatemala*, 7–8. By 1792, the viceroy had agreed, writing that "el sitio de Chapultepec . . . tiene [proporciones] más ventajosas en las partes llanas, montanosas y escarpadas de su corto recinto para el Jardín Botánico" (the Chapultepec location has, in the flat, mountainous, and steep areas of its small enclosure, very advantageous proportions for the Botanical Garden). Díaz, "El Jardín Botánico de Nueva España," 73. See also Rickett, *The Royal Botanical Expedition*, 18–19.

57. See Cañizares-Esguerra, "How Derivative Was Humboldt?," 148–165; and Linnaeus, "On the Increase of the Habitable Earth," 90.

58. He also praised Constanzó's engineering prowess and cited Alzate's work numerous times, if critically. Humboldt, *Political Essay on the Kingdom of New Spain*, IV, 215, 340; I, 219. In another work, he specifically mentions having visited "the gardens of Chapultepec near Mexico City" but does not offer much detail beyond this. Humboldt, *Views of the Cordilleras and Monuments of the Indigenous Peoples of the Americas*, 136.

59. Humboldt and Bonpland mainly spent their time "researching in a wealth of Mexican archives, libraries, and botanical gardens never before open to non-Spaniards." Pratt, *Imperial Eyes*, 115, 129.

60. Humboldt, *Essay on the Geography of Plants*, 64.

61. Jackson, "Instruments Utilized in Developing the *Tableau physique*," 221–226; Bourguet, "Measurable Difference," 285.

62. Humboldt, *Essay on the Geography of Plants*, 86.

63. Ibid., 66.

64. Another example is found in his discussion of the effect of light on both plant and animal functions: "It is well known that light exerts a powerful influence on the vital functions of plants, especially on their breathing, on the formation of their coloring part that has a resinous character, and . . . on the fixation of nitrogen in their starch. . . . In my work on nerves, I cited some experiments in which solar light seems to produce stimulating effects on nervous fibers that would be difficult to attribute solely to heat." Ibid., 109, 114. On Cuvier's work, which privileged function (e.g., respiration in general) over form (e.g., gills or lungs), see Foucault, *The Order of Things*, 287–304.

65. On the transition from the three-kingdom model of natural history (animals, vegetables, minerals) to the two-kingdom model of biology (organic, inorganic), see Foucault, *The Order of Things*, 251–252.

66. Humboldt, *Essay on the Geography of Plants*, 69–70.

67. Humboldt, *Personal Narrative of Travels*, I, xiv.

68. Humboldt, *Essay on the Geography of Plants*, 72, 70 (translation altered).

69. Ibid., 75.

70. Humboldt, *Personal Narrative of Travels*, I, 135–136.

71. Silva, *Toward a Global Idea of Race*, 107.

72. On Humboldt as a "crucial link" in Foucault's story, see Nicolson, "Alexander von Humboldt," 167. Silva shows that race was central for Cuvier, especially with regard to his attempt to understand man's relation to other animals. His exploration of the "conditions of existence" posited a global division of racialized bodies, subject to what Silva calls "the productive *nomos*" of life in divergent ways. See Silva, *Toward a Global Idea of Race*, 101–107.

73. Foucault, *The History of Sexuality*, 149.

74. Foucault, *"Society Must Be Defended,"* 258. Here I am drawing on Alexander Weheliye's sharp critique in *Habeas Viscus*, chap. 4.

75. See Balibar, "Is There a Neo-Racism?," 22–23.

76. For example, Outram, *The Enlightenment*, 76; and Banton, *Racial Theories*, 5–6. See my discussion in the introduction of the "historiographical" paradigm of race in colonial Latin American studies.

77. Silva, *Toward a Global Idea of Race*; Stoler, "Racial Histories and Their Regimes of Truth."

78. Cañizares-Esguerra, "New World, New Stars," 66–68.

79. Pratt makes the important observation that Humboldt's work was equally useful to European colonizers and American Creoles, though perhaps in different ways. My analysis here shows that one point of intersection was precisely the authority of the White body. See Pratt, *Imperial Eyes*, 110.

### EPILOGUE

1. A video and transcript of the speech are available at Calderón, "El Presidente Calderón en la fundación del Nuevo Juan de Grijalva."

2. Khalili, *Time in the Shadows*, 172–212; Sackley, "The Village as Cold War Site," 501–502.

3. One of the most complete studies of the *ciudades rurales* project to date is a report prepared by the San Cristóbal de las Casas–based organizations Red por la Paz Chiapas and the Colectivo de Análisis e Información Kolectiva (CAIK). The report includes a detailed analysis of the transnational corporate and state interests associated with the land around the sites chosen for the new settlements. See Red por la Paz Chiapas, *De la tierra al asfalto*. See also Wilson, "Notes on the Rural City," 1000; and Contreras et al., "Ciudades rurales sustentables," 141.

4. Wilson, "The Urbanization of the Countryside," 228–229.

5. Wilson, "Notes on the Rural City," 999–1004 (emphasis in original).

6. Foucault, *"Society Must Be Defended,"* 50–51.

7. "What matters here is that . . . a state of emergency linked to a colonial war is extended to an entire civil population. The camps are born not out of ordinary law . . . but out of a state of exception and martial law." Agamben, *Homo Sacer*, 166–167.

8. Khalili, *Time in the Shadows*, 4–5, 234–235.

9. This is also the case with mass incarceration in the United States today,

which primarily targets Black communities and other communities of color. Alexander Weheliye importantly notes that Agamben's focus on martial law and the state of exception as the operative logic of the concentration camp blinds him to the everyday workings of racialized mass incarceration, which constitutes nothing less than the edifice of the law. Weheliye, *Habeas Viscus*, 86.

10. My reading of racialization resonates in certain ways with the influential work of Michael Omi and Howard Winant, who define racialization as *"the extension of racial meaning to a previously racially unclassified relationship, social practice, or group."* Still, it seems important to account for ongoing processes of racialization that either transform racial meanings or reconfigure the relationships, social practices, or groups to which they are ascribed. Moreover, while acknowledging that race has a history, Omi and Winant's definition seems to take for granted the reality and contours of these groups, without reckoning with the possibility that groupness may itself be produced through the material reorganization of life. See Omi and Winant, *Racial Formation in the United States*, 3rd ed., 111 (emphasis in original). Oddly, this keyword appears only in the first and third editions, published in 1986 and 2015, respectively, but is absent from the more widely read second edition from 1994.

11. Marx, *Capital*, I, 915.

12. Federici, *Caliban and the Witch*, 63–64 (emphasis in original).

13. Marx, *Capital*, I, 873.

14. Ibid., 874–875; Harvey, *The New Imperialism*, 137–182. On the "propensity in human nature . . . to truck, barter, and exchange," see Smith, *An Inquiry into the Nature and Causes of the Wealth of Nations*, I, 16.

15. See, for example, Drucker, *The Practice of Management*, 106, who calls it "a favourite story at management meetings." Calderón offers a different lineage, telling the audience that the story came from his father: "una anécdota, una historia que relataba mi padre, que era gran soñador" (an anecdote or story that my father, who was a great dreamer, used to tell).

16. Wilson, "Notes on the Rural City," 1003; Contreras et al., "Ciudades rurales sustentables," 147.

17. Wilson, "The Urbanization of the Countryside," 229–230.

BIBLIOGRAPHY

ARCHIVES

Archivo General de la Nación (AGN), Mexico City, Mexico
Archivo General de Indias (AGI), Seville, Spain
Archivo Histórico Nacional (AHN), Madrid, Spain

PUBLISHED MATERIALS

Acosta, José de. *De procuranda indorum salute.* Edited by Luciano Pereña. Madrid: CSIC, 1984–1987.
Agamben, Giorgio. *Homo Sacer: Sovereign Power and Bare Life.* Translated by Daniel Heller-Roazen. Stanford, CA: Stanford University Press, 1998.
Alzate, José Antonio. *Gacetas de literatura de México.* Puebla, Mexico: Reimpresas en la Oficina del Hospital de San Pedro, 1831.
———. "Un indio de la Nueva España, ¿qué especie de hombre es, y cuáles sus caracteres morales y físicos?" In *Memorias y ensayos,* 154–165. Edited by Roberto Moreno. Mexico City: UNAM, 1985.
Balibar, Etienne. "Is There a Neo-Racism?" In *Race, Nation, Class: Ambiguous Identities,* by Etienne Balibar and Immanuel Wallerstein, 17–28. London: Verso, 1991.
Banton, Michael. *Racial Theories.* 2nd ed. Cambridge: Cambridge University Press, 1998.
Bentancor, Orlando. "La disposición de la materia en la *Información en derecho de Vasco de Quiroga.*" In *Estudios transatlánticos postcoloniales II: Mito, archivo, disciplina: Cartografías culturales,* edited by Ileana Rodríguez and Josebe Martínez, 171–207. Barcelona: Anthropos Editorial, 2011.
———. "Matter, Form, and the Generation of Metals in Álvaro Alonso Barba's *Arte de los metales.*" *Journal of Spanish Cultural Studies* 8, no. 2 (2007): 117–133.
Berlant, Lauren. *Cruel Optimism.* Durham, NC: Duke University Press, 2011.
Bernal García, María Elena, and Ángel Julián García Zambrano. "El altepetl colonial y sus antecedentes prehispánicos: Contexto teórico-historiográfico." In *Territorialidad y paisaje en el altepetl del siglo XVI,* edited by Federico Fernández Christlieb and Ángel Julián García Zambrano, 31–113. Mexico City: Fondo de Cultura Económica, 2006.
Bernand, Carmen. "Los nuevos cuerpos mestizos de la América colonial." In *Retóricas del cuerpo amerindio,* edited by Manuel Gutiérrez Estévez and Pedro Pitarch, 87–116. Madrid: Iberoamericana, 2010.
Bleichmar, Daniela. *Visible Empire: Botanical Expeditions and Visual Culture in the Hispanic Enlightenment.* Chicago: University of Chicago Press, 2012.
Bonilla-Silva, Eduardo. *Racism without Racists: Color-Blind Racism and the Persistence of Racial Inequality in the United States.* 2nd ed. Lanham, MD: Rowman and Littlefield, 2006.

Bourguet, Marie-Noëlle. "Measurable Difference: Botany, Climate, and the Gardener's Thermometer in Eighteenth-Century France." In *Colonial Botany: Science, Commerce, and Politics in the Early Modern World*, edited by Londa Schiebinger and Claudia Swan, 270–286. Philadelphia: University of Pennsylvania Press, 2005.

Bravo Rubio, Bernise, and Marco Antonio Pérez Iturbe. "Tiempos y espacios religiosos novohispanos: La visita pastoral de Francisco Aguiar y Seijas (1683–1684)." In *Religión, poder, y autoridad en la Nueva España*, edited by Alicia Mayer and Ernesto de la Torre Villar, 67–83. Mexico City: UNAM, 2004.

Brewer-García, Larissa. "Bodies, Texts, and Translators: Indigenous Breast Milk and the Jesuit Exclusion of Mestizos in Late Sixteenth-Century Peru." *Colonial Latin American Review* 21, no. 3 (2012): 365–390.

Buffon, Comte de. *Histoire naturelle, générale et particulière, avec la description du Cabinet du Roi.* Vol. 14. Paris: L'Imprimerie Royale, 1766.

———. *Historia natural, general y particular.* Translated by Joseph Clavijo y Fajardo. 21 vols. Madrid: La Viuda de Don Joaquín Ibarra, 1785.

Burkhart, Louise M. "The 'Little Doctrine' and Indigenous Catechesis in New Spain." *Hispanic American Historical Review* 94, no. 2 (2014): 168–206.

Burns, Kathryn. *Colonial Habits: Convents and the Spiritual Economy of Cuzco, Peru.* Durham, NC: Duke University Press, 1999.

Cabello Carro, Paz. "Spanish Collections of Americana in the Late Eighteenth Century." In *Collecting across Cultures: Material Exchanges in the Early Modern Atlantic World*, edited by Daniela Bleichmar and Peter C. Mancall, 217–235. Philadelphia: University of Pennsylvania Press, 2011.

Calderón, Felipe. "El Presidente Calderón en la fundación del Nuevo Juan de Grijalva, ciudad rural sustentable." September 17, 2009. http://calderon.presidencia .gob.mx/2009/09/el-presidente-calderon-en-la-fundacion-del-nuevo-juan-de -grijalva-ciudad-rural-sustentable/.

Cañizares-Esguerra, Jorge. "How Derivative Was Humboldt? Microcosmic Nature Narratives in Early Modern Spanish America and the (Other) Origins of Humboldt's Ecological Sensibilities." In *Colonial Botany: Science, Commerce, and Politics in the Early Modern World*, edited by Londa Schiebinger and Claudia Swan, 148–165. Philadelphia: University of Pennsylvania Press, 2005.

———. *How to Write the History of the New World: Histories, Epistemologies, and Identities in the Eighteenth-Century Atlantic World.* Stanford, CA: Stanford University Press, 2001.

———. "New World, New Stars: Patriotic Astrology and the Invention of Indian and Creole Bodies in Colonial Spanish America, 1600–1650." *American Historical Review* 104, no. 1 (1999): 33–68.

Carrera, Magali M. *Imagining Identity in New Spain: Race, Lineage, and the Colonial Body in Portraiture and Casta Paintings.* Austin: University of Texas Press, 2003.

*Cartas de Indias.* Madrid: Imprenta de Manuel G. Hernández, 1877.

Castañeda Delgado, Paulino. "El Colegio de San Juan de Letrán de México (Apuntes para su historia)." *Anuario de estudios americanos* 37 (1980): 69–126.

Cervantes de Salazar, Francisco. *Life in the Imperial and Loyal City of Mexico in New Spain.* Edited by Carlos Eduardo Castañeda. Translated by Minnie Lee

Barrett Shepard. Austin: University of Texas Press, 1953. Includes a facsimile of the Latin original.

Césaire, Aimé. *Discourse on Colonialism*. Translated by Joan Pinkham. New York: Monthly Review Press, 2000 [1955].

Chance, John K., and William B. Taylor, "Estate and Class in a Colonial City: Oaxaca in 1792." *Comparative Studies in Society and History* 19, no. 4 (1977): 454–487.

Chen, Chris. "The Limit Point of Capitalist Equality: Notes toward an Abolitionist Antiracism." *Endnotes* 3 (2013): 202–223. http://endnotes.org.uk/en/chris -chen-the-limit-point-of-capitalist-equality.

Chimalpahin Quauhtlehuanitzin, Don Domingo de San Antón Muñón. *Annals of His Time*. Edited and translated by James Lockhart, Susan Schroeder, and Doris Namala. Stanford, CA: Stanford University Press, 2006.

Chorba, Carrie C. *Mexico, from Mestizo to Multicultural: National Identity and Recent Representations of the Conquest*. Nashville, TN: Vanderbilt University Press, 2007.

Clark, Fiona. "'Read All About It': Science, Translation, Adaptation, and Confrontation in the *Gazeta de Literatura de México*, 1788–1795." In *Science in the Spanish and Portuguese Empires, 1500–1800*, edited by Daniela Bleichmar, Paula De Vos, Kristin Huffine, and Kevin Sheehan, 147–177. Stanford, CA: Stanford University Press, 2009.

Clavijo y Fajardo, Joseph. "Prólogo del traductor." In *Historia natural, general y particular*, by Comte de Buffon, vol. 1, iii–lxxii. Translated by Joseph Clavijo y Fajardo. Madrid: por D. Joachín Ibarra Impresor de Cámara de S.M., 1785.

Cline, Howard F. "Civil Congregations of the Indians in New Spain, 1598–1606." *Hispanic American Historical Review* 29, no. 3 (1949): 349–369.

Clover, Joshua. *Riot. Strike. Riot: The New Era of Uprisings*. London: Verso, 2016.

Colmeiro, Miguel. *Bosquejo histórico y estadístico del Jardín Botánico de Madrid*. Madrid: Imprenta de T. Fortanet, 1875.

Contreras, Karela, Rosaluz Pérez, Miguel Pickard, Abraham Rivera, and Mariela Zunino. "Ciudades rurales sustentables, despojo y contrainsurgencia en Chiapas." In *Planes geoestratégicos, desplazamientos y migraciones forzadas en el área del proyecto de desarrollo e integración de Mesoamérica*, edited by Juan Manuel Sandoval Palacios, Raquel Álvarez de Flores, and Sara Yaneth Fernández Moreno, 141–158. Mexico City: Seminario Permanente de Estudios Chicanos y de Fronteras, 2011.

Cope, R. Douglas. *The Limits of Racial Domination: Plebeian Society in Colonial Mexico City, 1660–1720*. Madison: University of Wisconsin Press, 1994.

Cortés, Hernán. *Letters from Mexico*. Edited and translated by Anthony Pagden. New Haven, CT: Yale University Press, 2001.

Crenshaw, Kimberlé. "Mapping the Margins: Intersectionality, Identity Politics, and Violence against Women of Color." *Stanford Law Review* 43 (1991): 1241–1299.

Cuevas, P. Mariano. *Documentos inéditos del siglo XVI para la historia de México*. Mexico City: Tallers del Museo Nacional de Arqueología, Historia y Etnología, 1914.

Deans-Smith, Susan. "Creating the Colonial Subject: Casta Paintings, Collectors, and Critics in Eighteenth-Century Mexico and Spain." *Colonial Latin American Review* 14, no. 2 (2005): 169–204.

De Certeau, Michel. *The Practice of Everyday Life*. Translated by Steven Rendall. Berkeley: University of California Press, 1984.

Del Valle, Ivonne. "José de Acosta: Entre el realismo político y disparates e imposibles, o por qué importan los estudios coloniales." In *Estudios transatlánticos postcoloniales II: Mito, archivo, disciplina: Cartografías culturales*, edited by Ileana Rodríguez and Josebe Martínez, 291–324. Barcelona: Anthropos Editorial, 2011.

———. "On Shaky Ground: Hydraulics, State Formation, and Colonialism in Sixteenth-Century Mexico." *Hispanic Review* 77, no. 2 (2009): 197–220.

Descartes, René. *Discourse on the Method for Conducting One's Reason Well and for Seeking Truth in the Sciences*. Translated by Donald A. Cress. 3rd ed. Indianapolis: Hackett, 1998 [1637].

De Vos, Paula. "Natural History and the Pursuit of Empire in Eighteenth-Century Spain." *Eighteenth-Century Studies* 40, no. 2 (2007): 209–239.

Díaz, Lilia. "El Jardín Botánico de Nueva España y la obra de Sessé según documentos mexicanos." *Historia Mexicana* 27, no. 1 (1977): 49–78.

Drayton, Richard. *Nature's Government: Science, Imperial Britain, and the "Improvement" of the World*. New Haven, CT: Yale University Press, 2000.

Drucker, Peter F. *The Practice of Management*. Oxford: Butterworth-Heinemann, 2007 [1955].

Durston, Alan. *Pastoral Quechua: The History of Christian Translation in Colonial Peru, 1550–1650*. Notre Dame, IN: University of Notre Dame Press, 2007.

Dussel, Enrique. *Philosophy of Liberation*. Translated by Aquilina Martínez and Christine Morkovsky. Maryknoll, NY: Orbis Books, 1985.

Easterling, Keller. *Extrastatecraft: The Power of Infrastructure Space*. London: Verso, 2014.

Eddy, J. H. "Buffon, Organic Alterations, and Man." *Studies in the History of Biology* 7 (1984): 1–45.

Edgerton, Samuel Y. *Theaters of Conversion: Religious Architecture and Indian Artisans in Colonial Mexico*. Albuquerque: University of New Mexico Press, 2001.

Edwards, Paul N. "Infrastructure and Modernity: Force, Time, and Social Organization in the History of Sociotechnical Systems." In *Modernity and Technology*, edited by Thomas J. Misa, Philip Brey, and Andrew Feenberg, 185–225. Cambridge, MA: MIT Press, 2003.

Elden, Stuart. "Government, Calculation, Territory." *Environment and Planning D: Society and Space* 25 (2007): 562–580.

Elliott, J. H. *Spain and Its World, 1500–1700*. New Haven, CT: Yale University Press, 1989.

Escamilla González, Iván. "El siglo de oro vindicado: Carlos de Sigüenza y Góngora, el Conde de Galve, y el tumulto de 1692." In *Carlos de Sigüenza y Góngora: Homenaje, 1700–2000*, edited by Alicia Mayer, vol. 2, 179–203. Mexico City: UNAM, 2002.

Esposito, Roberto. *Bíos: Biopolitics and Philosophy*. Translated by Timothy Campbell. Minneapolis: University of Minnesota Press, 2008.

Estrada Torres, María Isabel. "Fronteras imaginarias en la ciudad de México: Parcialidades indígenas y traza española en el siglo XVII." In *Las ciudades y sus estructuras: Población, espacio, y cultura en México, siglos XVIII y XIX*, edited by Sonia Pérez Toledo, René Elizalde Salazar, and Luis Pérez Cruz, 98–107. Mexico City: Universidad Autónoma Metropolitana-Iztapalapa, 1999.

Everdell, William R. *The First Moderns: Profiles in the Origins of Twentieth-Century Thought*. Chicago: University of Chicago Press, 1997.

Federici, Silvia. *Caliban and the Witch*. New York: Autonomedia, 2004.

Fields, Sherry. *Pestilence and Headcolds: Encountering Illness in Colonial Mexico*. New York: Columbia University Press, 2008.

Figueroa, Marcelo Fabián. "Packing Techniques and Political Obedience as Scientific Issues: 18th-Century Medicinal Balsams, Gums, and Resins from the Indies to Madrid." *HOST: Journal of History of Science and Technology* 5 (2012): 49–67.

Foucault, Michel. *The History of Sexuality, Volume 1: An Introduction*. Translated by Robert Hurley. New York: Pantheon, 1978.

———. "The Incorporation of the Hospital into Modern Technology." Translated by Edgar Knowlton Jr., William J. King, and Stuart Elden. In *Space, Knowledge, and Power: Foucault and Geography*, edited by Jeremy W. Crampton and Stuart Elden, 141–151. Aldershot, UK: Ashgate, 2007.

———. "Nietzsche, Genealogy, History." In *Language, Counter-Memory, Practice: Selected Essays and Interviews*, edited by D. F. Bouchard, 139–164. Ithaca, NY: Cornell University Press, 1977.

———. "'Omnes et Singulatim': Toward a Critique of Political Reason." In *Essential Works of Foucault, 1954–1984: Power*, edited by James D. Faubion, 298–325. Translated by Robert Hurley. New York: The New Press, 2000.

———. *The Order of Things: An Archaeology of the Human Sciences*. New York: Routledge, 2002.

———. "The Political Technology of Individuals." In *Essential Works of Foucault, 1954–1984: Power*, edited by James D. Faubion, 403–417. Translated by Robert Hurley. New York: The New Press, 2000.

———. *Security, Territory, Population: Lectures at the Collège de France, 1977–78*. Translated by Graham Burchell. New York: Palgrave Macmillan, 2007.

———. *"Society Must Be Defended": Lectures at the Collège de France, 1975–76*. Translated by David Macey. New York: Picador, 2003.

———. "The Subject and Power." In *Essential Works of Foucault, 1954–1984: Power*, edited by James D. Faubion, 326–348. Translated by Robert Hurley. New York: The New Press, 2000

Furlong, Kathryn. "STS Beyond the 'Modern Infrastructure Ideal': Extending Theory by Engaging with Infrastructural Challenges in the South." *Technology in Society* 38 (2014): 139–147.

Galli, Carlo. *Political Spaces and Global War*. Edited by Adam Sitze and translated by Elisabeth Fay. Minneapolis: University of Minnesota Press, 2010.

García Icazbalceta, Joaquín, ed. *Códice Franciscano*. Mexico City: Imprenta de Francisco Díaz de León, 1889.

———. *Códice Mendieta: Documentos franciscanos, siglos XVI y XVII*. Mexico City: Imprenta de Francisco Díaz de León, 1892.

García Martínez, Bernardo. *Los pueblos de la sierra: El poder y el espacio entre los indios del norte de Puebla hasta 1700.* Mexico City: El Colegio de México, 1987.

Gerhard, Peter. "Congregaciones de indios en la Nueva España antes de 1570." *Historia Mexicana* 26, no. 3 (1977): 347–395.

———. "La evolución del pueblo rural mexicano: 1519–1975." *Historia Mexicana* 24, no. 4 (1975): 566–578.

———. *A Guide to the Historical Geography of New Spain.* Cambridge: Cambridge University Press, 1972.

Gibson, Charles. *The Aztecs under Spanish Rule: A History of the Indians of the Valley of Mexico, 1519–1810.* Stanford, CA: Stanford University Press, 1964.

Gilmore, Ruth Wilson. *Golden Gulag: Prisons, Surplus, Crisis, and Opposition in Globalizing California.* Berkeley: University of California Press, 2007.

Gómez, Fernando. *Good Places and Non-Places in Colonial Mexico: The Figure of Vasco de Quiroga (1470–1565).* New York: University Press of America, 2001.

Gómez Canedo, Lino. *La educación de los marginados durante la época colonial: Escuelas y colegios para indios y mestizos en la Nueva España.* Mexico City: Editorial Porrúa, 1982.

Gómez Ortega, Casimiro. *Curso elemental de botánica, dispuesto para la enseñanza del Real Jardín de Madrid . . . Parte práctica.* 2nd ed. Madrid: Imprenta de la Viuda é Hijo de Marin, 1795.

———. *Instrucción sobre el modo mas seguro y económico de transportar plantas vivas por mar y tierra á los paises mas distantes.* Madrid: Joaquín Ibarra, 1779.

Gonzalbo Aizpuru, Pilar. "El nacimiento del miedo, 1692: Indios y españoles en la ciudad de México." *Revista de Indias* 68, no. 244 (2008): 9–34.

González Bueno, Antonio. "La aclimatación de plantas americanas en los jardines peninsulares." In *La agricultura viajera: Cultivos y manufacturas de plantas industriales y alimentarias en España y la América virreinal,* edited by Joaquín Fernández Pérez and Ignacio González Tascón, 37–51. Madrid: CSIC, 1990.

———. "Plantas y luces: La botánica de la Ilustración en la América hispana." In *La formación de la cultura virreinal, vol. 3: El siglo XVIII,* edited by Karl Kohut and Sonia V. Rose, 107–128. Madrid: Iberoamericana, 2006.

González Casanova, Pablo. "Internal Colonialism and National Development." *Studies in Comparative International Development* 1, no. 4 (1965): 27–37.

Greenleaf, Richard E. "San Juan de Letrán: Colonial Mexico's Royal College for Mestizos." In *Research and Reflections in Archaeology and History: Essays in Honor of Doris Stone,* edited by E. Wyllys Andrews, 113–148. New Orleans: Middle American Research Institute, 1986.

Guerra, Francisco. "The Role of Religion in Spanish American Medicine." In *Medicine and Culture,* edited by F. N. L. Poynter, 179–188. London: Wellcome Institute of the History of Medicine, 1969.

Harvey, David. *The New Imperialism.* Oxford: Oxford University Press, 2003.

Hassig, Ross. *Trade, Tribute, and Transportation: The Sixteenth-Century Political Economy of the Valley of Mexico.* Norman: University of Oklahoma Press, 1985.

Henderson, John. *The Renaissance Hospital: Healing the Body and Healing the Soul.* New Haven, CT: Yale University Press, 2006.

Herzog, Tamar. *Defining Nations: Immigrants and Citizens in Early Modern Spain and Spanish America.* New Haven, CT: Yale University Press, 2003.

Hill, Ruth. "Between Black and White: A Critical Race Theory Approach to Caste Poetry in the Spanish New World." *Comparative Literature* 59, no. 4 (2007): 269–293.

———. *Hierarchy, Commerce, and Fraud in Bourbon Spanish America: A Postal Inspector's Exposé.* Nashville, TN: Vanderbilt University Press, 2005.

Holler, Jacqueline. *Escogidas Plantas: Nuns and Beatas in Mexico City, 1531–1601.* New York: Columbia University Press, 2005.

Holt, Thomas C. *The Problem of Race in the Twenty-First Century.* Cambridge, MA: Harvard University Press, 2000.

Horn, Rebecca. *Postconquest Coyoacan: Nahua-Spanish Relations in Central Mexico, 1519–1650.* Stanford, CA: Stanford University Press, 1997.

Humboldt, Alexander von. *Personal Narrative of Travels to the Equinoctial Regions of America during the Years 1799–1804.* Translated by Thomasina Ross. Vol. 1. London: Henry G. Bohn, 1852 [1814].

———. *Political Essay on the Kingdom of New Spain.* London: printed for Longman, Hurst, Rees, Orme, and Brown, 1811.

———. *Views of the Cordilleras and Monuments of the Indigenous Peoples of the Americas: A Critical Edition.* Edited by Vera M. Kutzinski and Ottmar Ette and translated by J. Ryan Poynter. Chicago: University of Chicago Press, 2012 [1810–1813].

Humboldt, Alexander von, and Aimé Bonpland. *Essay on the Geography of Plants.* Edited by Stephen T. Jackson and translated by Sylvie Romanowski. Chicago: University of Chicago Press, 2009 [1807].

Hyland, Sabine. "Illegitimacy and Racial Hierarchy in the Peruvian Priesthood: A Seventeenth-Century Dispute." *Catholic Historical Review* 84, no. 3 (1998): 431–454.

Hyslop, Jonathan. "The Invention of the Concentration Camp: Cuba, Southern Africa, and the Philippines, 1896–1907." *Southern African Historical Journal* 63, no. 2 (2011): 251–276.

*Instrucciones que los virreyes de Nueva España dejaron a sus sucesores.* Mexico City: Imprenta de Ignacio Escalante, 1873.

Jackson, Stephen T. "Instruments Utilized in Developing the *Tableau physique.*" In *Essay on the Geography of Plants,* by Alexander von Humboldt and Aimé Bonpland, 221–226. Edited by Stephen T. Jackson and translated by Sylvie Romanowski. Chicago: University of Chicago Press, 2009.

Kagan, Richard L. *Urban Images of the Hispanic World, 1493–1793.* New Haven, CT: Yale University Press, 2000.

Katzew, Ilona. *Casta Painting: Images of Race in Eighteenth-Century Mexico.* New Haven, CT: Yale University Press, 2004.

Khalili, Laleh. *Time in the Shadows: Confinement in Counterinsurgencies.* Stanford, CA: Stanford University Press, 2013.

Klor de Alva, J. Jorge. "Sahagún and the Birth of Modern Ethnography: Representing, Confessing, and Inscribing the Native Other." In *The Work of Bernardino de Sahagún: Pioneer Ethnographer of Sixteenth-Century Aztec Mexico,* edited by J. Jorge Klor de Alva, H. B. Nicholson, and Eloise Quiñones Keber, 31–52. Austin: University of Texas Press, 1988.

Koerner, Lisbet. *Linnaeus: Nature and Nation*. Cambridge, MA: Harvard University Press, 1999.

Konetzke, Richard. *Colección de documentos para la historia de la formación social de Hispanoamérica, 1493–1810*. Madrid: CSIC, 1953.

Kubler, George. *Mexican Architecture of the Sixteenth Century*. Vol. 1. New Haven, CT: Yale University Press, 1948.

Lafuente, Antonio, and Nuria Valverde. "Linnaean Botany and Spanish Imperial Biopolitics." In *Colonial Botany: Science, Commerce, and Politics in the Early Modern World*, edited by Londa Schiebinger and Claudia Swan, 134–147. Philadelphia: University of Pennsylvania Press, 2005.

Larkin, Brian. "The Politics and Poetics of Infrastructure." *Annual Review of Anthropology* 42 (2013): 327–343.

———. *Signal and Noise: Media, Infrastructure, and Urban Culture in Nigeria*. Durham, NC: Duke University Press, 2008.

Latour, Bruno. *Science in Action: How to Follow Scientists and Engineers through Society*. Cambridge, MA: Harvard University Press, 1987.

Lefebvre, Henri. "An Interview with Henri Lefebvre." *Environment and Planning D: Society and Space* 5 (1987): 27–38.

———. *The Production of Space*. Translated by Donald Nicholson-Smith. Oxford: Blackwell, 1991.

———. *The Urban Revolution*. Translated by Robert Bononno. Minneapolis: University of Minnesota Press, 2003.

Leibsohn, Dana. "Primers for Memory: Cartographic Histories and Nahua Identity." In *Writing without Words: Alternative Literacies in Mesoamerica and the Andes*, edited by Elizabeth Boone Hill and Walter Mignolo, 161–187. Durham, NC: Duke University Press, 1996.

Leonard, Irving. *Don Carlos de Sigüenza y Góngora: A Mexican Savant of the Seventeenth Century*. Berkeley: University of California Press, 1929.

Lewis, Laura A. *Hall of Mirrors: Power, Witchcraft, and Caste in Colonial Mexico*. Durham, NC: Duke University Press, 2003.

Linnaeus, Carl. *Linnaeus' Philosophia Botanica*. Translated by Stephen Freer. Oxford: Oxford University Press, 2005.

———. "The Oeconomy of Nature." In *Miscellaneous Tracts Relating to Natural History, Husbandry, and Physick*, by Carl Linnaeus et al., 39–129. Translated by Benjamin Stillingfleet. London: J. Dodsley, 1775.

———. "On the Increase of the Habitable Earth." In *Select Dissertations from the Amoenitates Academicae: A Supplement to Mr. Stillingfleet's Tracts Relating to Natural History*, by Carl Linnaeus et al., 71–127. Translated by F. J. Brand. London, 1781.

Lockhart, James. *The Nahuas after the Conquest: A Social and Cultural History of the Indians of Central Mexico, Sixteenth through Eighteenth Centuries*. Stanford, CA: Stanford University Press, 1992.

Lodares, Juan R. "Languages, Catholicism, and Power in the Hispanic Empire (1500–1770)." In *Spanish and Empire*, edited by Nelsy Echávez-Solano and Kenya C. Dworkin y Méndez, 3–31. Nashville, TN: Vanderbilt University Press, 2007.

Lomnitz, Claudio. *Death and the Idea of Mexico*. New York: Zone Books, 2005.

López, Rick A. "Nature as Subject and Citizen in the Mexican Botanical Garden, 1787–1829." In *A Land between Waters: Environmental Histories of Modern Mexico*, edited by Christopher R. Boyer, 73–99. Tucson: University of Arizona Press, 2012.

Lund, Joshua. *The Mestizo State: Reading Race in Modern Mexico*. Minneapolis: University of Minnesota Press, 2012.

Mariátegui, José Carlos. *Siete ensayos de interpretación de la realidad peruana*. Caracas: Biblioteca Ayacucho, 1979 [1928].

Martínez, María Elena. *Genealogical Fictions: Limpieza de Sangre, Religion, and Gender in Colonial Mexico*. Stanford, CA: Stanford University Press, 2008.

Marx, Karl. *Capital: A Critique of Political Economy*. Vol. 1. New York: Penguin Books, 1976.

———. *The Eighteenth Brumaire of Louis Bonaparte*. New York: International, 1975.

Mbembe, Achille. "Necropolitics." *Public Culture* 15, no. 1 (2003): 11–40.

McCaa, Robert, Stuart B. Schwartz, and Arturo Grubessich. "Race and Class in Colonial Latin America: A Critique." *Comparative Studies in Society and History* 21, no. 3 (1979): 421–433.

McDonough, Kelly S. *The Learned Ones: Nahua Intellectuals in Postconquest Mexico*. Tucson: University of Arizona Press, 2014.

Melamed, Jodi. *Represent and Destroy: Rationalizing Violence in the New Racial Capitalism*. Minneapolis: University of Minnesota Press, 2011.

Melvin, Karen. *Building Colonial Cities of God: Mendicant Orders and Urban Culture in New Spain*. Stanford, CA: Stanford University Press, 2012.

Mendieta, Gerónimo de. *Historia eclesiástica indiana*. Edited by Joaquín García Icazbalceta. Mexico City: Antigua Libreria, 1870.

Merrim, Stephanie. *The Spectacular City, Mexico, and Colonial Hispanic Literary Culture*. Austin: University of Texas Press, 2010.

Mignolo, Walter D. *The Darker Side of Western Modernity: Global Futures, Decolonial Options*. Durham, NC: Duke University Press, 2011.

Milton, Cynthia, and Ben Vinson III. "Counting Heads: Race and Non-Native Tribute Policy in Colonial Spanish America." *Journal of Colonialism and Colonial History* 3, no. 3 (2002). doi:10.1353/cch.2002.0056.

Morales, Francisco. *Ethnic and Social Background of the Franciscan Friars in Seventeenth-Century Mexico*. Washington, DC: Academy of American Franciscan History, 1973.

More, Anna. *Baroque Sovereignty: Carlos de Sigüenza y Góngora and the Creole Archive of Colonial Mexico*. Philadelphia: University of Pennsylvania Press, 2013.

Moreiras, Alberto. "Ten Notes on Primitive Imperial Accumulation: Ginés de Sepúlveda, Las Casas, Fernández de Oviedo." *Interventions* 2, no. 3 (2000): 343–363.

Moreno de los Arcos, Roberto. *Linneo en México: Las controversias sobre el sistema binario sexual, 1788–1798*. Mexico City: UNAM, 1989.

———. "Los territorios parroquiales de la ciudad arzobispal." *Cuadernos de arquitectura virreinal* 12 (1992): 4–18.

Mörner, Magnus. "La afortunada gestión de un misionero del Perú en Madrid en 1578." *Anuario de estudios americanos* 19 (1962): 247–275.

Motolinía, Toribio de Benavente. *Memoriales de Fray Toribio de Motolinía.* Edited by Luis García Pimentel. Mexico City: En casa del editor, 1903.

Moziño, José Mariano. *Tratado del xiquilite y añil de Guatemala.* Edited by María Isabel Casín and Santiago Montes. San Salvador, El Salvador: Ministerio de Educación, 1976.

Mühlhahn, Klaus. "The Concentration Camp in Global Historical Perspective." *History Compass* 8, no. 6 (2010): 543–561.

Mumford, Jeremy Ravi. *Vertical Empire: The General Resettlement of Indians in the Colonial Andes.* Durham, NC: Duke University Press, 2012.

Mundy, Barbara E. "The Images of Eighteenth-Century Urban Reform in Mexico City and the Plan of José Antonio Alzate." *Colonial Latin American Review* 21, no. 1 (2012): 45–75.

———. *The Mapping of New Spain: Indigenous Cartography and the Maps of the Relaciones Geográficas.* Chicago: University of Chicago Press, 1996.

Muriel, Josefina. "Una nueva versión del motín del 8 de junio de 1692." *Estudios de Historia Novohispana* 18 (1998): 107–115.

Nemser, Daniel. "Archaeology in the Lettered City." *Colonial Latin American Review* 23, no. 2 (2014): 197–223.

———. "Eviction and the Archive: Materials for an Archaeology of the Archivo General de Indias." *Journal of Spanish Cultural Studies* 16, no. 2 (2015): 123–141.

———. "Primitive Spiritual Accumulation and the Colonial Extraction Economy." *Política Común* 5 (2014). http://quod.lib.umich.edu/p/pc/12322227.0005.003/--primitive-spiritual-accumulation-and-the-colonial-extraction?rgn=main;view=fulltext.

———. "'To Avoid This Mixture': Rethinking *Pulque* in Colonial Mexico City." *Food and Foodways* 19 (2011): 98–121.

Newson, Linda A. "Medical Practice in Early Colonial Spanish America: A Prospectus." *Bulletin of Latin American Research* 25, no. 3 (2006): 367–391.

Nicolson, Malcolm. "Alexander von Humboldt, Humboldtian Science, and the Origins of the Study of Vegetation." *History of Science* 25, no. 2 (1987): 167–194.

Nirenberg, David. "Race and the Middle Ages." In *Rereading the Black Legend: The Discourses of Religious and Racial Difference in the Renaissance Empires*, edited by Margaret R. Greer, Walter D. Mignolo, and Maureen Quilligan, 71–87. Chicago: University of Chicago Press, 2007.

Nixon, Rob. *Slow Violence and the Environmentalism of the Poor.* Cambridge, MA: Harvard University Press, 2011.

O'Gorman, Edmundo. "Reflexiones sobre la distribución urbana colonial de la ciudad de México." *Boletín del Archivo General de la Nación* 9, no. 4 (1938): 787–815.

———. "Sobre los inconvenientes de vivir los indios en el centro de la ciudad." *Boletín del Archivo General de la Nación* 9, no. 1 (1938): 1–33.

O'Hara, Matthew D. *A Flock Divided: Race, Religion, and Politics in Mexico, 1749–1857.* Durham, NC: Duke University Press, 2010.

Olsen, Bjørnar. *In Defense of Things: Archaeology and the Ontology of Objects.* Lanham, MD: AltaMira, 2010.

Omi, Michael, and Howard Winant. *Racial Formation in the United States*. 2nd ed., New York: Routledge, 1994; 3rd ed., New York: Routledge, 2015.

O'Toole, Rachel Sarah. *Bound Lives: Africans, Indians, and the Making of Race in Colonial Peru*. Pittsburgh: University of Pittsburgh Press, 2012.

———. "The Work of Race in Colonial Peru." In *Ethnicity as a Political Resource: Conceptualizations across Disciplines, Regions, and Periods*, edited by the University of Cologne forum "Ethnicity as a Political Resource" (transcript), 209–219. Bielefeld, Germany, 2015.

Outram, Dorinda. *The Enlightenment*. 3rd ed. Cambridge: Cambridge University Press, 2013.

Overmyer-Velázquez, Rebecca. *Folkloric Poverty: Neoliberal Multiculturalism in Mexico*. University Park: Pennsylvania State University Press, 2010.

Oviedo, Gonzalo Fernández de. *General y natural historia de las Indias*. Madrid: Atlas, 1959.

Pagden, Anthony. *European Encounters with the New World: From Renaissance to Romanticism*. New Haven, CT: Yale University Press, 1994.

———. *The Fall of Natural Man: The American Indian and the Origins of Comparative Ethnology*. Cambridge: Cambridge University Press, 1986.

———. "Identity Formation in Spanish America." In *Colonial Identity in the Atlantic World, 1500–1800*, edited by Nicholas Canny and Anthony Pagden, 51–93. Princeton, NJ: Princeton University Press, 1987.

Palau y Verdera, Antonio. *Explicación de la filosofía, y fundamentos botanicos de Linneo*. Madrid: Antonio de Sancha, 1778.

Parry, Bronwyn. *Trading the Genome: Investigating the Commodification of Bio-Information*. New York: Columbia University Press, 2004.

Phelan, John Leddy. *The Millennial Kingdom of the Franciscans in the New World*. Berkeley: University of California Press, 1970.

Pineda, Juan de. *Diálogos familiares de agricultura cristiana*. Edited by Juan Meseguer Fernández. Madrid: Ediciones Atlas, 1963.

Poole, Stafford. "Church Law on the Ordination of Indians and *Castas* in New Spain." *Hispanic American Historical Review* 61, no. 4 (1981): 637–650.

———. *Pedro Moya de Contreras: Catholic Reform and Royal Power in New Spain, 1571–1591*. 2nd ed. Norman: University of Oklahoma Press, 2011.

Pratt, Mary Louise. *Imperial Eyes: Travel Writing and Transculturation*. 2nd ed. New York: Routledge, 2008.

Prebisch, Raúl. *The Economic Development of Latin America and Its Principal Problems*. Lake Success, NY: United Nations Department of Economic Affairs, 1950.

Prieto, Andrés I. *Missionary Scientists: Jesuit Science in Spanish South America, 1570–1810*. Nashville, TN: Vanderbilt University Press, 2011.

Puerto Sarmiento, Francisco Javier. *Ciencia de cámara: Casimiro Gómez Ortega (1741–1818), el científico cortesano*. Madrid: CSIC, 1992.

———. *La ilusión quebrada: Botánica, sanidad y política científica en la España ilustrada*. Madrid: CSIC, 1988.

Puga, Vasco de. *Prouisiones, cedulas, instrucciones de Su Magestad*. Mexico City: En casa de P. Ocharte, 1563.

Quijano, Aníbal. "Coloniality of Power, Eurocentrism, and Latin America." *Nepantla: Views from the South* 1, no. 3 (2000): 533–580.

Quiroga, Vasco de. "Informacion en derecho del licenciado Quiroga, sobre algunas provisiones del Consejo de Indias (1535)." In *Colección de documentos inéditos relativos al descubrimiento, conquista y organización de las antiguas posesiones españolas de América y Oceanía*, edited by Luis Torres de Mendoza, vol. 10. Madrid: Imprenta de J. M. Pérez, 1868.

Rabasa, José. *Writing Violence on the Northern Frontier: The Historiography of Sixteenth-Century New Mexico and Florida and the Legacy of Conquest*. Durham, NC: Duke University Press, 2000.

Rama, Ángel. *La ciudad letrada*. Montevideo: Arca, 1998.

Ramírez Ruiz, Marcelo, and Federico Fernández Christlieb. "La policía de los indios y la urbanización del altepetl." In *Territorialidad y paisaje en el altepetl del siglo XVI*, edited by Federico Fernández Christlieb and Ángel Julián García Zambrano, 114–167. Mexico City: Fondo de Cultura Económica, 2006.

Rankin, William J. "Infrastructure and the International Governance of Economic Development, 1950–1965." In *Internationalization of Infrastructures*, edited by Jean-François Auger, Jan Jaap Bouma, and Rolf Künneke, 61–75. Delft, Holland: Delft University of Technology, 2009.

Rappaport, Joanne. *The Disappearing Mestizo: Configuring Difference in the Colonial New Kingdom of Granada*. Durham, NC: Duke University Press, 2014.

Read, Jason. *The Micro-Politics of Capital: Marx and the Prehistory of the Present*. Albany: State University of New York Press, 2003.

Real Academia Española. *Diccionario de la lengua castellana*. Madrid: Por la Viuda de Francisco del Hierro, 1726–1739.

*Recopilación de leyes de los reynos de las Indias*. Madrid: Por Julián de Paredes, 1681. http://fondosdigitales.us.es/fondos/libros/752/14/recopilacion-de-leyes-de-los-reynos-de-las-indias/.

Red por la Paz Chiapas. *De la tierra al asfalto: Informe de la misión civil de observación de la Red por la Paz Chiapas y CAIK al programa ciudades rurales sustentables*. San Cristóbal de las Casas, Mexico: Red por la Paz Chiapas, 2012.

Ricard, Robert. *The Spiritual Conquest of Mexico: An Essay on the Apostolate and the Evangelizing Methods of the Mendicant Orders of New Spain, 1523–1572*. Translated by Lesley Byrd Simpson. Berkeley: University of California Press, 1966.

Rickett, Harold William. *The Royal Botanical Expedition to New Spain*. Waltham, MA: Chronica Botanica, 1947.

Robles, Antonio de. *Diario de sucesos notables*. Edited by Antonio Castro Leal. Mexico City: Editorial Porrúa, 1946.

Sackley, Nicole. "The Village as Cold War Site: Experts, Development, and the History of Rural Reconstruction." *Journal of Global History* 6, no. 3 (2011): 481–504.

Saignes, Thierry, and Therese Bouysse-Cassagne. "Dos confundidas identidades: Mestizos y criollos en el siglo XVII." *Senri Ethnological Studies* 33 (1992): 14–26.

Saldívar, Emiko. "'It's Not Race, It's Culture': Untangling Racial Politics in Mexico." *Latin American and Caribbean Ethnic Studies* 9, no. 1 (2014): 89–108.

Sánchez Santiró, Ernest. "El *nuevo orden* parroquial de la ciudad de México: Población, etnia y territorio (1768–1777)." *Estudios de Historia Novohispana* 30 (2004): 63–92.

Scardaville, Michael C. "(Hapsburg) Law and (Bourbon) Order: State Authority, Popular Unrest, and the Criminal Justice System in Bourbon Mexico City." In *Reconstructing Criminality in Latin America*, edited by Carlos A. Aguirre and Robert Buffington. Wilmington, DE: Scholarly Resources, 2000.

Schiebinger, Londa. *Plants and Empire: Colonial Bioprospecting in the Atlantic World*. Cambridge, MA: Harvard University Press, 2004.

Schmitt, Carl. *The* Nomos *of the Earth in the International Law of the* Jus Publicum Europaeum. Translated by G. L. Ulmen. New York: Telos, 2006.

———. *Political Theology: Four Chapters on the Concept of Sovereignty*. Translated by George Schwab. Cambridge, MA: MIT Press, 1985.

Schroeder, Susan. *Chimalpahin and the Kingdoms of Chalco*. Tucson: University of Arizona Press, 1991.

Schwartz, Stuart B., and Frank Salomon. "New Peoples and New Kinds of People: Adaptation, Readjustment, and Ethnogenesis in South American Indigenous Societies (Colonial Era)." In *The Cambridge History of the Native Peoples of the Americas, vol. 3: South America, Part 2*, edited by Frank Salomon and Stuart B. Schwartz, 443–501. Cambridge: Cambridge University Press, 1999.

Seed, Patricia. "Social Dimensions of Race: Mexico City, 1753." *Hispanic American Historical Review* 62, no. 4 (1982): 569–606.

Sepúlveda, Juan Ginés de. *Tratado de las justas causas de la guerra contra los indios*. Mexico City: Fondo de Cultura Económica, 1987.

Sigüenza y Góngora, Carlos de. *Alboroto y motín de México del 8 de junio de 1692*. Edited by Irving Leonard. Mexico City: Talleres Gráficos del Museo Nacional de Arqueología, Historia y Etnografía, 1932.

Silva, Denise Ferreira da. *Toward a Global Idea of Race*. Minneapolis: University of Minnesota Press, 2007.

Silva Prada, Natalia. *La política de una rebelión: Los indígenas frente al tumulto de 1692 en la Ciudad de México*. Mexico City: El Colegio de México, 2007.

Silverblatt, Irene. *Modern Inquisitions: Peru and the Colonial Origins of the Civilized World*. Durham, NC: Duke University Press, 2004.

Simone, AbdouMaliq. "People as Infrastructure: Intersecting Fragments in Johannesburg." *Public Culture* 16, no. 3 (2004): 407–429.

Singh, Nikhil Pal. *Black Is a Country: Race and the Unfinished Struggle for Democracy*. Cambridge, MA: Harvard University Press, 2004.

Sitze, Adam. "Editor's Introduction." In Carlo Galli, *Political Spaces and Global War*, edited by Adam Sitze and translated by Elisabeth Fay, xi–lxxxv. Minneapolis: University of Minnesota Press, 2010.

Smith, Adam. *An Inquiry into the Nature and Causes of the Wealth of Nations*. London: W. Strahan and T. Cadell, 1776.

Spary, E. C. *Utopia's Garden: French Natural History from Old Regime to Revolution*. Chicago: University of Chicago Press, 2000.

Star, Susan Leigh. "The Ethnography of Infrastructure." *American Behavioral Scientist* 43, no. 3 (1999): 377–391.

Stepan, Nancy Leys. *"The Hour of Eugenics": Race, Gender, and Nation in Latin America*. Ithaca, NY: Cornell University Press, 1991.

———. "Race and Gender: The Role of Analogy in Science." *Isis* 77, no. 2 (1986): 261–277.

Stern, Steve J. "Feudalism, Capitalism, and the World-System in the Perspective of Latin America and the Caribbean." *American Historical Review* 93, no. 4 (1988): 829–872.

Stoler, Ann Laura. *Carnal Knowledge and Imperial Power: Race and the Intimate in Colonial Rule.* Berkeley: University of California Press, 2002.

———. *Race and the Education of Desire: Foucault's History of Sexuality and the Colonial Order of Things.* Durham, NC: Duke University Press, 1995.

———. "Racial Histories and Their Regimes of Truth." *Political Power and Social Theory* 11 (1997): 183–206.

Telles, Edward E. "Race and Ethnicity and Latin America's United Nations Millennium Development Goals." *Latin American and Caribbean Ethnic Studies* 2, no. 2 (2007): 185–200.

Terraciano, Kevin. *The Mixtecs of Colonial Oaxaca: Ñudzahui History, Sixteenth through Eighteenth Centuries.* Stanford, CA: Stanford University Press, 2001.

Tone, John Lawrence. *Guerra y genocidio en Cuba, 1895–1898.* Translated by Nicolás Santos and Rocío Westendorp. Madrid: Turner, 2008.

———. *War and Genocide in Cuba, 1895–1898.* Chapel Hill: University of North Carolina Press, 2006.

Torquemada, Juan de. *Primera parte de los veinte i un libros rituales i monarchia indiana.* Madrid: En la oficina de Nicolás Rodríguez Franco, 1723.

Torre Villar, Ernesto de la. *Las congregaciones de los pueblos de indios: Fase terminal, aprobaciones y rectificaciones.* Mexico City: Instituto de Investigaciones Históricas, 1995.

Toussaint, Manuel. *Información de méritos y servicios de Alonso García Bravo, alarife que trazó la ciudad de México.* Mexico City: UNAM, 1956.

Twinam, Ann. *Purchasing Whiteness: Pardos, Mulattos, and the Quest for Social Mobility in the Spanish Indies.* Stanford, CA: Stanford University Press, 2015.

Valadés, Diego. *Retórica cristiana.* Translated by Tarsicio Herrera Zapién. Mexico City: Fondo de Cultura Económica, 1989.

Van Deusen, Nancy E. *Between the Sacred and the Worldly: The Institutional and Cultural Practice of Recogimiento in Colonial Lima.* Stanford, CA: Stanford University Press, 2001.

Verdesio, Gustavo. "Invisible at a Glance: Indigenous Cultures of the Past, Ruins, Archaeological Sites, and Our Regimes of Visibility." In *Ruins of Modernity,* edited by Julia Hell and Andrea Schönle, 339–353. Durham, NC: Duke University Press, 2010.

Vetancurt, Agustín de. *Teatro mexicano.* Mexico City: Imprenta de I. Escalante, 1870–1871.

Viqueira, Juan Pedro. *Propriety and Permissiveness in Bourbon Mexico.* Translated by Sonya Lipsett-Rivera and Sergio Rivera Ayala. Lanham, MD: SR Books, 2004.

Vitoria, Francisco de. *Political Writings.* Edited and translated by Anthony Pagden and Jeremy Lawrence. Cambridge: Cambridge University Press, 1991.

Wallerstein, Immanuel. *Historical Capitalism.* London: Verso, 1983.

Weheliye, Alexander G. *Habeas Viscus: Racializing Assemblages, Biopolitics, and Black Feminist Theories of the Human.* Durham, NC: Duke University Press, 2014.

Weyler, Valeriano. *Mi mando en Cuba.* Madrid: F. González Rojas, 1910–1911.

Williams, Raymond. *Marxism and Literature*. Oxford: Oxford University Press, 1977.

Wilson, Japhy. "Notes on the Rural City: Henri Lefebvre and the Transformation of Everyday Life in Chiapas, Mexico." *Environment and Planning D: Society and Space* 29 (2011): 993–1009.

———. "The Urbanization of the Countryside: Depoliticization and the Production of Space in Chiapas." *Latin American Perspectives* 40, no. 2 (2013): 218–236.

Winant, Howard. *The World Is a Ghetto: Race and Democracy since World War II*. New York: Basic Books, 2001.

Withers, Charles W. J. *Placing the Enlightenment: Thinking Geographically about the Age of Reason*. Chicago: University of Chicago Press, 2007.

Zubillaga, Félix. "Tercer Concilio Mexicano, 1585: Los memoriales del P. Juan de la Plaza, S.I." *Archivum Historicum Societatis Iesu* 30 (1961): 180–244.

Page numbers in italics indicate illustrations.

Mestizos (*continued*)
182n13; social construction and,
68–69; wage labor and, 6–7, 66–67,
80–81, 100. See also *mestizaje*; race
Mexico City, 17, 21–22, 33–34, 38, 47,
65, 69, 75, 98, 101–132, 138, 149–
150, 151–153, 157, 173n14, 187n33,
187n39, 193n58; *barrios* of, 102–
103, 106, 117, 122, 125, 129; *cuarteles* (wards) of, 131; gridded layout
of, 33, 38, 102; as model for congregated towns, 34, 38; parishes of,
113–114, 119–123, 124, 131–132; riot
of 1692 and, 101–132; *traza* of, 21,
65, 102–103, 106, 107–118, 120, 122,
124–125, 129, 131; urban economy
of, 115–118, 122–123, 129, 131. *See
also* botanical garden: of Mexico;
Chapultepec Hill; segregation
Mignolo, Walter, 6, 174n16
More, Anna, 105–107, 185–186n2
More, Thomas, 36, 179n27
Moreiras, Alberto, 165, 171
Motolinía, Toribio de Benavente, 25,
26, 50–51, 58, 63
Moya de Contreras, Pedro, 87–88, 98
Mulatto as racial category, 99, 124–125,
127, 173–174n13, 187–188n40
Muñoz, Juan Bautista, 150
Muslims, 8, 68, 187n24

natural history, 4, 125, 133–136, 138–
139, 151–153, 162, 193n65
nature: vs. culture, 93–97, 100, 126,
160, 167, 170; external determination and, 137, 146, 154–156, 158–162;
as "laboratory," 156; as "natural resources," 35, 138; science and study
of, 134–135, 142, 152–153; state of,
15, 73–74. *See also* natural history;
race
Nazi Germany, 14, 168
necropolitics, 15–16, 48, 63. *See
also* biopolitics; race; surplus
population
Nirenberg, David, 9, 174n20
Nochixtlan, *33*, 33–35

O'Gorman, Edmundo, 130, 186n8
Omi, Michael, and Howard Winant,
10–11, 175n26, 195n10
Oviedo, Gonzalo Fernández de, 142–
143, 145

*padrones* (ecclesiastical censuses), 103,
118–124, *121*, 125, 129, 132, 186n8.
*See also* biopolitics
Palau y Verdera, Antonio, 140–142
Palestine, Israeli occupation of, 16
parishes: and *derechos* (fees), 113–114;
in Europe vs. in colonial space, 119;
Indian, 103, 113–114, 119, 123, 132;
non-Indian, 114; secularization of,
131–132. *See also* pastoral power; religious orders
pastoral power, 12–14, 30–31, 78–80,
106–107, 112, 114, 119–124; in Europe vs. colonial space, 119; and
modern biopolitics, 12–14, 107; salvation and, 31, 36, 49–50, 112, 125,
129. *See also* biopolitics; police
Pesquera, Gregorio de, 74–75, 86, 91,
182–183n21
Philip II, 32, 72, 97–99
Pineda, Juan de, 94
plant geography, 22, 156–162. *See also*
botany; Humboldt, Alexander von
plants: as analogous with animals, including humans, 133–136, 159–160,
162, 190n6; epistemological precedence of, in eighteenth century,
133, 136, 139; in Europe vs. in the
Americas, 142–149, 160; and race,
22, 133–136, 159–164, 190n6; vs. vegetation, 159. *See also* botanical garden; botany
Plaza, Juan de la, 88–91, 97, 100
Plebe, 22, 104–105, 115, 124–131; as defined by mixture, 22, 104–105, 127–
128, 130; in Europe vs. in colonial
Mexico, 127–128; Indians as included in, 128–129; as surplus population, 105, 107, 128. *See also*
intersectionality; racialization; surplus population